The Table-Rappers

THE VICTORIANS AND THE OCCULT

RONALD PEARSALL

SUTTON PUBLISHING

This book was first published in 1972 by Michael Joseph Ltd

This edition first published in 2004 by
Sutton Publishing Limited · Phoenix Mill
Thrupp · Stroud · Gloucestershire · GL5 2BU

British Library Cataloguing in Publication Data
A catalogue record for this book is avialble from the British
Library.

ISBN 0 7509 3684 3

Printed and bound in Great Britain by
J.H. Haynes & Co. Ltd, Sparkford.

Contents

The Table-Rappers

Introduction

... the veil
Is rending, and the Voices of the day
Are heard across the Voices of the dark

ALFRED LORD TENNYSON

Spiritualism was tailor-made for the nineteenth century. Beneath the rationalism and the optimism of Victorian England, there was a wide feeling of unease. God had been dismissed from His universe, and had left a yawning chasm.

Without a unique combination of circumstances, it is doubtful whether spiritualism would have achieved such a hold, a hold that has persisted until the present. To begin with, it was the first movement to be imported from the United States. Today it is customary for trends first to show themselves in America before being transplanted wholesale in Britain, but in 1852 this was something new.

The United States was then regarded as a not particularly important overseas power. Its population was still considerably less than that of the United Kingdom. However, the middle classes considered that anything that emanated from the United States carried an added kudos, and the rapturous reception given to Mrs Hayden, the first spiritualist medium to arrive in Britain, was totally out of proportion to the phenomena she produced.

Although anything from America was guaranteed attention, it was not necessarily guaranteed success. The 'bloomer' movement – trousers for women – died a quick death in Britain after its import from the United States.

The arrival of Mrs Hayden was timely, for an interest in the occult had been gathering force for several years. In 1848 Mrs Crowe had published *The Night Side of Nature,* a ramshackle collage of ghosts and mysterious happenings, and in 1851 the

9

Ghost Club had been formed at Cambridge University for the purpose of investigating supernatural phenomena.

There were four main factors that underwrote spiritualism: the passive interest in the occult needed a focal point; the established church was losing touch with its public; the mesmerism movement was there to provide practitioners and a nucleus of apostles; and Queen Victoria approved, and herself practiced table-turning. From the first there was a conflict between those who saw spiritualism as a pastime and those who viewed it as a religion. Spiritualism certainly made the supernatural respectable; but at times the *raison d'être* of spiritualism – communication with the dead – was forgotten beneath a welter of parlour tricks, and believers were side-tracked and confused by antagonistic clergymen writing such books as *Table-moving tested and proved to be the result of Satanic Agency,* by professional conjurors, and by scientists who were more interested in having a knot produced in a sealed coil of rope than in spirit forms.

Spiritualism was a haven for the repressed, the unsatisfied, and the bereaved, and was held together only by commitment and a desire to believe. The more fervent supporters would not be detracted from their course by incompetent mediums and the cases of clumsy fraud that received wide coverage in the columns of the newspapers.

Efforts were made to form spiritualism into a coherent compact movement, for, as Stainton Moses, one of the leading non-professional mediums of the day, admitted: 'We are emphatically in need of discipline and education'. The loose-knit nature of spiritualism meant that splinter groups were constantly breaking away, the most important of these being theosophy, though there were also many adherents to the French breakaway movement called spiritism of which reincarnation was a basic tenet.

How important was spiritualism to the Victorian age?

Never so important as its supporters thought. In many ways it was an easy option. Most of its supporters retreated into spiritualism rather than ventured into it. It did little to inculcate moral qualities, as did Nonconformism on the one hand and the High Church movement on the other.

It was never sufficiently important to influence the course to Victorian life, and, significantly, the spiritualist movement failed to produce one literary masterpiece, whereas occultism produced several, from *Wuthering Heights* and *A Christmas Carol* to Bulwer Lytton's *The Haunters and the Haunted,* all published in the 1840s and 1850s.

Whereas spiritualism contributed little to the sum of human knowledge, except in indicating the extent of human credulity, its investigators, and in particular the Society for Psychical Research, formed 1882, pursued enquiries that have yielded a rich haul. Lacking evidence of what spiritualism considered its apex of achievement – the materialisation of the spirit form – the SPR turned its attention to clairvoyance and the world of extra-sensory perception. The debt of today's experimenters in the field cannot be repaid to that dedicated body of Victorians who began the objective observation of the paranormal.

*Mesmerism and the
Growth of Spiritualism*

1. Mesmerism

In the early years of the Victorian period the technological revolution born of the industrial revolution was providing new means of probing the unknown. It is perhaps not surprising that there arose against this background certain cult words. One of them was electricity, and another was magnetism, especially that variety known as animal magnetism. In the wave of optimism, old concepts, old notions, were reviewed, and in particular the supernatural came under scrutiny.

In the preface to *The Night Side of Nature* a collage of ghost stories, legends, and myths, Catherine Crowe, a hack novelist, author of the forgotten *Lilly Dawson*, declared, 'The contemptuous scepticism of the last age is yielding to a more humble spirit of inquiry.' Although *The Night Side of Nature* is a muddle, Mrs Crowe was in the van regarding the interest in the supernatural; another manifestation of this interest was the formation in 1851 of the Ghost Club among undergraduates of the University of Cambridge, who sent out questionnaires and interviewed likely people almost in the spirit of the twentieth century.

With the new technological equipment at their command, it was thought that many phenomena would yield to a fresh examination, and that science would unravel the mysteries of this world and the next. The only snag was that the numbers of the scientists were small, those of the hangers-on and the entrepreneurs anxious to jump on the band-wagon large, and the multitude of new concepts only served to confuse. It was not a long step to the stage where what were originally specific ideas and theories were all lumped together, until animal magnetism was indistinguishable from mesmerism and mesmerism indistinguishable from clairvoyance. This confusion persisted, and in the 1883 edition of the *Encyclopaedia Britannica* J. G. McKendrick began his article on animal magnetism by saying:

'The terms *animal magnetism, electro-biology, mesmerism, clairvoyance, odylic* or *odic force,* and *hypnotism* have been used to designate peculiar nervous conditions in which the body and mind of an individual were supposed to be influenced by a mysterious force emanating from another person'. T. P. Barkas in March 1889 was even more categorical: 'Mesmerism, electro-biology, Braidism, hypnotism and somnambulism are all one and the same thing.'

But are they? Hypnotism and mesmerism certainly are, and so is the little-used term Braidism (Braid was one of the pioneers of hypnotism in Britain) but one does not know what was meant by electro-biology – it was just a handy term at the time, conjured up in 1850 by two American lecturers.

The ability to control the minds of others has always been a powerful stimulus for those with occult inclinations, who were only too pleased if their successes were termed supernatural and such phenomena have always received widespread publicity.

The first man to formulate any kind of theory about mind over mind was Franz Anton Mesmer, born near Lake Constance in either 1733 or 1744. He studied medicine in Vienna, took a degree, and began practice; his examination thesis had been on the influence of planets on people, and he supposed that this force was electrical. The key property in all electrical investigation was the magnet, and Mesmer believed that by stroking a diseased body with a magnet a cure would ensue; such is the power of suggestion, such was the magical effect of a magnet amongst the ignorant, that cures were effected; but when he met up with John Gassner, a Roman Catholic priest who believed that all disease arose from demoniacal possession, he discarded his magnets, observing Gassner's successes. He drew the conclusion that the power lay in the man rather than the accessories.

However, the magnets had made Mesmer a celebrity in Vienna; the Viennese ladies wore 'magnetised clothes' and ate from 'magnetised plates'. The demand for his services had become so great that he evolved what he called a *baquet,* a wooden tub in which magnetised iron filings were put, and from which protruded flexible metal rods which touched a number of patients. Admittedly, some of Mesmer's astonishing cures back-fired. He cured the daughter of one of the empress's secretaries of blindness;

the girl had been something of a protégée of the empress on account of her piano-playing. Now she could see, she discovered that she could not play the piano so well, and somewhat ungraciously complained. The empress had made her an allowance, and this would probably stop. The girl's father went for Mesmer with a drawn sword. Conveniently the girl went blind again.

Mesmer decided that Vienna was too provincial for him and went to the centre of the civilized world, Paris, where he was taken up by society, though scientists treated him as a charlatan. Louis XVI immediately appointed a commission to investigate mesmerism. The commission came out against it and also produced a secret report, suggesting that mesmerism or animal magnetism might disrupt public morality. The medical faculty of the University of Paris was warned against having any connection with mesmerism – individual members would be expelled for dabbling. However, the rumour had it that the government itself was not sure and offered 20,000 francs for Mesmer's secret.

Mesmer's methods encouraged the accusations of charlatanism. Mesmer had his consulting rooms hung with mirrors, and dimly lit, while soft music seeped through the rooms and perfumes were wafted in and out. The patients sat round a vat in which mystic ingredients bubbled, holding each others' hands or joined by cords. Although Dr F. C. Hake was writing a hundred years later, his strictures might well apply to Mesmer at this time: 'This hypnotism is only the old witchcraft restored, renovated, and adapted.'[1]

The patients sat in expectancy, and then Mesmer entered, dressed as a magician, making passes, touching, or merely looking. Women had fits, men had seizures. Like later spiritualistic mediums, Mesmer overplayed his hand; his genuine gifts were forgotten amidst the tricks, and animal magnetism became disreputable, the more so because of the frauds and poseurs who took it up. Society people withdrew their patronage, and Mesmer retired to Karlsruhe and in 1793 to Vienna, where he was thrown into prison as a French spy for two months. Mesmer moved to Switzerland, dying in 1815.

He had made his disciples, in particular the Marquis de Puységur who initiated the modern movement of hypnosis, having eschewed the theatrical methods of Mesmer, finding that gentle manipulation causing sleep was equally as effective. However, Puységur differed from the Victorian mesmerists in his belief that patients had supernatural powers when they were hypnotised – the Victorians would have assured him that only they, the mesmerists, were vouchsafed this.

Another of Mesmer's disciples, Deleuse, discovered the ability to make an hypnotic suggestion that would be acted upon when the subject came out of his trance; it was this aspect of mesmerism that made it such a popular theatrical venture in the nineteenth century. A new stage was reached when a Dr Oudet extracted teeth from a patient while he was hypnotised, but this promise of hypnotism as a useful servant of medicine came to an untimely end with the discovery of chloroform.

Mesmerism was introduced to Britain shortly before the accession of Queen Victoria, and its enthusiasts were split into two camps, those who thought that the mesmerist himself was the agent, and those who considered that an intervening object, the magnet, was responsible. Thus was the confusion engendered between animal magnetism and mesmerism. The early practitioners in Britain were level-headed men, far removed from the sensationalism of Mesmer.[2] John Elliotson was a doctor of many talents, the friend of the novelist Thackeray, one of the first men to use a stethoscope, and one of the founders of University College Hospital. He was converted to mesmerism in 1837, and this cost him the professorship at London University which he had held since 1831. In 1843 he started the magazine the *Zoist* devoted to mesmerism and allied subjects, which ran for thirteen years. In 1842 a man had his thigh amputated under hypnosis, and showed no pain. When an account of the case was read to the learned Royal Medical and Chirurgical Society, some of the members suggested that the man had been trained not to show pain. Nine years after he left the University of London, Elliotson was still in the wilderness and was stigmatised in the *Lancet* as a professional pariah.

In 1841, James Braid, an Edinburgh-trained doctor working in Manchester, decided to investigate the claims of mesmerism. Starting off as a sceptic he became convinced of its validity, though he was somewhat at a loss to fit it into a theoretical setting – the title of his book *Magic, Witchcraft, Animal Magnetism, Hypnotism* affirms this. Braid was influenced by the work of

Baron von Reichenbach, part scientist, part occultist, who in 1845 announced his concept of the odylic force, or od-force. Certain crystals, magnets, human bodies, developed 'imponderables' or 'influences'. Persons sensitive to odyl saw luminous phenomena near the poles of magnets or surrounding people; the association with the haloes of Christianity was eagerly grasped, a new word sprang into prominence, 'sensitive' as a noun. To be a sensitive was to be the member of an elect assembly.

The English translation in 1850 of von Reichenbach's *Researches on Magnetism, &c., in relation to Vital Force* had a great effect, not only on convinced mesmerists such as Braid. 'We are in the present day upon the trace of a great many important facts relating to the imponderable agencies employed in nature,' wrote a journalist in *Household Words* in 1852. 'Light, heat, and electricity are no longer the simple matters, or effects of matter, that they have aforetime seemed to be. New wonders point to more beyond.'

In complex matters, therefore, it seemed advisable for the layman to reserve his judgment. For the sceptical this was not easy. They were told by von Reichenbach and his followers that certain persons, either those with a disordered nervous system or possessing a nervous temperament, were especially sensitive to magnetism. How was one to tell whether one had the appropriate temperament? Simple: confront the budding sensitive with a magnet:

A lady upwards of fifty-six years of age, in youth a somnambulist, but now in perfect health, and wide awake having been taken into a dark closet, and desired to look at the poles of the powerful horse-shoe magnet of nine elements, and describe what she saw, declared, after looking a considerable time, that she saw nothing. However, after I told her to look attentively, and she would see fire come out of it she speedily saw sparks, and presently it seemed to her to burst forth, as she had witnessed an artificial representation of the vocano of Mount Vesuvius at some public gardens. Without her knowledge, I closed down the lid of the trunk which contained the magnet, but still the same appearances were described as visible.[3]

Clearly not a sensitive to have much faith in.

The same kind of self-induced hallucination was noted by Braid. A woman would see light streaming from a magnet owned by her husband. Braid related: 'I had had a *fourteen pound lifting magnet*, with the armature unattached, *in my side pocket next to the lady* – and that was a magnet of *more than double the power of her husband's;* and yet *no visible* effect was produced by *my powerful* but *unsuspected* magnet'.[4]

In India, Dr Esdaile had read about hypnotism; he had to perform an operation on a Hindoo convict, and although he doubted his own powers as a hypnotist he tried it and succeeded. The Deputy Governor of Bengal appointed a commission to look into Esdaile's methods, the upshot being that Esdaile was appointed superintendent of a small Calcutta hospital where he could pursue his interests. Before he left India, Esdaile had performed three hundred painless operations using hypnotism. He found the Indians receptive, and related one interesting case using telepathic hypnosis: 'I have also entranced a blind man, and made him so sensitive, that I could entrance him *however employed* (eating his dinner for instance), by merely making him the object of my attention for ten minutes. He would gradually cease to eat, remain stationary a few moments, and then plunge, head foremost, among his rice and curry.'[5]

But for the discovery of chloroform, hypnotism might well have contributed more than it has done towards the well-being of the human race.

The two streams of the hypnotism – animal magnetism complex for a time ran parallel, but while the more sensational stream flourished, the quieter healing stream dried up for a time. The possibilities of hypnotism as a medical adjunct revived dramatically in 1882 when an obscure French physician, Liébeault, cured with hypnosis a chronic case of sciatica. The patient had been under the care of a famous neurologist, Bernheim, who was so impressed that he changed the whole course of his career, and the course of international hypnotism, by founding with Liébeault the celebrated Nancy school. They discarded the impedimenta that had dogged the pioneers of hypnotism, the magnets, the tricks, and although the Nancy school languished in obscurity for some time the work gradually came to the notice of the great neurologist, Charcot, who drew the attention of

Sigmund Freud to hypnosis, and hypnosis became one of the therapeutic weapons of psychoanalysis.

The sensationalists and occultists were, however, attracting popular attention, and the od-force or odyl dreamed up by von Reichenbach was treated with immense respect by metaphysicians and scientists; despite the failures of sensitives to see under laboratory conditions the od-force streaming from the poles of magnets, or of the camera to capture it.

Von Reichenbach believed that the od-force would succeed in scotching traditional superstition, and was particularly interested in settling the vexed question: what were ghosts? The sensitives saw flames emanating from magnets, phosphorescence from people. Odyl was generated among other things by heat and by chemical action, and von Reichenbach reasoned from this that it was generated in extra strength in the decomposition of the human body. He was explicit about this:

The desire to inflict a mortal wound on the monster, Superstition, which, from a similar origin, a few centuries ago, inflicted on European society so vast an amount of misery, and by whose influence not hundreds, but thousands, of innocent persons died in tortures, on the rack and at the stake; – this desire made me wish to make the experiment, if possible, of bringing a highly sensitive person, by night, to a churchyard. I thought it possible that they might see, over graves where mouldering bodies lay, something like that which Billing had seen.[6]

(Billing was a clergyman who had seen 'the delicate appearance of a fiery ghost-like form'. When the ground was dug up there was a skeleton covered with lime.)

The sensitive von Reichenbach discovered for his experiment was Madamoiselle Reichel. He took her to a churchyard and she saw on a grave mound a delicate, fiery, breathing flame. He then took her to a large cemetery near Vienna where many burials were carried out; the girl saw 'masses of fire' lying about, only over new graves. On many graves the flames were four feet high; when she put her hand in it was like a dense fiery cloud.

Von Reichenbach's theorising is a good deal less ludicrous than many, and in historical terms is an advance on previous conjectures – 'The old doctrine of "ghosts" regarded them as actual "spirits" of the dead, freed from the flesh or from the grave. This view, whatever else may be said for it, represents the simple philosophy of the savage, which may be correct or erroneous.'[7]

It was not von Reichenbach's fault that his accounts of his experiments were overloaded with those adjectives associated with the Gothic horror stories then in vogue; these verbal excesses one must lay at the door of his translator, Dr Gregory. And his air of certainty, almost smugness, was no more offensive than the complacent obtuseness of his colleagues and critics. The more acute of the scientists realised that von Reichenbach was wading out into the muddy reaches of pseudo-science, but even a scientific genius like Faraday was impressed enough to look into animal magnetism. Faraday did not treat it with the scorn he later reserved for spiritualism; he thought that magnetism had a great effect on the day to day business of living, and took von Reichenbach seriously enough to oppose him on a specific issue. (Von Reichenbach maintained that men sleep better with the head to the north, Faraday that body was 'dio-magnetic' and was most comfortable east – west).

Just as in the eighteenth century, it was found that the od-force and its related subjects mesmerism and animal magnetism were wonderful baits for dupes and gulls, and that people would believe anything if it was in some way related to these marvels. Mesmerised water had a vogue; this was done by breathing on the water, and waving the fingers over it. It was then used in the treatment of sores, the patients having been persuaded that it was as effective as nitric acid. The fact that mesmerism *did* work helped along the od-force; many thought that mesmerism *was* the od-force, 'a thought-stamped, nervous fluid, sent to the brain of the subject'.[8]

Those who were mesmerised could see things that ordinary mortals could not. One mesmerised girl saw 'small insects in the water fall down is if struck by electricity; but this could not be confirmed, as no one but herself could discern insects so minute.'[9] The Reverend R. A. Temple, mesmerised, saw a bucket of cold water become agitated and, to all appearances, boil, when it stood on a kitchen table.

When spiritualism burst forth in the late 'forties in America and in the early 'fifties in Britain, those who were associated with mesmerism for profit turned their attentions to this new field. The mesmerists became mediums overnight, and the tricks of their trade were transplanted wholesale into the new craze. Even the technical vocabulary of the movement could be used, with a shift of emphasis, and 'mesmeric' became a multi-purpose adjective that could have no relation at all to hypnosis. At a seance a young lady could touch the table and it would begin to rap. A mesmerist cum medium told her that he 'thought the tapping largely mesmeric, remarking that she was probably a sensitive'. He added: 'I have also discovered a strong man so susceptible to mesmeric control, that, without contact or speech, I dared not look at him without his falling in an unconscious mesmeric trance on the floor, and refrained from thinking intently about him lest he should fall unconscious.'

The mere idea of mesmerism powerfully reinforced the usual suggestibility of sitters at seances, and the neurotic pounced on garbled bits of theory and adapted them for their own private purposes, such as the man who was convinced he had been taken over by Satan, and heard voices: 'The voices loudly and clamorously spoke of all my misdeeds, and taxed me with sins of which I had not been guilty.' He thought that this was due to animal magnetism, and the weird way in which this operated throws light on the manner in which theories and ideas were stretched and distorted to suit the individual psyche. He had been 'magnetised by a nautical compass which had belonged to my father'.[10]

To professional mediums and those with a bias towards throwing sensational shows, the existence of sensitives in such large numbers was a gift. This culminated in purely theatrical shows such as the performance of Miss Abbott 'the magnetic lady' at the Alhambra Theatre in 1891. Some interesting and amusing performances were put on at the Progressive Library in Southampton Row, London, presided over benignly by Mr Burns, the editor of a psychic newspaper. Ostensibly these were serious scientific investigations, but the objective could get a good deal of honest fun out of them.

One of the disdainful was the Reverend Charles Maurice Davies. He noted that 'lady mediums and mesmerisers are so apt to run to eighteen stone, or be old and frumpish'. When the medium – mesmeriser was young and pretty the response of the sensitives in the audience was magical. 'When Miss Chandos invited patients to put themselves in her hands I thought the room had risen en masse. Everybody wanted to be mesmerised.' One victim 'seemed to like it immensely, and smiled a fatuous smile as those taper fingers lighted on his head'. When Miss Chandos was not getting the results she wanted she was severe with the audience: 'Somebody at the back of the room is exercising control. I shall be glad if they will refrain.' Another girl greatly amused the Reverend Mr Davies when she sang 'The Slave Girl's Love' ('I cannot love, because I *ham* a slave...'). 'She broke down in the middle of this aspiring ditty, and then personated a Jew old clo' man, a woman "selling ornaments for your firestoves", and various other characters, all of which she overacted considerably.' Mr Burns, the promoter, sat on a table and yawned. Mr Davies asked himself 'whether I should have stayed three mortal hours in that stuffy room, and I frankly own I came to the conclusion I should *not*'.[11]

Mesmerism had a great appeal to that numerous class of Victorian women, the professional invalid. One of the first to acclaim it was Harriet Martineau, one of the larger-than-life characters of the nineteenth-century scene, economist, agnostic, journalist, who, with her celebrated ear trumpet, can be found in most memoirs of the age. Suffering, as she thought, from an internal cancer, she took to mesmerism, which wrought such an incredible cure that within months she could walk fifteen miles in a day, and inspired her to write *Letters on Mesmerism* (published well in advance of the works by Braid which promoted mesmerism in Britain).

Jane Carlyle, wife of the sage and philosopher, was one of her confidantes. Although Mrs Carlyle was not averse to trying any of the panaceas of the scientific age, particularly those that came in bottles, she drew the line at mesmerism:

We here are sick of hearing about it. Harriet Martineau expects that the whole system of Medicine is going to be flung to the dogs presently; and that henceforth, instead of Physicians, we are to have Magnetisers! May be so; but 'I as one solitary individual' (my Husband's favourite Phrase) will in that case prefer my sickness to the cure. One knows that sickness, at all events, comes from God; and is not at all sure that *such* cure does not come from the Devil. The wonder is that sensible people who have heard tell, ever since they were born, of Witchcraft and Demoniacal possession, and all that sort of thing, should all at once fall to singing *Te Deum*s over Magnetism as if it were a new revelation! Nay, anybody that had ever seen a child tickled might have recognised the principle of Animal Magnetism without going further![12]

Elizabeth Barrett was more receptive. She was reluctant to 'give one's specific convictions to general sweeping testimonies, with a mist all round them,' though she did 'lean to believing this *class* of mysteries. . . . If it is credible that a person in a mesmeric sleep can taste the sourness of the vinegar on another person's palate, I am ready to go the whole length of the transmigration of senses'.

One of her sisters went into a swoon, and could not open her eyes. This was hideous and detestable to Miss Barrett's imagination. A friend of hers tried to get her to supply a lock of hair to send to 'a celebrated prophet of mesmerism in Paris'. She drew the same conclusion as Mrs Carlyle: it savoured of witchcraft and diabolical possession. If she had yielded, 'I should have felt the steps of pale spirits treading as thick as snow all over my sofa and bed, by day and night'.

She realised that she would be susceptible to mesmerism: 'I who was born with a double set of nerves, which are always out of order; the most excitable person in the world, and nearly the most superstitious. I should have been scarcely sane at the end of a fortnight, I believe of myself!'[13]

Far removed from the world of female neurotics was Charles Dickens. In 1838 he made friends with John Elliotson. In August 1840 Dickens dined with Elliotson and met the Reverend Chauncey Hare Townshend, whose life was spent searching for health in Europe and who had recently returned from studying mesmerism in Antwerp. At this meeting, Elliotson promised to instruct Dickens in the craft, and Dickens became an adept, practising successfully on his wife and his sister-in-law. He brought the new fad to the notice of Lady Blessington, whose salon at Gore House (which stood where the Albert Hall now stands) was a centre of early Victorian society, and who was ever eager to entertain her guests with new tricks.

A few years later Dickens and his family were in Italy, and whilst in Genoa they met the de la Rue family. Mr de la Rue was a banker carrying on business there, his wife was, according to Dickens, an 'affectionate, excellent little' woman. Mrs Dickens watched the friendship grow with misgivings; when Mrs de la Rue told Dickens about her hallucinations, the phantom which spoke to her, the crowd of creatures that pursued her with veiled faces, Dickens was convinced that he could help her with hypnotism, and when he and his family left Genoa Mrs de la Rue was concerned in case Dickens had attracted to himself her phantoms. All was grist to Dickens, and his venture into the occult spurred him to write *The Chimes*.

They met up again in Rome at the same hotel, and Dickens once more devoted much of his time to mesmerising Mrs de la Rue. Her worst times were between one and two in the morning; one night at this time, Mrs Dickens awoke, to find her husband pacing the floor in obvious terror. A night or two later about the same time, the banker knocked at their bedroom door; his wife needed help immediately. Dickens went with him, and found Mrs de la Rue 'rolled up into an apparently impossible ball. I only knew where her head was by following her long hair to its source'.[14] He treated her by stroking her, which caused her to unwind.

There was no question that Dickens had the true mesmeric personality. When his readings from his novels became as popular as the novels themselves, he could dominate an audience in the same way as the Calvinist Spurgeon could dominate his. His intense grip on an audience could result in hysteria on the part of the more suggestible, and before his rendering of the murder scene from *Oliver Twist* (Bill Sikes versus Nancy) a doctor warned him 'that if only one woman cries out when you murder the girl, there will be a contagion of hysteria all over the place'.[15]

In 1850 Charlotte Brontë met Harriet Martineau. Miss Martineau's interests in mesmerism were now being shared by cow-keeping experiments on a two-acre farm, but the author of *Jane Eyre*, plain, past thirty, with expressive grey eyes, was relentlessly canvassed. She was asked if she had been converted. 'Scarcely,' she replied, 'yet I heard miracles of its efficacy and could hardly discredit the whole of what was told me. I even underwent a personal experiment; and though the result was not absolutely clear, it was inferred that in time I should prove an excellent subject.'[16]

This uncritical attitude towards mesmerism, using the term as an umbrella under which to shelter the most widely differentiated ideas, was even adopted by the organ of the mesmerist movement, the *Zoist*, which provided a convenient platform for all sorts of cranks, mainly, the philosopher Herbert Spencer considered, because there was not enough mesmerist material available to fill its pages. During the early years of spiritualism, when table rapping was the standard method of communication by the spirits, mesmerists were inclined to think that the manifestations were a form of mesmerism; thus G. Sandby writing in the *Zoist* that 'this action of the table, induced by continued contact with a chain of human fingers, is nothing but simple mesmerism, developing itself in an unexpected phase'.

When the experts could not agree amongst themselves, when they persisted in muddling all kinds of causes with all kinds of effects, it was not to be surprised that the intermediaries between them and the public – the journalists – should also be flummoxed. The confusion was only amplified when a new term for mesmerism, electro-biology, was invented. Two journalists, Hamilton Aïdé and Alphonse Kerr, were flabbergasted when at a seance the table tilted and lifted and the lamp on it did not fall off. 'Either we were all "electrobiologised" – as the imposition of one will upon others was then termed – into believing we had seen this thing, or we had actually witnessed a phenomenal exhibition of magnetic force, reversing all the laws that have hitherto been understood to govern it.'

That people under hypnosis can be induced to say, and do, odd things, could be accepted, even by the periodicals and newspapers of the establishment. But that under hypnosis they could know things which they did not know before – this the respectable press would not stomach. The woman under hypnosis who sang the slave girl's song would have had to know the song beforehand. The medical journal the *Lancet* considered that mesmerism flourished 'wherever there are clever girls, philosophic Bohemians, weak women, weaker men'. The clairvoyance ostensibly shown by the mesmerized, suggested *Punch* ironically, could surely be adapted to practical ends. Could not a mesmerist officiate at the customs house so that it would no longer be necessary to open parcels and strew the contents all over the floor? The mesmerist would be able to see inside the parcels and save a lot of trouble. *Punch* regarded mesmerism much as did the *Lancet*: 'A new system of theology, and mental and moral philosophy, is making some progress in the world, especially among a portion of the superior classes, whose sense of pleasure is exhausted by enjoyment, and in whom an enthusiastic temperament is combined with a feeble understanding. This species of revelation is derived from the mouths of soothsayers who are generally either nervous and epileptic youths, or females afflicted with hysteria.'[17]

The link between mesmerism and spiritualism in the 'fifties was very close, and *Punch*'s fulminations above were to be repeated many times in many papers when spiritualism got under way. The operators and the audiences not only seemed the same – they were the same. The leisured classes found it all agreeably diverting, and only when spiritualism gave more sophisticated pleasures than table-rapping did mesmerism as entertainment languish.

2. The Birth of Spiritualism

The main story of spiritualism dates from 1848, when curious raps occurred in the presence of the Fox family of Rochester, New York. The pattern of these raps betrayed an intelligent source, said to be a murdered pedlar. The two principals in this tableau were the Fox sisters, who were fêted and encouraged to demonstrate their abilities in less parochial surroundings. This they did. One of them later recanted, and stated that she had made the noises by voluntarily cracking her knee joints.

In 1852, Mrs Hayden, the wife of a New England journalist, brought the movement to England. The middle classes took her to their hearts. 'In those days,' wrote a journalist nostalgically in 1856, 'you were invited to "Tea and Table Moving" as a new excitement, and made to revolve with the family like mad round articles of furniture.'

Initially, spiritualism was a parlour pastime, of no more religious significance than mesmerism. Its advent in England was nicely timed. There was a body of workers already trained in mesmerism and animal magnetism, together with their audience, conditioned to accepting miracles and cosmic phenomena. The idea of communicating with the dead was naturally more interesting to the merely curious than flames streaming from magnets or the singular ability of certain men and women to put other men and women into a trance, and spirit circles were an amusing way to spend the long winter evenings. It must be remembered that there were few rival entertainments; the theatre had been in decline since the days of Garrick; the melodramas and gimcrack shows of the time were not spectacles which the sensitive and the discerning would flock to. Although there were dozens of lectures going on all over London any day of the week, these were mainly directed at those classes – the lower-middle – most avid for knowledge.

The main opposition (in terms of entertainment) came from

the church, then passing through a gloriously mixed-up phase. Certain preachers received the same kind of idolisation now reserved for television performers. The Reverend Robert Alfred Vaughan was a parish vicar, but 'there were persons who travelled great distances, some more than a hundred miles on a Saturday, that they might be present at his Sabbath-day's service, returning home on the Monday'.[1] The news that the hell-fire-and-damnation preacher C. H. Spurgeon was to preach at the Surrey Music Hall on October 19th 1856, passed rapidly throughout London. 'In the squares, the streets, the lanes, the alleys, as well as in the workshops and counting-houses, all the chief places of concourse, it has been, through each successive day, the one great object of thought and converse.'[2]

One of Spurgeon's friends declared that ecclesiastically viewed it was one of the most eventful nights that had descended on London for generations, that it was the largest congregation a Nonconformist minister had ever had.

The *Saturday Review* observed sardonically: 'This hiring of places of amusement for Sunday preaching is a novelty, and a powerful one. It looks as if religion were at its last shift. It is a confession of weakness rather than a sign of strength.' A year or two later, Spurgeon preached in the Crystal Palace before 23,654 people.

Religion was big business. Theatre-owners and promoters of all kinds were envious of the money Spurgeon had taken at the turnstiles – £675 – and Spurgeon could afford to ignore the strictures of the established church, which classified him as one of 'the Barnums of the pulpit who draw large gatherings, collect large amounts, and preach many sermons'. The Church of England was not lacking in energy. Between 1826 and 1856 two hundred new churches were built in London alone.

The clergy had a captive audience, but did not realise that they were in danger of losing it. Tractarianism had split the clergy. Even those attracted to the High Church movement were uncertain whether to put up a picture of the Virgin Mary and have the bishops down on them, or to play it safe, hear confessions in secret, but drone on in the pulpit in the same old way.

This inner confusion transmitted itself to the congregation. The relentless religion of Spurgeon, smoking his cigars to the glory of God and revelling in his fame, was too much for them, the small-budget evangelical movements later to erupt into the Salvation Army were too austere, and there was a conservative aversion to comfortable but close-knit religious groups such as the Quakers. Those repelled by the High Church movement but anxious to stay within the fold of the Church of England found the Broad Church movement dogged with complicated theory; these were the days of the Higher Criticism imported from Germany, and the intellectual clergy were too preoccupied in trying somehow to incorporate fashionable philosophy, in particular that of Comte, into nineteenth-century Christianity, to bother about whether what they were preaching was relevant for, or indeed intelligible to, their congregation.

Spiritualism was not yet a religion but was all set up to be taken from a secular field. Just as spiritualism itself stemmed from America, so did its religious aspect follow thence. Astute clergymen recognised that spiritalism could offer something that nineteenth-century Christianity could not. Comte believed that all religion sprang from an attempt to explain the phenomena of the universe, but a new school of theologians denied this: 'it was not a philosophical want of a *theory*, but a moral want of a *revelation*, that prompted religious systems'.[3]

Spiritualism offered both. If communication with the dead was possible, then surely those on earth would have access to sources which would give a full explanation of all mysteries? As for revelations, these would presumably never end. The clergymen who viewed spiritualism as a religion first of all made certain that they got their messages from the top. St John, St Paul, and the prophet Daniel were among personages present at one of the first forays into religious spiritualism, the Apostolic circle of Auburn, New York.

The leading light in the Apostolic movement was Thomas Lake Harris. Born in 1823 in Fenny Stratford, Buckinghamshire, he went to America at the age of three. The movement had already acquired its ultramundane character when he joined it, but he speedily took control, persuading the others that he was a 'chosen vessel' and claiming to have visited celestial regions in trance. There was an outcry against this, and he moved from New York to Mountain Cove, Virginia, guided by Isaiah. He started a sect based on the common ownership of property. But Harris's divine gifts did not extend to keeping his colony going;

the families broke up, and money ran short. Harris found more disciples in New York, repurchased Mountain Cove, but the community did not flourish, and in 1861, shortly after returning from a preaching session in Britain, he started up again at Wassaic, New York, where he was joined by about sixty converts, including the Englishman, Laurence Oliphant, novelist, poet, member of parliament.

It is not surprising that the phenomena of spiritualism were *assumed* to have religious significance, long before spiritualism was generally regarded as a religious movement. The syllogism was simple: if the phenomena were not natural they were supernatural, if they were supernatural they came either from above or below, if they came from heaven they were good, if they came from the devil they were bad. Dr Charles Cowan in his *Thoughts on Satanic Influence, or Modern Spiritualism Considered* thought they belonged to the latter. 'Satanic Agency ... is at least equal to the production of the effects.'

It was an age of fervent religious controversy. In October 1850, a Papal Bull re-establishing the hierarchy of the Roman Catholic Church in England created a furore. The Prime Minister, Lord John Russell, wrote to the Bishop of Durham, denouncing the recent measures of the Pope as 'a pretension of supremacy over the realm of England, and a claim to sole and undivided sway, which is inconsistent with the Queen's supremacy'.

The piping screams of the new-born spiritualistic religion were scarcely heard amidst such a tumult. It was sniped at by narrow-minded clergymen who thought it spawned by Satan, and the fashionable society preacher Stopford Brooke dismissed the whole thing as a cheat, but some clergymen, disenchanted with the Church of England, found that they could associate themselves with spiritualism if they indulged in a little theological sophistry.

Spiritualism as a religious movement insinuated itself, it bent to the prevailing wind. Bishop Wilberforce's condemnation of spiritualism as savouring of witchcraft was gently ignored. Had the spiritualists been as arrogant as the Roman Catholics, had they proclaimed in the learned journals their divergences from Anglican theology, the forces of the establishment unquestionably would have paid more – and sterner – attention. Sitting in a darkened room listening to the voices of the dead was, in the abstract, more contrary to the dictates of protestant Christianity than the practices of the Roman Catholic Church. Many seances might well have been a kind of auricular confession. But by developing from a parlour game with occult overtones, spiritualism avoided any direct confrontation with the state religion, and when in 1855 the first spiritualist newspaper with avowedly religious aspirations started up – the *Yorkshire Spiritual Telegraph* – it was merely treated as one more organ of a Nonconformist movement that drained off some believers but was not a serious threat to the Church of England.

3. Table-rapping

The earliest spiritualist phenomena were table-rapping and table-turning. The operation was simple; a suitable atmosphere was conjured up, questions were asked, and the table replied in code, usually one knock or tilt for a no, three knocks or tilts for a yes. Table-rapping and table-tilting or turning were therefore very much the same.

An early enthusiast was Elizabeth Barrett Browning. Wintering in Florence, she wrote to a friend, 'Do your American friends write ever to you about the rapping spirits? I hear and would hear much of them. It is said that at least fifteen thousand persons in America, of all classes and society, are *mediums*, as the term is. Most curious these phenomena'.[1] Mrs Browning asked another friend, Miss Haworth, if anything of the kind had appeared in England. It had in Paris, where the tables were speaking 'alphabetically and intelligently'.

The entrepreneurs were cashing in on the occult mood. In Florence 'guaranteed' turning tables were being sold with the tag 'It Moves!' In London, crystal balls were all the rage, and the 'original' was bought by Lady Blessington from an 'Egyptian magician', though she admitted that she never got the hang of it. An optician in London was turning them out by the dozen. Lord Stanhope said, 'Many people use the balls, without the moral courage to confess it'.

When Mrs Hayden disembarked in 1852, she was acclaimed before she had transmitted a single tap. Her audience was undemanding. They were advised not to ask leading questions, but to accept what they got. Mrs Hayden was young, intelligent, yet simple in her manners, and was invited to perform before a select gathering in Cavendish Square. The audience included Mrs Crowe, Mrs Milner Gibson, Mr Colley Gratton, and Robert Chambers.

Mrs Crowe, the author of *The Night Side of Nature*, had a

vested interest in the supernatural, the source of her greatest success. Born in 1800, she spent most of her later life in Edinburgh. Of a morbid and despairing disposition, her interests in the occult fostered these tendencies, and she was frequently on the border of insanity. She had at least one major attack of mania. Mrs Milner Gibson was a fashionable hostess among the cognoscenti, and her *soirées* to meet the spirits were extremely popular as, narrated the journalist Edmund Yates, 'a substantial supper was a feature of the evening'. Her husband was an energetic politician who opposed the Crimean War. While his wife was prodding the spirits into action, he was engaged in getting the newspaper tax repealed; whether his wife appreciated this is debatable: newspapers found that debunking spiritualism was unfailingly good copy.

Colley Gratton was a minor writer, author of the completely forgotten *High Ways and Bye Ways*. On the other hand, Robert Chambers was a man of substance. Co-founder of the publishing house that bears his name, he was a person of great energy and talents, the author of seventy books, and the compiler of that marvellous medley of anecdote and fact, *Chamber's Book of Days*. At the gathering at Cavendish Square he reserved his judgment. During his lifetime he collected a mass of material relating to spiritualism, and wrote an inquiry into it which he never published. His final summing-up was this: 'The phenomena of spiritualism may be the confused elements of a new chapter of human nature, which will only require some careful investigation to form a respectable addition to our stock of knowledge. Such, I must confess, is the light in which it has presented itself to me, or rather the aspect which it promises to assume.'[2]

Prying journalists were surprised by the status of those actively encouraging Mrs Hayden in her taps, which were, declared Professor de Morgan, the mathematician, like 'ends of knitting-needles . . . if dropped from a small distance upon a marble slab, and instantly checked by a damper of some kind . . . Our readers would be astonished were we to lay before them the names of several of those who are unflinching believers in it, or who are devoting themselves to the study or reproduction of its marvels. Not only does it survive, but it survives with all the charm, and all the stimulating attractiveness of a secret society'.[3]

The addicts were even grander than the writer of the above

realised. Table-turning was a parlour amusement for Queen Victoria and Prince Albert. As early as 1846 the Queen had taken an interest in the occult; only by the existence of a watch with a curious inscription are we aware of these dabblings. The inscription reads, 'Presented by Her Majesty to Miss Georgiana Eagle for her Meritorious and Extraordinary Clairvoyance produced at Osborne House, Isle of Wight. July 15th 1846'. (Georgina Eagle died before the watch was presented, and the watch later went to an American voice medium Etta Wriedt).

The select gatherings at Mrs Hayden's sessions were well aware that there was 'secret society air about the whole thing',[4] and many of the participants were anxious to keep it that way. Even more keen to do so was the medium; three types of sitter were suspect: the sceptic, the journalist, and another medium or medium's confederate. In several instances a rival medium's confederate penetrated a seance to wreck the act. Being the first in the field, Mrs Hayden was for a time untroubled by professional jealousy, but before she left England in 1853 competitors had arisen. By then the earlier manifestations were becoming rather passé as other mediums were providing more of a show and were transmitting more elaborate messages than a mere yes or no. By May 1853, reported *Chambers's Journal*, the 'alphabet [was] used successfully behind the medium's back'.

Some of the rival mediums were not so prepossessing as Mrs Hayden, and sitters had to be persuaded that no fraud or trickery was involved. Miss Jennie Homer had her wrists encircled and her hands tied, foreshadowing the 'sixties and the 'seventies when mediums were subjected to all kinds of indignities: they were searched down to their drawers, they were handcuffed, with their necks in metal collars, and mild electrical currents were run through them so that if they broke the contact everyone would know. One medium, Mrs Roberts, considered that attack was the best method of defence. She had 'genuine spirit messages from the poet Shelley, containing many sentiments of a distinctly religious character', and also messages of more moment with regard to her professional career: 'Woe to you who believe in Mrs Hayden! Her spirits are false and wicked.' Mediums were now more discriminating in pairing spirits with subjects: for instance, Miss Eliza Finch decided that the Duke of Kent was a suitable spirit for Robert Owen, of whom the Reverend Stopford Brooke wrote, 'He took to spirit rapping at the close of his life, and I know no history which so clearly points out that atheism and credulity are brother and sister'.[5]

There were other sceptics. Sir David Brewster went to Cox's Hotel with Lord Brougham, aged and faintly disreputable, and there he saw 'several mechanical effects which I was unable to explain. But though I could not account for all these effects, I never thought of ascribing them to spirits stalking beneath the drapery of the table, and I saw enough to satisfy myself that they could all be produced by human hands and feet, and to prove to others that some of them at least had such an origin'.[6] He related this in the columns of the *Morning Advertiser*. He was speedily rebuked by others who had been at the session. William Cox maintained that Brewster had said to him, 'Sir, this upsets the philosophy of fifty years'. A stalwart of the spiritualist movement, Benjamin Coleman, introduced into the controversy a report of a dialogue he and Brewster were involved in:

Coleman: Do you think these things were produced by trick?
Brewster: No, certainly not.
Coleman: Is it delusion, think you?
Brewster: No, that is out of the question.
Coleman: Then what is it?
Brewster: I don't know, but Spirit is the last thing I will give in to.

This note of acrimony persisted when Sir David Brewster set out a theory for the mysterious raps: 'the repeated displacement of the tendon of the peroneus longus muscle, in the sheath in which it slides behind the external malleolus'. Three medical professors of the University of Buffalo in America had earlier come to the same conclusion when they had investigated the Fox sisters. They were convinced that the noises came from the deliberate dislocation and replacement of the knee joint; there were no raps when Professor Lee held the knees at the side (over the dress, one might add), or when the girls' legs were outstretched, the feet not touching. That this method of making the sounds was a reasonable hypothesis was confirmed from other sources, having nothing to do with spiritualism. In an account of one of his insane patients, Dr Forbes Winslow reported that 'rapid successive cracking of the joints of the fingers would be heard resembling slight electrical discharges; they were exerted by movements of flexion and circumduction, which she unceasingly performed'.[7]

It might be argued that intelligent sitters would surely realise what was happening; that at least they would know from which direction the sounds were coming. But in a darkened room in a tense atmosphere it was almost impossible to determine whence a specific sound came. Even at light seances a direction of the attention towards where the sounds *should* be coming from was sufficient. And where gadgetry was being used (a hollow boot heel, a battery beneath the medium's position under the floor-board with a metal plate, pressure on which would make or break a contact, an accomplice in the room below transmitting 'raps' through a hollow table leg) the production of the most exotic raps was child's play.

How were the raps produced? Even among the mediums there was a divergence of opinion. The most sophisticated view was that raps were caused by a protrusion from the medium's body of a long rod of substance having properties that distinguished it from all other forms of matter, namely ectoplasm. These rods of ectoplasm were invisible to the human eye but not to the sensitive chemicals on a camera plate, and could conduct energy in such a manner as to make sounds and strike blows, even at a distance. This hypothesis could account for raps that occurred in far corners of the room or on objects apparently picked out in an arbitrary fashion. 'These tiny indications of an influence ulterior to our own,' wrote Florence Marryat, 'are not necessarily confined to a table. I have received them through a cardboard box, a gentleman's hat, a footstool, the strings of a guitar, and on the back of my chair, even on the pillow of my bed.'[8]

In his book *Metaphysical Phenomena*, a Dr Maxwell explored in some depth rappings that occurred on or in his umbrella :

The raps in the open umbrella are extremely curious. We have heard raps on the woodwork and on the silk at one and the same time; it is easy to perceive that the shock actually occurs in the wood, that the molecules of the latter are set in motion. The same thing occurs with the silk; and here observation is even more interesting still; each rap *looks* like a drop of some invisible liquid falling on the silk from a respectable height. The stretched silk of the umbrella is quickly and slightly but surely dented in; sometimes the force with which the raps are given is such as to shake the umbrella.

When the raps occurred in the immediate neighbourhood of the medium, the concept of ectoplasmic rods was unnecessary. Mrs de Morgan described her sensation: 'As such raps seemed to be shot through my arm it was accompanied by a feeling like a slight blow or electricity and an aching pain extending from the shoulder to the hand which remained for more than an hour after they had entirely ceased.' The theory of rods of ectoplasm was also unnecessary when the raps merely served as a background noise, as in the novel *The Mediums* by J. H. Powell serialised in the *Spiritual Times* of 1864: '.... how he was to obtain an intelligible communication without putting interrogations was to him a most profound mystery. He lay a considerable time perplexing his brain with this problem. Meanwhile the unseen visitants kept up a serenade of rappings in all parts of his room.'

Powell is a partisan of the theory that the rappings were self-operating phenomena not needing the services of a medium, but most spiritualists preferred to think that when they sat around a table with their fingers pressed against the top they were helping to evoke the sounds. 'The table will appear to throb or vibrate under the hands as if charged with a kind of electricity. Do not attend to the supposition that this arises only from pulsation at the finger-ends produced by pressure.'[9] After the vibration the table would 'crack or creak' (Mrs de Morgan), 'make a very small throbbing or patting sound' (at Mrs Hayden's seances), or 'give a sort of crunch and bubble' (Mrs Everitt's seances). This was a prelude to either table-rappings or table-movements.

One should remember that the basic table of the table-rapping period was oval or more rarely circular, on a heavy single carved column. The top was slotted on to a platform fixed to the base, and kept in position by two or four long screws. Unlike tables on four legs, such tables always had a certain amount of play, and would naturally creak if uneven pressures were applied around the perimeter of the top.

Table-moving was a good deal more spectacular than rapping, and it became a centre piece in the performances of the early and middle period mediums. The most popular mediums were those who could guarantee spectacular shows, and some of them did not scruple to deceive. A cunning way with small tables was this: the medium had a ring, slit half way. There was a strong pin in the centre of the table. The medium edged the pin into the ring, and the table was easily moved. The larger tables, such as dining-room tables were also capable of dramatic movements. A confederate had a stout leather band around the wrist; this could conceal a strong iron rod which fitted into a small projection under the table, or into a slot. For very heavy tables the force needed was much greater, but a leather strap around the neck terminating in a sharp hook just above the bottom of the waistcoat could accomplish much. When the medium went into 'trance' he could convincingly drop over the edge of the table. The hook would catch the underside of the table, and the table could be tilted at will. The hands could be displayed, and the sitters would marvel. In seances lit by a flickering gas light this trick could be eerily impressive. It was common practice amongst fraudulent mediums to have the gas turned down before they began operations; frequently the gas was turned down too low, and went out. Before it was lit, probably in a fumbling nervous fashion by a confederate, the medium could organise his *modus operandi.* When there were two confederates, two blackened threads could work wonders. It was only a question of applying sufficient force at the right place.

This paraphernalia of conjurers and tricksters, or even the placing of hands on the table, was not always necessary to make tables move. A characteristic illustration was furnished by Mrs de Morgan: the table moved without being touched, and moved so energetically that a sceptic was pushed back against the sofa calling out, 'Hold! Enough!' At a session with D. D. Home, Mrs de Morgan saw 'the *thrilling* of the table', and a spiritualistic surgeon was moved to say that it was 'exactly like what takes place in that affection of the muscles called *subsultus tendinum*'. One of the most extraordinary narratives concerns two of the most intensely committed of spiritualists, the Reverend Stainton Moses and Serjeant E. W. Cox. On June 2nd 1873, Moses went to see Cox at his house in Russell Square. They had half an hour spare, and while Cox opened letters, Moses read *The Times*. During this half-hour there were frequent loud rappings on the table. Moses held the paper with both hands, put his one arm on the table, which responded with an 'ague fit', swayed to and fro, and went forward three inches. Would the table move without contact? The two men stood to the side of the table, poised their hands above it eight inches from the table. The table moved a little, rocked violently, moved a little more, then rose three inches one side and three inches the other. Moses held his hands four inches over the end of the table, and asked the table to touch his hands three times. The table obediently did this.

Although table-rapping was not susceptible to any great advances, it continued to be popular until the end of the century. As a way of transmitting messages from the dead, though, it was slow and tedious compared to the more dramatic ways of communicating with the hereafter which were found. The ultimate, of course, was the materialisation of the dead themselves.

With table-rapping and table-turning came the formal seance.

4. Seance

The seance is central in understanding the especial appeal of spiritualism. Rules for spirit circles were formally laid down, though it is doubtful whether all spirit circles conformed to them. The people who composed the circles should be of opposite temperaments, 'as positive and negative', not marked by repulsive disease, not obviously struggling under mental handicap. The number of persons should be not less than three, not more than twelve, eight being the ideal number. No person of a strong magnetic temperament should be present, as he or she would quash the power of the spirits. The room should not be over-heated, and should be well-ventilated; bright light was anathema to successful dealings with spirits.

The seance should open with a prayer or a song sung in chorus, and general subdued conversation was better than a wearisome silence; but sitters were requested to keep the talk cool, not to fly into discussion or argument. Pencil and paper should always be kept at hand, and once the sitters were there they should stay and not drift in and out of the room. Unpunctual people should be kept out. No seance should last longer than two hours (unless the spirits ask for an extension). A circle sitting for 'mutual development' should bar all sitters of bad habits and those of a violent or disputatious disposition; sitters should be prepared for anything to happen, and if they felt like singing, dancing, writing, or gesticulating, they should give in to these feelings.

Sitters were advised not to attribute falsehoods to lying spirits, as mistakes frequently happened. Finally, sitters should be aware that only one in seven had the requisite mediumistic qualities. 'The faculty often accompanies the sparkling dark eyes and hair of what phrenologists call the nervous-bilious temperament,' wrote Mrs de Morgan. 'Blue eyes and fair hair are also generally favourable, but great exercise of mediumship is likely to ex-

haust the more delicate constitution of the nervous sanguine.'[1]
Mrs de Morgan agreed with all the formulae laid down for the
best spirit circles, confirming that 'if one of the party becomes
drowsy as if mesmerised, and then falls either into a trance or
a series of strange contortions and movements, there is no cause
for fear'.

In the early seances, there was no need, ostensibly, for any
special arrangements, but when 'the earlier and most material
forms of mediumship, such as rapping and table moving [did]
not seem to be susceptible of any great change or refinement,'[2]
additional equipment was needed. For materialisation seances the
most dramatic piece was the cabinet, flippantly named the 'Punch
and Judy' cabinet. The medium remained in this, went into a
trance, and the 'spirit' emerged. This became the most popular
type of seance, for reasons that are not very difficult to see; it
was the area in which the most spectacular denouements and
disclosures of fraud were carried out. On a slightly more mundane plane was the face seance, at which spirit faces appeared
at a cut-out in a curtain or in the cabinet.

A typical set-up was one recorded in 1880 in Newcastle. It
was a cabinet seance, with the cabinet, measuring three and a
half feet by three feet in the corner of the room, reaching from
the floor to the ceiling. The frame was of wood, the panels
were of gauze, and there was a door, secured by two large screws,
the heads facing the sitters. A curtain was hung between the
cabinet and the sitters, who were grouped between seven and
ten feet from the cabinet. There was sufficient light to read a
watch by.

A manifestation seance without props occurred in February
1880, at the rooms of Mr Blackburn in Museum Street, Blooms-
bury. The medium was his protégée, Florence Cook, who lay
on a sofa close to a wall, the light behind her. The nearest
sitter was four or five feet away; the lights were turned down
very low, just sufficiently for the sitters to see white woollen
around the neck of the medium.

A typical run-of-the-mill provincial seance took place in East
Jarrow on January 13th 1889. The medium was a Mr Bowen,
and the sitters comprised eleven men, four women, and three
children. The medium's hands were tied to his chair legs; on
the floor were a banjo, a violin, a bell, and two slates. After

some singing and prayer the circle joined hands, the lights were put out, the slates floated about, the bell tinkled, the banjo was placed on two sitters' knees, the keys of the piano were struck, and the sitters were touched with a paper tube. The women and one man had their boots unlaced and taken off, and the boots were taken to sitters opposite. The whole session lasted one hour and twenty minutes. A refinement in the seances of Alfred Smedley, where the medium was a Mrs Wigley, was the provision of a padded box for the medium's feet. Mrs Wigley's hands were locked in stocks. During a dark seance bells rang and musical instruments played, which impressed Mr Smedley.

The sort of music used to evoke a sympathetic atmosphere could be tedious. The new disciple Lord Amberley suggested instead of a hymn a rollicking song, 'We won't go home till morning,' but although the spirits approved with agreeing taps, the spiritualists themselves were not so sure: 'His lordship is apparently a member of that section termed "jolly dogs", and to whom a "free-and-easy" is more congenial than a solemn seance.'[3] (Lord Amberley retorted that mediums were jugglers of the most vulgar order.) At another seance, William Crookes suggested 'For he's a jolly good fellow' on the logical grounds that this was the only tune the whole company knew. Again, the spirits approved, and joined the chorus with 'a sort of anvil accompaniment' on chairs and tables and things on the tables.

Seances quickly attracted cynical and amused observers. Charles Dickens found comical both seances and the people connected with them. His account of Mr and Mrs S. C. Hall, two fervent but humourless personages associated with spiritualism, sums up a certain species of Victorian. When asked whether Mr and Mrs Hall ever unbent, Dickens said, 'I believe that, once a year or so, they exchange a wink'.

Dr Alfred Schofield was an adventurous and lively doctor who knew many of the participants in spiritualism. He had come out against spiritualism, saying that the small portion of it that was not fraudulent was unmistakably evil. He and three other Harley Street doctors had been invited by W. T. Stead, the first of the tabloid journalists who had gone religious, to a house that had been lent to Stead in Regent's Park. The week before, two American spiritualists had produced Stead's dead son in his own house. To prove there was no fraud, Stead had borrowed a 'clean' house. The mediums, a man and his wife, were stripped to the skin and searched by two of the doctors; the man was then dressed in the footman's clothes, his wife in blouse, skirts, stockings and slippers. The woman was placed in a cabinet, the man placed in the middle of the audience. The audience all sat down, about seventy all told, professors from Oxford, spiritualists, society people always eager to sample any new stunt of Stead's. Schofield's account is laconic and precise.

I sat next to a well-known Duchess, and we all had to remove our gloves, and clasp each other's hands for over two hours. The gas was lowered, and several hymns were sung more or less discordantly; it was a treat to see the Oxford Professors and some of my learned friends doing their best. The first bomb-shell was then dropped into our midst by the new 'footman', who, evidently moved by the spirit of truth, stood up and declared that neither he nor his wife were spiritists but were society entertainers, and that he then offered £100 to any hospital in London if anyone could produce the phenomena that he would show them that afternoon.

No one moved, for the spell of collective hypnotism was already working. Mr Stead, however, rose on my left, and told us not to mind the man, for they *were spiritists*, though they didn't know it, and that he had a message from Mr F. W. H. Myers on the other side that the seance would be a wonderful one.[4]

The gas was lowered, and Stead suggested that the audience in couples should hold hands and go into the cabinet to see that there was no fraud. The duchess and Schofield went in, and he asked the medium to give them a good show; she replied, 'That will be all right'. When the audience was satisfied that there was no fraud, the husband called out, 'Are you there, colonel?' A hoarse voice from the cabinet replied, 'All right'. What looked like quicksilver to Schofield appeared in front of the cabinet. It was a luminous foot, and it was followed by a silver leg. The medium came out 'shining all over' (with phosphorus paint) . . . Mr Stead looked at her very steadily, and at last seemed to recognise his aunt. He explained that this was her materialised figure from the other side, and that the medium was sitting in the cabinet all the time. And then the second bomb-shell fell. In a clear voice the luminous figure said: 'No, I ain't, I'm here.'

The medium came out of the cabinet three times, and then the audience was allowed to go one by one and peer in at her while she contorted her face (transfigurations). Schofield suggested to Stead that the medium had taken some gauze and luminous paint into the cabinet with her, and Stead was furious, especially as he had been informed by the spirit of Myers that the whole thing had been a wonderful manifestation.

An interesting sceptical account came from an anonymous journalist in 1871:

> I went boldly in, and found myself in a small, stuffy front parlour, over a bookseller's shop. It was a room divided with folding-doors, and provided, as Houdini would have arranged it, with two means of exit. There were two long tables in the front rooms, a piano in one corner, and a sofa. The windows were carefully closed, and the evening being very hot, the atmosphere was naturally oppressive. On the walls were some crazy-looking pictures, some of clouds that here and there disclosed a lurid-coloured face, others that looked like geometric puzzles. On the tables, which were much dinted at either end, as if from blows, were several speaking-trumpets, of a funnel shape, and constructed of stiff brown paper, in one or two instances covered with gold tinsel, which rendered them theatrically impressive.[5]

The audience totalled fourteen; they were 'wandering about the apartment in a hot, nervous, altogether uneasy manner, though trying to appear perfectly accustomed to the spiritual world. Some looked at the pictures with vague wonder; while the sceptics took up the tubes, and talked through them in corners in hoarse and assumed voices'.

The two mediums had been mingling with the crowd, and eventually separated themselves. One had a cast in the eye and a strong accent, both had large, red, muscular hands 'strong enough to help the spirits in supporting any reasonable table'. The mediums divided the sceptics from the believers, seating them round separate tables – it would improve the conditions, they said. The lights were put out, and there was a deal of hysterical laughing and nervous inquiry. One of the mediums began to groan and gurgle, the gas was turned up, and the believers declared that the spirits were starting their work. A lady suggested a hymn, and 'Power of Love Enchanting' was sung, 'adapted to some feeble spiritualistic words'. It was getting hotter, and raps broke out under the table, and one of the sceptics was hit very hard on the head with a speaking-tube. There was a plethora of raps, and kicks, and someone exclaimed, 'Rest, rest perturbed spirit'. A small mild man was attacked with the speaking-tube about the face and head, but made no effort to ward off the blows, though whiningly imploring the spirit to leave off. 'The spirits did not patronise those who were seated near the middle of the table and farthest from the mediums, unless a wildly-flung antimacasar sofa-pillow or table-cloth happened occasionally to reach them, and keep them going.' Some of those not favoured complained; one of the mediums spoke up: 'If I were the spirits, I'd throw a bucket of water over you there!'

Two hard objects struck the table. The lights were turned up. To the journalist they reminded him of ornaments he had seen earlier on the mantelpiece. He was struck in the face by a cushion, but kept silent, though everyone else who was suffering was cooing with delight. He felt spirit legs probing at him under the table, but said nothing. He had heard that mediums prophecied sudden death and mayhem. He did not want to be involved, longed for the end of the session, and was not stimulated when one of the mediums announced that the best condition for seances was frostiness – and, of course, the ten-shilling seances were better than the half-crown ones. 'I had heard and seen strange things,' ended off the journalist ironically, 'and yet, somehow or other, they hardly seemed supernatural.'

The Reverend Charles Maurice Davies was fortunate enough to see many of the celebrated manifestation mediums of the early 'seventies. Mrs Holmes of Old Quebec Street encouraged sceptics, and at one of her circles where she was 'sitting for faces', twenty-seven persons were present. Mrs Holmes was tied to her chair, and violins, guitars, tambourines and bells flew about. Davies had a violin bow stuck down his back and a guitar in his lap, a tambourine around his neck and one up his arm. But these were only hors d'oeuvre to the main course, the face seance. The folding doors between the front and rear rooms at Mrs Holmes's house had been replaced by a large black screen with a peephole eighteen inches square in the middle. The doors were dramatically locked, and the audience waited for things to happen within that peephole. They did not have long to wait. There was a 'ghostly-looking child's face', and a face with a 'strange leaden look about the eyes'. A young man 'surveyed his resuscitated papa calmly through a double-barrelled opera glass'.[7] Summing face seances up, Davies wrote, 'Spirit faces no longer interest me; for I seek among them in vain the lineaments of my departed friends. Spirit hands I shake as unconcernedly as I do those of my familiar acquaintances at the club or in the street'.

In the early eighteen-fifties when spiritualism first came to England, the circles were select and the participants knew and could vouch for each other. As the years went by, the number of mediums and circles grew, and audiences were admitted more casually. Audiences naturally looked for a good show; the potential for exploitation was obvious. The Dialectical Society sponsored an inquiry into spiritualism in the late 'sixties; at their seances they advocated orderliness in the conduct of the seances, a quiet, but not particularly passive demeanour, quietude in the house – servants in bed and domestic noises stilled – and a 'somewhat moderate' supply of light.

As for the quiet, let us consider a seance held under the aegis of the celebrated Mrs Marshall. A spiritualist enquirer, Hain Friswell, stated to the Dialectical Society investigation committee that the party at the table 'foamed at the mouth and shook each other. They then began to talk nonsense and to prophesy'. It may be possible to reconcile this with the suggestion in the rules that persons at a seance should feel free to dance, sing, or gesticulate when the mood took them. Mrs Marshall had her own viewpoint; she denied that foaming at the mouth had occurred, and, indeed, at any of her seances the shaking of other members of the party was not condoned. 'The only approach to it was on one occasion when a person calling himself Captain Stuart, and a party of friends came to our house, and after obtaining some striking phenomena, they pretended to be greatly affected; one

48

of them rolled about the floor, tore his hair, and foamed at the mouth; but we found afterwards that Captain Stuart was a well-known actor, who with his friends, had come to amuse themselves by imposing upon our credulity.'[8]

The performances of 'Captain Stuart' may well have made the evening memorable to the more credulous of Mrs Marshall's sitters. But such occasions were frolicsome, and there was no intention of wrecking a seance. Much more of a danger to the well-tempered seance were the deliberate attempts of rival mediums to disrupt seances. This could be a hazardous business; if the medium was in a trance it could injure her. At the very least it could spoil her programme, alienate her audience, ruin her professionally.

Although they were assailed with advice ('Mediums! don't be content in ignorance because you are mediums. Make yourself worthy of the companionship and inspiration of exalted spirits, who seek to raise humanity from grovelling vice, materialism, and superstition'[9]), the mediums did not need anyone to tell them their trade. Ultimately they had to have results. If they did not get them their paying audience would desert them, or – if they were unpaid mediums (and even some of the most blatant frauds were unpaid) – they would lose a cherished reputation. There was professional rivalry, professional hatred.

In the 'seventies, a three-cornered battle broke out between Mrs Guppy, Florence Cook, and the Holmeses. The Holmes family, though they did not endear themselves to the Reverend Mr Davies, had a high reputation, though when they returned to America they suffered a good deal of indignity by being 'exposed'. In January 1873, Mrs Guppy called on them to gain their co-operation in a crazy scheme to fix the prettier and more successful Florence Cook. Three of Mrs Guppy's myrmidons were to attend a seance of Miss Cook's, wait for a favourable opportunity, and then throw vitriol into the 'spirit's' face, hoping thereby to ruin Florence's features. Mrs Guppy confessed to Holmes that Miss Cook had taken all her friends away from her, friends on whose patronage Mrs Guppy depended. Holmes declared that while Mrs Guppy was telling him this she seemed to be possessed by a legion of fiends, and that her rage at Florence Cook and her 'doll face' was fearful. Holmes ordered her out of his house, and wrote to Mr Guppy, a very minor figure whose duty was to write up his wife's manifestations saying how wonderful they were, declaring that she was not to go to his house again. When Guppy called with tears in his eyes to smooth things over, Holmes remained steadfast.

So Mrs Guppy turned against the Holmeses. A month later, James Clark, one of the three men who was to have thrown vitriol at Miss Cook, turned up at a Holmes session. Manifestations were going nicely, there were instruments floating and being played in mid-air, when Clark lit a match. The instruments fell. Clark was staring fixedly; Holmes went to him, and asked him who had told him to light the match. Clark retorted, 'I told myself'. Holmes ordered him out of the room, then changed his mind and detained him. The sequence of the events was noted by Stainton Moses, who wrote in his notebook that he had been brought into it and that he denounced Clark as a cheat. Mrs Guppy intended to go one better, by having the Holmes cabinet broken up by a gang headed by a photographer named Henderson.

Holmes naturally felt like revenging himself on Mrs Guppy, and threatened to expose her. His comment makes a most interesting footnote to the spiritualist scene: 'If necessary, I can give you the details of the infamous transactions of Mrs Guppy with Miss Emily Berry, 1 Hyde Park Place, also why Mrs Guppy used her pretended mediumship for base purposes, and gave seances solely for assignation meetings to better certain disreputable parties to further carry out their lewd propensities.'[10]

This is a case of dog eating dog with a vengeance. By the time Holmes had made these insinuations, he and his wife were back in America. The implications are pretty clear. Mrs Guppy was using her seance rooms as an introducing house, which, with the night-house, was such a feature of the Victorian scene. There was a deal of clandestine activity at seances. Frequently the sexual element was explicit. It was widely believed that the scientist William Crookes had an extended affair with Florence Cook before and during the period when Mrs Crookes was having her tenth child, and that he was party to Miss Cook's deception, though this is still the subject of learned disputation. It is certainly true that Myers's interest in young lady mediums was not solely due to their spiritualistic talents.

Florence Cook and her sister Kate were doubly at an advantage in that they not only had a sympathetic and influencial manager in William Crookes but also a rich backer in Charles Blackburn. But this may have made them bold, and therefore vulnerable. In January 1880, Florence Cook was giving a seance under the auspices of the British National Association of Spiritualists. To this seance went Sir George Sitwell and his friend Carl von Buch; it was the third one of Miss Cook's they had been to. The first was negative, at the second the spirit of 'Marie', Miss Cook's control, appeared, but Sir George detected a corset beneath the ghostly garb. As Marie was supposed to be twelve years old, this seemed strange. On the third visit Sir George was accompanied by John Fell, an engineer, and when Marie appeared she was grabbed, the curtains that separated the medium from the audience were drawn aside, the medium was found to be gone leaving behind stockings, boots, and other clothes. Miss Cook was certainly Marie.

The *Daily Telegraph* took the opportunity to indulge its sense of righteousness. 'Spiritualism as an imposture is the more shameful because it trades on grief. From small beginnings and an obscure propaganda it now impudently assumes the dignity of a religion. "Professors" live by it, indulging themselves in idleness and luxury at the expense of public credulity.' The *Telegraph* could have pointed a portentous finger at American seance events :

Smash! Down came a black-jack on the head of a man who tried to force open the cabinet, which, by this time, was found to be barricaded by a heavy wooden partition and secured by means of a stout spring lock. It resisted the united efforts of three men who tried to kick it down. The two men who had been inside succeeded in dragging out the woman and stripped her of a cheap, cheese-cloth garment with an elastic neck-band and short sleeves of such a size as might be worn by a girl of sixteen.

Whack! Smash came a stove-lifter down on the head of a curiously disposed individual, while three or four sluggers in the employ of the establishment made a grand rush to cut off further investigation.[11]

In his comment on this tableau, Frank Podmore wrote, 'This, it must be remembered, was at a spiritualistic seance, where, if ever, the most elevating of all the soul's aspirations are supposed to be centred'. The defrocking of mediums pretending to be spirits became such a regular occurrence, that even the most gullible spiritualists were forced to admit that no materialising medium was above suspicion. W. T. Stead, a fairly recent convert and editor of *Borderland* and therefore doubly committed, almost conceded defeat.

> The phenomena of spiritualism, at least so far as relates to the materialising of spirits, seems to be much less frequent in London at present than they were some years ago. During these investigations I have made great efforts to obtain the services of a trustworthy materialising medium who has not at any time been detected in fraud ... The net result of my inquiries came to this: that, in the whole of the United Kingdom, so far as was known to the spiritualist community, there was only one person of undoubted materialising faculty and undoubted character who could almost always secure the presence of phenomena, and who had never been detected in a trick of any kind ... I refer to Mrs Mellon, late of Newcastle-on-Tyne whose success as a materialising medium is undoubted.[12]

Stead could hardly have fastened on a more unfortunate choice. Mrs Mellon had been investigated as early as 1875, when, as Miss Fairlamb, she had done a double turn with Miss Wood. The investigators were Sidgwick, Myers, and Gurney, later to form the nucleus of the Society for Psychical Research. There was some minor inconclusive phenomena, a small form that might have been a doll or drapery, a rather larger form that might, suggested Mrs Sidgwick, be a woman on her knees, a brightish irregularly shaped object, that might have been the pillow provided for one of the mediums. Miss Fairlamb refused to be searched on one occasion; when reminded that she was flouting the pre-set conditions of the seance series, she said that she had agreed to be searched but only *before* a session, not afterwards.

One of the guards against trickery was a tape around the ankle. After one seance, the tape was creased, strained, dirty, apparently handled and pulled. The 'indications of deception were palpable and sufficient, and we were not surprised to hear a few months later that a more aggressive investigator had violated the rules of the seance, and captured Miss Wood personating the "spirit" '. Myers was always prepared to make allowances if the mediums were young and pretty. He wrote to Sidgwick in December 1876, 'Miss Fairlamb is supposed to be somewhat distraite at present on account of an *amoureux* with whom she often wants to be going out instead of sitting: – but thus small, thus natural, thus transparent, seem to be the workings of the mediums' hearts and minds!'

When Miss Fairlamb married Mr Mellon, she continued her career, but the doubts entertained by Barrett and his colleagues were shared by her new audience, who collectively suspected that the spirit forms Mrs Mellon was showing off were really Mrs Mellon herself. At a seance on October 12th 1894, a Mr Henry suddenly seized Mrs Mellon in the guise of a spirit emerging from a cabinet; she was on her knees, with a muslin-like material around her head and shoulders. She struggled while Henry asked for the light to be turned up; someone struck matches, and it could be seen that she had a mask of black material over her face, sleeves up above the elbows, skirt hitched up, and her feet bare. The matches were blown out, and two or three men attacked Henry, Mrs Mellon's husband, grabbing at his throat and tearing off his tie. Inside the cabinet was a false beard, a small black shawl, some old muslin, shoes, stockings, and a cotton bag nine inches square with black tapes attached to it.

Well might Frank Podmore comment that 'the history of materialisation, so far as professional mediums are concerned, is practically one unbroken line of fraud'.

The entire pattern of the Victorian seance was predictable, almost a mirror of the social pattern. First of all cosy and simple, then quasi-religious, then heavy and ostentatious leading to extravagance and exoticism, finally falling into confusion in the 'nineties, with the investigators honing their weapons on the unfortunate mediums, the religious element being trodden underfoot, and the instruments of science dealing harshly with what had been unexampled phenomena. There was also a turning away from physical phenomena; psychical researchers were moving towards what is now known as ESP. Extensive experiments with thought transference under reasonable test conditions were being carried out, and these did not engross the general public who had been so feverishly interested in the uncanny and in the promise of life after death.

The collapse of the seance formula was also predictable. As soon as qualified investigators moved in after the formation of the Society for Psychical Research in 1882, investigators who would not be emotionally upset if the phenomena were true or false, the intense and hysterical atmosphere of the traditional seance was dispersed. The medium Mrs Everitt might write nine hundred words in six seconds under trance in the provinces – in Japanese at that – but she would have been hard put to it to do the same thing before the eagle eye of perhaps the best investigator of them all, Mrs Sidgwick. A fellow member of the Society for Psychical Research, Professor Barrett, wrote, 'Mrs Sidgwick's adverse testimony is the most damaging blow which Spiritualism, or rather a certain class of Spiritualistic phenomena, has yet received'.[13]

Mrs Sidgwick could spell sudden death to the fraudulent medium. A typical case is the medium Edward Bullock, operating in 1876. Mrs Sidgwick was at a series of four seances; at the first three nothing happened. Mrs Sidgwick suggested that this was because the medium was accompanied by his mother who warned him that conditions were unfavourable for fraud. On the fourth occasion, Mrs Sidgwick placed herself so that she could see the medium outlined against a background as daylight was filtering into the seance room. The sitters held hands round a drop-leaf table, the medium twitched, leaned forward over the table, but kept his hands held by adjacent sitters. On the table were a musical box, a tambourine, and a bell. They were moved about, and the inner and outer lids of the musical box were opened and shut. Mrs Sidgwick thought that the medium had done this with his nose and teeth. The tambourine floated in the air; the medium's head and body moved from side to side with an object like the tambourine projecting from his mouth. Mrs Sidgwick considered Bullock to be deliberately cheating.

This dark seance was followed by a so-called light one. The medium's hands rested on his knees. He sat behind a curtain, disclosing to the sitters his legs up to the hands. 'Presently we perceived that a handkerchief was placed on the left knee so as to bear a coarse resemblance to a hand, and subsequently by looking closely, the hand on the right knee was discerned to be a left hand. Lights then appeared, tambourine and bell were vigorously moved about in the cabinet, &c. Afterwards, in the course of futile attempts to draw the musical box into the cabinet, an arm was exhibited with a sleeve very like the medium's. We then observed the handkerchief slowly removed and the hand substituted, and the seance was at an end. Just before the removal of the handkerchief, it was observed that the hand on the right knee was now a right hand.'[14]

Mrs Sidgwick noted ironically that probably Bullock was not a really skilful performer, and may have acted wisely when he dropped the role of medium and acquired that of exposer of spiritualism. When the renowned medium Williams was confronted with the formidable Sidgwick family he chose discretion, and over seven seances only one thing occurred, the transposition of an ornament from mantelpiece to table at the very time when Sidgwick let go the medium's hand to greet a latecomer to the circle. Yet amongst the provincials, Williams's name was one to conjure with, and at a seance with Alfred Smedley of Belper, there were lights over the room, a bell left the table, small child-like hands touched the sitters, an armchair was magically transported on top of a table, there was a slightly illuminated cloud, and the upper portion of a man holding a light. Still, Smedley could be impressed by anything, even a musical box that played the bass notes only and not the treble.

Not surprisingly, there was panic among the mediums, and the agonised hysteria spread to devotees of the cause. The editor of the *Occult Review* obviously had a vested interest in the continued success of spiritualism: 'I know, for I have proved Spiritualism to be true. And though every medium now living should recant, and every Spiritualist of the age desert the pure white standard of its faith, I will uphold that standard, if I must do so alone. I will proclaim the truth of Spiritualism with my latest breath on earth, and the first I draw in the spirit world.'[15]

At times, it seemed as if every medium then living *was* recanting. A great blow fell on spiritualism when the first heroine of the movement, one of the Miss Foxes who had heard those rappings long ago in 1848 in provincial New York State, turned on her heel and proclaimed, 'Spiritualism is humbug from beginning to end. It is the greatest rubbish of the century . . . Every so-called manifestation produced through me in London or anywhere else was a fraud. Many a time have I wept, because, when I was young and innocent, I was led into such a life'. With friends like this, spiritualism did not need many enemies. Wearily, those same defenders of the faith who had explained that when mediums personated spirits it was during somnambulism informed the laughing sceptics that Miss Fox, now Mrs Jencken, did not know what she was saying, that she was sodden with drink, that her outbursts meant nothing.

But the seances went on. There remained a core of believers for whom recantations and exposures were evidence that Satan was still there, fighting against the true religion, and like the editor of the *Occult Review* they would proclaim the truth of spiritualism with their last breath on earth, confident that they would be drawing fresh breaths in the hereafter. They were a good deal more sanguine, one might say fortunate, than Henry Sidgwick; after twelve years close and persistent research, he came to the reluctant conclusion that life after death was a dubious hypothesis.

5. The Appeal of Spiritualism

Spiritualism and the resurgence of the occult found fertile soil in Victorian England: the sophisticated and educated classes *wanted* to be credulous, the unsophisticated and uneducated classes *were* credulous. They wanted marvels and wonders, things that never were on land or sea, and because Victorian England was a capitalist country subsisting on the law of supply and demand, they got them. A Mr Corsterphine of Glasgow was near the mark when he wrote, 'Much of the success of the spiritual movement will depend upon the phenomenal – the people seem anxious for it. They have been lectured, preached to and at, and the literature has been scattered broadcast among them, but the cry is "Show us our dead!" '[1] Spiritualism provided a respectable fulfilment of this desire.

When bored audiences asked for something more dramatic, they were sneered at as vulgar and sensation-mongers. Not surprisingly they sniped back: 'An individual in search of a little amusement might advantageously turn [to a spiritualist church] were it not for the preliminaries in the way of mysterious invocations and hymn singing that have to be borne . . .'[2]

In mesmerism, the favoured person was the sensitive; the exact parallel in spiritualism was the medium. As spiritualism spread, it was discovered that more people than might be expected had mediumistic gifts. More to the point, those that had none thought they had. There is a grudging tone in Mrs de Morgan's account of seances with a medium named Jane, who was 'always most successful when sitting beside me, and is I judged from that circumstance that *some* share of the power of transmission belonged to myself'.

This desire to share the kudos of mediumship was especially pronounced when the medium belonged to one of the lower echelons of society, as Jane did. Mrs de Morgan sneered at Jane's education. No matter from whom the message was emanating the spelling was Jane's ('butiful' 'riting') 'except on some rare occasions when educated persons were present whose strong medium power, as I conjecture, overcame hers'. Mrs de Morgan took a shrewd look at Jane, as a phrenological object. 'The organ called "individuality" was small in her.' She compared ill with Mrs Hayden. In Mrs Hayden's forehead 'all the perceptions were large and full'. It was a comfort rather than otherwise when Jane died from consumption, but as the lower classes could not be trusted to tell the truth, Mrs de Morgan was gratified when shortly before her death Jane solemnly swore that the messages she had transmitted were really from the other side. Whatever lower class mediums received in the way of messages or visions, they were sure to be raw and unworked and needing the civilised attention of their betters. Jane talked of visions and curious dreams, and these appeared to Mrs de Morgan 'to convey a splendid symbolism, the application of which she did not understand, but was able to appreciate when it was explained to her'. Many of the mediums were also stupid. The scientist Baron Rayleigh was particularly harsh on Mrs Jencken, who, as Miss Fox, was the earliest of the early birds (she sparked off the spiritualist movement in America in 1848): 'Mrs Jencken seems to me to be rather a fool, and if this be so the phenomena must be genuine, as no fool could do them as tricks.'[3]

When mediums were of gentle birth they were appreciated to a greater extent than their innate talent warranted. Perspicacious mediums who realised that their background did not suit their image clothed it in mystery. If they were slack in tying up the minor details, utter confusion could result, as it did in the case of Miss Goodrich-Freer, who invented a suitable background with more enthusiasm than discretion. Operating for some time under the portentous pseudonym 'Miss X', Miss Goodrich-Freer tried to impress her more class-conscious clients with the information that she was the first woman to be a Fellow of the Royal Society (untrue), that she had county connections (untrue), and that she walked between six and twelve miles every day in all weathers (also untrue – the Victorians were great walkers and climbers and the lie was well designed to impress).

Her most careless error in inventing a false autobiography was uncertainty about her date of birth. Her obituary in the magazine *Folklore* gave it as 1870. If that were so she could hardly have been friendly with Jane Welsh Carlyle (died 1866) as she claimed, though this applies to, if one considers her more reliable birth-date (1857).

Miss Goodrich-Freer was beset by a difficulty common to mediums of sensibility: would she be treated as an equal in the houses she visited or would she be treated as a sort of part-time domestic, someone with a status between a housemaid and a housekeeper? It was small wonder that she threw herself with gusto into the affairs of the newly-formed Society for Psychical Research, for when she went investigating on their behalf she was assured of some social standing; she was not a guest who was not quite *persona grata,* and she was not a parlour entertainer.

The gap that separated the mediums from the class they particularly wanted to impress could not be bridged, no matter how fervently this was desired by both groups. It was the golden summer of the English upper classes, and the assurance and confidence they exuded acted on the mediums as a goad. They became pretentious and pompous, and the exhortations and mystical addresses that had proved so efficacious when dealing with the middle classes sounded empty and flatulent. The middle classes, especially those sections aping the upper classes, were no more ready to accept the mediums as their social equals, but they were more easily imposed upon.

The continuous appeal of spiritualism was in reverse ratio to a group's sophistication. The fact that Queen Victoria and her court experimented with table rapping gave spiritualism a cachet, but her particular clique was considered decidedly *passé* compared with the salons of the fashionable society hostesses, Lady Blessington in earlier days, Lady Molesworth and Lady Waldegrave later.

The tendency of all nineteenth-century movements was towards the institutionary: tenets needed to be codified, methods of procedure had to be formalised. But institutionalisation leads to schism. Just as this happened in nineteenth-century socialism in Britain, which split off into the Social-Democratic Federation and Fabianism, it happened in theosophy, from which splinter groups, such as the Hermetic Society were constantly breaking. Positivism was more integrated; it had a following of intellectuals, and its propagation was principally through the salon, the leading one of which was Mrs Hertz's in Harley Street, operating from 1875 onwards.

Had the spiritualist movement been directed with single-minded purpose there is little doubt that it would have achieved more than it did, but its disciples had come into it with widely diverse aims and backgrounds. To the more modest, it was a development of Christianity, a more progressive form in tune with the times; to the speculative spiritualism could be equated with the traditional Christian sects. For Catholics, it could be the time-honoured formulae in a fresh guise, as it was to Isobel, Lady Burton, writing on Boxing Day, 1879: 'However, as I am a Catholic, and Catholicism is the *highest order* of Spiritualism, what to "Scrutator" is a force or spirit is to me simply my angel guardian, and who is to me an *actual presence,* to whom I constantly refer during the day, and who directs everything I ask him to.'

Yet there were others for whom spiritualism was a substitute for Christianity: 'Theology has much to answer for, the teachings of the sects have paralysed the true springs of the human soul, and given it in exchange nothing but dogmatic garbage. There is a thick crust of materialistic doubt clinging to all religious faith, and we fail to see the spiritual realities around and about us, because we have been blinded by prejudice and dogmatism.'[4]

Not surprisingly, splits in the movement occurred at fairly regular intervals, and the various splinter groups were catered for by a wide range of spiritualist newspapers and periodicals, some of which branched out in eccentric ventures of their own, trying to integrate into the movement Egyptian mythology, vegetarianism, anti-vaccination and anti-vivisection. The main element of spiritualism – the reality of an afterlife – seemed sometimes forgotten, or deliberately ignored in favour of personal aggrandisement. The columns of self-congratulation on the part of editors of spiritualist newspapers are endless. The efforts by James Burns to instil the idea into his readers that he was a long-suffering martyr sacrificing all home comforts for the benefit of the Cause are never less than ludicrous: 'We felt the shadow of years of suffering and toil enveloping us, and moved in our work, as the hands do on the face of the clock, with no purpose of their own, but obedient to the unseen power within.'

His colleagues were associate martyrs, never quite so important as Burns: 'Large number of brave men and women who have formed and held circles, organised public meetings, and given platform addresses, have kept the lamps which light poor blind mortals to the higher life, well trimmed and burning.'[5]

Nevertheless, the spiritualist newspapers performed a service for their cause by keeping a widely dispersed audience welded into some kind of cohesive body. Not that they kept the audience especially well informed; the ventures into peripheral matters such as vegetarianism assumed the proportion of hobby-horses, the rambling and abstruse speculations in theology had little appeal to the majority of the readers. But away from the heady waters of the metropolis, a large body of believers had sprung up, who never lost sight of the principal object of spiritualism — reunion with the dead.

When the dilettantes had dropped spiritualism for some other novelty, the army of believers culled from the labouring, artisan, and lower middle classes, went on, finding in spiritualism a meaning that was lacking in everyday life. Almost any future state would be better than the one they suffered now, and they were assured by platform speakers that if they struggled on all would be put right in the future. They fervently grasped this straw in the same way as their more mundane contempories in factories and mills were reacting to platform speakers promising them an idyllic existence when they banded together to form trade unions. There was a little nervous flirtation between spiritualism and grass-roots socialism.

James Burns was right when he said that there were men and women sacrificing a good deal to keep the lamps burning and well-trimmed. Some of the organisers of group circles, rallies, and meetings were altruistic; some knew that they would have their reward in the hereafter. They worked hard with sometimes intractable material, using methods adopted from evangelicalism. They shrewdly realised that the best way to get adherents was to catch them young, and there sprang up over the country a large number of lyceums, catering solely for young people. There was a certain amount of poaching from Sunday schools, but the existence of the lyceum did not represent a threat to the Sunday school movement (the Sunday school union was founded in 1802; in 1878 there were 4,204 schools, in 1892 6,162).

The programmes of the spiritualist lyceums were varied, but they included invariably calisthenics, marching, recitations, and lectures on subjects not normally associated with spiritualism – physiology, astronomy, geology. Some of the lectures were hard going for the youngsters – 'How the bony framework of man was constructed' and 'Bones of the skull' – and some were abtrusely irrelevant. The truth is that the lyceums operated on a shoe-string, and had to be content with what lecturers they could get, irrespective of subject.

The Victorian was an age desperately keen on education and self-improvement, a time when working men who had just done ten hours down a mine pored over English primers at Mechanics' Institutes. Nevertheless, the lyceum was never more than a partial success, the organisers were always lamenting poor attendances, and some of the reasons for lack of support were pathetic. Twenty-three 'scholars' turned up at a Bradford meet in January, 1889, instructed by seven 'officers', not enough for marching, so they sang a song, appositely titled 'Think gently of the erring one'. At the Middlesbrough lyceum there was a tangible reason for a low turn-out for a meeting in March 1889: 'We are sorry to see our number decreasing, owing to being without a harmonium player.'[6] A census was made in May 1889. Fifty-seven lyceums were asked to submit returns, thirty-eight did so; total children 2,457, total officers 437, and taking into account the lyceums who had failed to make returns, the estimated total was 4,353. Hardly the kind of figures to encourage those who believed the future of spiritualism lay in the coming generation.

Amongst the grass-roots supporters of spiritualism who sent their children to lyceums, who bought and sought succour in the pages of the spiritualist papers, who were glad that their kind of spiritualism still made obeissance to Christianity, there was no money to be spent on the materialisation mediums who caused such a stir in London. They had to rely on local talent, whose manifestations were pale copies of those occurring in London. At one provincial seance frequented by a goggling parish reporter a 'piece of cardboard shaped like the back of a hair-brush suddenly moved from the table and began to float about over our heads. Once I noticed that it came in contact with the chandelier, but beyond a slight recoil there was no perceptible check to its movements'.[7] He also had his leg pinched, the host's smoking-cap thrust on his head, and unseen hands played an American organ in a corner of the room. Where materialisations were carried out, they were almost parodies of the shows put on in the capital.

To cope with the mass demand for enlightenment, spiritualist institutes were formed, halls were rented, and open-air meetings were organised; the curricula were more secular than those of the spiritualist churches, but there was a similar formula. Very much the same thing was happening at the Miners' Old Hall, Hetton, as at the Spiritualists' Free Church, Macclesfield. Hymns and psalms were sung, there were inspirational addresses under or out of trance, there were educational lectures on subjects that came under the umbrella of spiritualism (phrenology was particularly popular), and there were evenings of clairvoyance. So far as the audience was concerned, the latter was the basic feature of the evening, and pagans at the meetings were willing to sit through a sequence of hymns and rambling, wheedling rhetoric to see what the clairvoyant would say. Institutional spiritualism still exists, the pattern unaltered in a hundred years.

Lectures could be informative, comforting, promising, exhorting. Typical titles for 1889 lectures were 'Be thou faithful unto death, and I will give thee a crown of life', 'Is Spiritualism a Fact or a Folly?' 'Life is a vessel, God the Captain, and the angels as sailors', and 'The good time coming'. In Newcastle-on-Tyne, the leading lecturer was Alderman Barkas, and he included Calvinist tenets in his addresses – men who behaved like animals would continue as animals in the afterlife, and there was some doubt whether they had a future life at all. Where messages were especially fatuous they could be ascribed to controls: 'Wisdom is what is wise. Wisdom is not folly, and folly is not wisdom. Wisdom is not selfishness, etc. Wisdom is not evil, etc. All is not wisdom; all is not folly.'[8] It hardly needed an oracle to enunciate these.

It might be supposed that nothing that happened at spiritualist meetings could offend, but there was a good deal of sniping from the local press and rival bodies, the Salvation Army being particularly energetic. In January, 1889, the *Middlesborough Watchtower*, the local organ of the Salvation Army, roundly declared that 'the Trinity of evils in Middlesborough is composed of ritualism, spiritualism, and gambling'. In the following month, the newspaper *North Star* poured scorn on 'the table-tipping white-sheeted trumpet-tootling medium performances of the professional entertainer, or the hysterical imaginings of very nervous people'.

The demand for mediums to cover the provincial circuit was great. In London there was no shortage of potential mediums, the only difficulty there being to keep them quiet and submissive in the face of genuine talent. The provincials were not so self-assertive, content to be an audience, and those who felt that they had the necessary psychic qualifications were encouraged. A. D. Wilson of Halifax urged them on. 'The best way to gain information and confidence touching this matter is to ask the opinion of various intelligent spirits, and if the replies coming through several media, all corroborative of each order, tend to encourage the sitter in the desired direction, then I should certain say, Persevere.'[9] (Note the plural form of medium.)

The mediums doing the provincial circuit were a collection of amiable hacks, spiritualist journalists, eccentrics, and mediums who for one reason or another had quit the London scene. There was little money to be made, even in the London suburbs. Between October 1888 and February 1889 the Notting Hill sector had held thirty-six services and two public debates. The cost had been £19 9s. 5½d., the receipts £19 12s. 0¾d. Adventurously, the Sunderland circle decided to buy an organ. With 232 regular enthusiasts, it might be supposed that this would be no difficult thing to accomplish, but they only managed to raise £8 6s. 11d.

There arose a kind of trade union of mediums. Certain mediums had their specialities, their pet lectures (Miss Walton of Keighley favoured 'Where are our dead?' which she used everywhere), and their rights were not infringed by their colleagues. They had their get-togethers. There was a tea-party for mediums at 92 Ashted Row, Birmingham, on March 7th 1889 (a shilling each). The centre piece of the party was the exposure of a photographic plate, and participants were invited to bring their own unopened plates to see what would transpire.

It was a precipitous existence, and most mediums were part-timers, keeping the details of their day to day life away from their audiences. Mr Vango of Islington was in constant demand on the London suburban circuit, but when he was thrown out of his job as a ledger clerk he decided that humiliation was preferable to indigence, and asked through the columns of a spiritualist newspaper for £10 so that he could start a newsagent's business, backed up by a fellow medium who asserted that he had most convincing proofs of an outside intelligence acting through Mr Vango.

The circuit was concerned when mediums failed to turn up at meetings, but mediums too had their complaints. They went to meetings only to find someone else holding court, and they plaintively totted up the cost of the train fare and other expenses, while new mediums had great difficulty in finding their venues, the most lordly-sounding meeting hall being hardly more than a shack down a grubby side-street. There was also concern when mediums who had ventured on circuit turned out to be not merely eccentric (eccentricity could be accommodated in this field as in no other) but downright mad. This was sometimes hinted at in spiritualist newspapers: 'The writer's peculiar symptoms show that he is one of those organisms to whom mediumship would be injurious rather than beneficial.'[10]

Mediums who were doing stout work, keeping the lamps trimmed and burning, were usually allowed their little quirks, their private theories. Miss S. A. Power of Birmingham had not endeared herself to the spiritualistic press as she had attacked them for pandering to the public, but her contention that every article of clothing that we have ever worn is waiting for us 'to redeem' in the afterlife was given a sympathetic hearing.

Provincial spiritualism was dogged by faults of communication between the platform and the audience. A full hall did not necessarily mean aspiration; it could mean that it was cold outside, that there was no rival entertainment, and that anything, even a session of hymns, was better than nothing. A New York pseudo-enthusiast put it bluntly in 1856: 'Come, let us go in and see Kate Fox. It will cost you nothing; Good show; cheap.' Provincial spiritualism needed lecturers with a charisma, someone like Charles Bradlaugh who invariably got good audiences when proclaiming atheism, or the society preacher Bellew with his lavender gloves. Too often they got stodge. The medium was not the message. The audience wanted the phenomenal, the magical, they wanted to be shown their dead, and so often they were disappointed and disillusioned.

The provincial groups started with a bang, ended with a

whimper. The West Hartlepool Institute was typical. Started in high excitement in May, by June the temperature had cooled: 'The night was exceedingly unpropitious, being stormy, wet, and cold. The room in which the meeting was held was very commodious, the attendance was meagre in the extreme, probably less than thirty adults. The singing, which should be an accomplishment that all Spiritualists should aspire to acquire, was not up to the mark. Such a combination of untoward circumstances could not fail to damp the spirit and enthusiasm of the meeting.'[11] This may serve as the obituary to many a brave spiritualist project.

6. D. D. Home's Gift

A wide gulf lay between provincial and metropolitan spiritualism, but this was not so wide as the one between the followers of the itinerant part-time mediums and the devotees of the fashionable society mediums of the time. No one took much notice of Miss Walton of Keighley or Miss Power of Birmingham except the spiritualist newspapers, but the famous mediums such as the Davenport Brothers or D. D. Home were fêted and reviled.

D. D. Home dominates English spiritualism from 1855, when he arrived in England from America, until 1870. These were the golden years of Victorian spiritualism, and after his retirement no one was able to take up his mantle. If only for one reason: Home was never detected in any fraud.

Men and women who scorned the vulgarities of lesser mediums cultivated Home. He did not make spiritualism respectable; he made it fashionable.

One of those who went to a seance with Home was H. T. Buckle, and he was sufficiently impressed to wish for further seances. Buckle had heard about Home through his journalist friend, Robert Bell, who covered spiritualism in a widely-read article in the *Cornhill Magazine*. Buckle had an intelligence of the highest order; master of eighteen languages, his *An Introduction to the History of Civilisation in England* represents Victorian scholarship at its best. At this seance, Home caused a circular dining-room table to leave the floor and float in mid-air. Buckle would not admit to the force being supernatural, but commented that he knew of no existing physical law that could account for the phenomenon. Home visited Buckle after the seance, anxious that the newcomer to spiritualistic phenomena would realise how much importance Home attached to his testimony. Buckle was willing to arrange further seances with Home, but the second volume of his *History of Civilisation* was being prepared for press and such further seances would have to be postponed until he had returned from an extensive trip on the Nile. On this trip Buckle died suddenly, and no further meetings had been possible in the meantime.

Another person of consequence who was prepared to pay more than passing attention to spiritualism was Edwin Arnold. Playwright, *Daily Telegraph* journalist, poet, and orientalist, Arnold's *The Light of Asia* was once considered a work of transcendental importance. Arnold was no cloistered poet; it was he who arranged for H. M. Stanley to discover the course of the Congo. Like Buckle, Arnold would have been a valuable ally to spiritualism. He was asked by the committee of the Dialectical Society to state his attitude towards spiritualism. In a letter dated July 10th 1869, Arnold stated that he regarded 'many of the "manifestations" as genuine, undeniable, and inexplicable by any known law, or any collusion, arrangement, or deception of the senses, and that I conceive it to be the duty and the interest of men of science and sense to examine and prosecute the inquiry as one which has fairly passed from the region of ridicule'.

Like Buckle, Arnold did not see why the phenomena should be supernatural, but they were demonstrations of 'mental and vital power' that should be further investigated. He agreed that there was so much fraud and folly about that there was a danger of throwing out the baby with the bath-water.

A writer of a quite different order, E. L. Blanchard went to a large number of seances given by Home and Mrs Marshall, and attested his interest and involvement in spiritualistic phenomena. Blanchard was a leader of the Bohemian theatrical set, a writer of pantomimes; in his late teens and early twenties he was a staff writer of the sharp and scabrous satirical weekly *The Town*. Acquainted with the underworld tricks of the London sharpsters, he was not the man to be taken in by clever legerdemain.

Less impressive is the adherence of Geraldine Jewsbury. When in her thirties and forties she wrote a series of novels that achieved a good deal of success, but she is best-known today as the twittering friend of Thomas Carlyle. John Ruskin also went to a number of Home's seances, and was claimed as a true believer by Mrs S. C. Hall, that avid collector of likely celebrities. Ruskin was anxious to obtain the spirits of the great Italian painters of the past, but there is no evidence that he ever succeeded. He was drawn into spiritualist circles by his friend and proxy-mother, Lady Mount-Temple, the former society hostess Mrs Cowper. At one seance Ruskin was impelled to recite a poem beginning 'O Christ, save my soul, if Thou think'st it worth the saving' while the table beat time, the sound, to Ruskin, being descriptive of the time when he memorised the poem, 'when the earth was as iron and the heavens were as brass to me'.[1]

To Ruskin, belief in the hereafter was no academic exercise. The spirits of the Italian painters may have been his ostensible target, but more important to him was the possibility of the ghost of Rose La Touche appearing. She was a young child with whom Ruskin was in love; her mother forbade Rose to have anything more to do with Ruskin, and the delicate and otherworldly girl died. In 1876 at Broadlands, the country seat of the Mount-Temples, her ghost was seen beside Lady Mount-Temple and Ruskin. In 1878 Ruskin had an attack of madness, and in 1881 he tried to evoke the dead girl, and 'got in my own evening thoughts into a steady try if I couldn't get Rosie's ghost at least alive by me, if not the body of her . . .'[2]

Lady Mount-Temple was anxious to keep out of the limelight, though she recruited her sister-in-law Lady Fanny Jocelyn and Lady Londonderry as seance sitters. Lady Fanny Jocelyn was one of Queen Victoria's Ladies-in-Waiting, the daughter of Lord Roden; she was related to Roden Noel, homosexual poet, friend of Oscar Wilde and a frequenter of fashionable seances. Lady Londonderry was one of the society queens of the period, comparable with Lady Jersey, but like Lady Fanny Jocelyn and Lady Mount-Temple did not think it desirable that the fashionable world should know that she had been to seances and seen tables dance (the most common phenomena of the society seances), though Lady Mount-Temple admitted that she felt no interest in worldly things, only the spirit-world.

Like his fellow-novelist Dickens, Thackeray was at one time a magazine editor. Under his auspices, Bell's celebrated article *Stranger Than Fiction* appeared in 1860 in the *Cornhill Magazine*. Dickens never let the chance go of poking fun at spiritualism, but Thackeray was less critical. No records exist of the seances Thackeray had with Home, but he unquestionably added considerable cachet to the movement.

In 1855 Home went to Florence. The English in Florence were

less hidebound than their contemporaries at home, and openly goggled at the phenomena Home was producing. One of those most impressed was the expatriate American sculptor, Hiram Powers, for whom Home produced spirit hands. At this time, Home had the entrée to the most influential cliques of London, and his sitters included Lady Hastings, and perhaps the most influential woman in the London of her period, Lady Walde-grave. She was the leading Liberal party hostess of the 'fifties and 'sixties, holding court at her house at Strawberry Hill, Twicken-ham. The fascination of Home also extended to the most im-portant society preacher of the day, J. M. Bellew, who introduced the painter Frith to his spirit circles.

W. P. Frith, the painter of *Derby Day* and a vast range of genre paintings, had acted as a confederate with the playwright Sothern in pretended seances, and an experience with the medium Mrs Marshall had made him sceptical about spiritualism. There is no doubt that Mrs Marshall was one of the most blatant cheats of the spiritualist circus, and Frith had caught her out. At a seance Mrs Marshall was assisted by a young woman she called her niece; the phenomena were very tame, consisting of a spirit, helped by a candle, dropping coins into a tumbler beneath the table. Frith looked beneath the table and saw the niece picking up the coins with her naked toes and dropping them into the tumbler.

Sothern, a practical joker of the most obstinate kind, went to see Mrs Marshall accompanied by a friend, John Toole, a comedy actor much in demand for droll roles. Sothern pretended to be awe-struck by the phenomena, rolled on the floor and foamed at the mouth (helped by a piece of soap), biting the aged medium's leg in the process.

Home made a Continental tour in the late 1850s, returning in 1859. His engagement book contained the names of the one-time Lord Chancellor, Lord Lyndhurst (born 1772 and thus almost a candidate for spiritship), Lord Dufferin, the painter Landseer, the politician Henry Grattan, Lady Downshire, the Duchess of Somerset, and Lady Salisbury. Landseer was suffic-iently pleased with Home to give him a painting of his dog. The society octopus was bringing in new seance members; Lady Londonderry brought in Lady Milford, and the foremost jour-nalists of the time were paying court to Home, including

Matthew Higgins of *The Times*. Home was taken up by Lady Shelley's set, and paid several visits to her home at Boscombe.

The distinction must be made between Home and the run of the mill mediums. Home was not only believed to have aristocratic connections – the anecdotalist J. O. Field roundly asserted that he was an illegitimate son of one of the Earls of Home – but he acted as if he had. He was at ease in the aristocratic circles in which he moved, whereas most other mediums were painfully aware that they were not. But the allegiance of his sitters was confirmed by the simple fact that he was never detected in any fraud or double-dealing.

Although she was an obvious partisan, the assertion of Home's widow that 'during the presence of Home in England, the interest of English society in spiritualism grew as rapidly as, on his departure, it declined,' was true. She went on to say that 'the void that he left there was none to fill,' and maintained in *The Gift of D. D. Home,* written in 1890, that the 'decaying feebleness' of spiritualism then contrasted sharply with its vigour in the days of her husband twenty or thirty years earlier. She felt that Home had been betrayed by English society, and that members of society had been battening on Home, that they were forcing him to live in a manner he could not afford, leading to the Mrs Lyon fiasco. Unquestionably, they got Home on the cheap; he did not charge for conducting seances. If he had, it would have been a commercial transaction and the names he wanted to cultivate would not have come.

A way was found to support Home. In the summer of 1866 the Spiritual Athenaeum was founded with Home as secretary. It was hoped that fashionable society would support this in an appropriate manner, and Home's friend Dr Gully of Malvern endeavoured to drum up custom. However, the 'stupid people' were afraid of having their names mentioned, and stipulated that if they did join it the Spiritual Athenaeum must be a secret society. Mrs S. C. Hall was anxious that the Athenaeum should assume a semi-religious character, that candidates should attest to their belief in orthodox Christianity, and that the reading-tables should contain only approved publications. Not surprisingly, society people were not over-excited by this prospect, and the five pounds a year subscriptions were slow in coming.

Had the Spiritual Athenaeum been differently constituted, had it been an institute for honest enquiry and experiment then it might have prospered as the Society for Psychical Research did fifteen years later. The SPR was never short of aristocratic members.

When the Lyon law suit broke in the years 1867 and 1868, the upper classes deserted Home in droves; their own ranks were racked with scandals, but they were scandals that were carefully kept hidden from the prying eyes of the world.

Mrs Lyon was seventy-five years old, hysterical, illegitimate, shabby. But she was rich. She had married in 1823, her husband had died in 1859; he left her a large sum of money, and she had between £15,000 and £20,000 of her own. Before he died, Lyon had told his wife that she would only survive him seven years. The seven years were now up. In an effort to avert this stroke of ill luck, Mrs Lyon went to see a man named Sims, who put her on to Home. Home had been on the scene for eleven years, and it was a critical time for him. He had joined the Roman Catholic Church, and had recently been expelled as a sorcerer. Two years before, Browning had castigated him in *Mr Sludge the Medium*:

> I know it's folly and worse
> I feel such tricks sap, honeycomb the soul,
> But I can't cure myself: despond, despair,
> And then, hey, presto, there's a turn o' the wheel. . . .

Mrs Lyon wrote to Home at the Spiritual Athenaeum in Sloane Street, but received no reply, and two or three days later she went there, and met Home. To her delight, Home got through immediately to her dead husband, and raps spelled out 'I live to bless you, my own precious darling'. Mrs Lyon gave Home a cheque for £30, and asked him to call on her at her lodgings in Westbourne Place. Home did so a few days later; the messages became more explicit. Home 'is to be our son; he is my son therefore yours,' and the table jumped with joy. And there was more to come. Home was to be independent. Somewhat parsimoniously Mrs Lyon gave him £50 but when the dead Mr Lyon came through a day or two later he indicated that £700 per annum was a more likely figure. At this stage, S. C. Hall, a pious spiritualist, editor of the *Art Journal* from 1839 to 1880, an immensely prolific producer of art coffee table books of the period (he and his wife edited and produced upwards of five hundred works of one kind or another), was brought into the business, and he and Mrs Lyon calculated that it would be necessary to transfer £24,000 to Home to establish this income. On October 10th 1866, Home and Mrs Lyon proceeded by cab from Bayswater to the City, accompanied by gleeful raps, and when the transaction was effected, Home went to Malvern, the home of the celebrated Dr Gully, part quack, part homeopathist.

Early in November, the spirit of Mr Lyon spoke again: Home was to take the name of Lyon; a month later Home had a bonus, £6,000 for a birthday present. The lawyers concerned with this transfer of money were bemused. Arthur Jones of Basinghall Street was there when the birthday gift was arranged, and he saw Mrs Lyon caressing Home and calling him 'dear boy'. When asked if he thought Mrs Lyon was mad, he was non-committal. It would be logical for him to think that Home was on to a very good thing.

In January 1867, mortgage securities to the value of £30,000 were transferred to Home, and fortified by this true independence, Home visited Hastings, Torquay and Plymouth. During this period Mrs Lyon seems to have had doubts about her adopted son, and from March Mrs Lyon ceased signing herself 'your affectionate mother'. The spirits settled her doubts about her husband's somewhat malignant promise that she would join him seven years after his death, and surely they would co-operate in this new situation?

Mrs Lyon was in two minds about it all, and when Home turned up on June 10th she was so affectionate, said Home, that he 'repulsed her'. The following day Mrs Lyon asked for the return of the trust deeds. She was in a state of great agitation and fear. Had not Home been expelled from the Church of Rome as a sorcerer, was he not by common consent the most powerful medium operating in the 'sixties? Spiteful acquaintances warned her that in all probability she would be killed in her bed, and advised her to lock her door. But Home was more concerned with the defection of his fairy godmother, and seeking to lower the temperature he wrote to her on June 12th, beginning 'My darling mother,' a letter Mrs Lyon did not deign to answer.

Four days later, Home tried again, this time addressing her as 'My dear mother,' and offering her peace terms: a four-part treaty by which she would acknowledge the personal honesty of Home in writing, Home would drop the appendage of Lyon, she would return the jewels he had given to her, while he would return two rings she had given to him and, finally, he would keep £30,000. This was not to Mrs Lyon's liking; on the following day Home was arrested and incarcerated in Whitecross Street prison.

The action at law was followed eagerly, and the reports of the trial received top billing in *The Times*. The court was crowded by sensation-seekers, by mountebanks who had been reviled by Home (no respecter of fraudulent colleagues), by friends of Home and by the fashionable. 'All the town is angry with the story,' said Mrs Hall.

Mrs Lyon cut a ludicrous figure in the witness box, and cross-examination made her seem to be utterly deranged. Here was a woman who had married the grandson of the eighth Earl of Strathmore, who had honeymooned at Glamis Castle, who was living in thirty shillings a week lodgings, and who was carrying on with a man young enough to be her grandson. The questioning took on a tone as if she were in the dock, and Mrs Lyon reacted violently, accusing the Lord Chancellor, not remembering letters she had written, and growing resentful when extracts from her private memorandum book were read out. (Home was, she wrote, 'a greedy, fawning, sneaking hypocrite'.) She interrupted witnesses who were hostile. When her affectionate behaviour on the occasion of Home's birthday present of £6,000 was being described, she screamed out, 'False, false, false!' Damaging evidence by a servant at the lodgings drove her to hysteria – the girl was a 'saucy, dirty, dangerous, story-telling slut'.

The opponents of spiritualism had their laughs. Mrs Fellowes related that once when she cracked a biscuit, Mrs Lyon called out, 'That's a spirit rapping!' Stumbling over the facts, the old woman became yet more disturbed when counsel probed the precise relationship between her and Home. She had once kissed him, but only on the forehead: 'You see, I am not so fond of kissing.' As for marriage, she found it repulsive and distasteful; she still cherished her husband's memory.

That the relationship between Home and Mrs Lyon was not as chaste as Mrs Lyon made out was hinted at by a witness, Gerald Massey: 'A more cynical looker-on might have surmised a something too fond or fervent;' while S. C. Hall detected a fierce possessiveness in Mrs Lyon's behaviour, reporting her as declaring 'I am his only mother; I have bought him with a price, and now he is my own'.

In between her tirades at hostile witnesses, Mrs Lyon pathetically attempted to establish her identity as an educated woman, claiming to have read Josephus and Bishop Colenso.

Although Home was being pilloried in public in a manner that in retrospect seems outrageous, although his personal life was being scrutinised in a manner reminiscent of the Inquisition, although his finances were being examined with cruel energy, he still managed to preserve an odd dignity. It might have been supposed that the trial would crack the enigma of Home, the only medium thus far never caught out in sharp practices. Yet it only confirmed Home as the most important figure in nineteenth-century spiritualism. Although the principal figure in the trial, he remained somehow outside it, a tall, thin man with broad, square shoulders, suggestive, according to Dicken's ace reporter W. G. Wills, 'of a suit of clothes hung upon an iron cross'. His hair was long and yellow, his teeth were large, glittering, and sharp, and his small, red-rimmed rolling eyes gave the impression of a medieval warlock.

It is probable that had Home remained an adoring pseudo-son, had he remained at the side of his 'mother' instead of departing to the west country when his independence had been confirmed with large sums of money, his financial future would have been secure. Likewise, had he been a less successful medium, the new mediums Mrs Lyon had visited, who had had bones to pick with Home, would not have been so malignant.

The truth about Home will never be known. If one dismisses the whole fabric of Victorian spiritualism as humbug, self-deception, and fraud, it is difficult to account for him. We will meet him again during the chapters on seance phenomena, and compared with the tawdry party tricks of his contemporaries his activities have an extraordinary assurance.

His pre-eminence in his field helped to bring him down. He rose high and he had a long way to fall.

With one blow spiritualism lost the allegiance of the aristocracy. Lesser mediums tried to appeal to the gentry by introducing apposite names into their spirit messages. Susan Horn, a medium from America, received a message from Prince Albert: 'I pass much of my time in dear Old England,' and Princess Alice, second daughter of Queen Victoria, 'hoped the kindergarten system of education for the young would be more generally adopted on earth, and that she herself had established one in the spirit land'.

Two men who were on the verge of receiving the society plaudits that Home had enjoyed were the Davenport Brothers. Ira was born in 1839 William in 1841, the sons of a police official in Buffalo, New York State. At early ages they succeeded in evoking raps, the movement of cutlery, and levitation. In 1857 a committee from Harvard University investigated them; the Davenport Brothers were beginning to make a speciality of untying themselves after being trussed up.

Several factors worked in their favour. They were men of presence; although not gentlemen they were polite and appeared to be more anxious to produce phenomena than take money; and they had a good public relations staff travelling with them, the Reverend Dr Ferguson, pastor of a large Nashville church, Mr Palmer, formerly an operatic manager, and William M. Fay, husband of a noted medium.

Their first London seance took place on October 11th 1864, in the house of Dion Boucicault. Boucicault was an important figure in mid-Victorian London; the author of 140 plays and adaptations, he was at the height of his fame. The audience at this seance was distinguished and the novelist Charles Reade and Lord Bury were present.

The difference between the Davenports and the other mediums of the time was that the Davenports put on a production. There was no dreary singing while the spirits were being materialised, and even their sternest critic, the conjurer J. N. Maskelyne, admitted that 'the Brothers did more than all other men to familiarise England with the so-called Spiritualism, and before crowded audiences and under varied conditions, they produced really wonderful feats. The hole-and-corner seances of other media, where with darkness or semi-darkness, and a pliant, or frequently a devoted assembly, manifestations are occasionally *said* to occur, cannot be compared with the Davenport exhibitions in their effect upon the public mind'.

The Davenport brothers began to give public seances at the Queen's Concert Rooms, Hanover Square, interspersed with private seances, and these continued for several months. They were taken up by the same people who had given their attention to Home, but their stock was lowered in February 1865 when they visited Liverpool. They were tied up in a manner that was described as cruel and savouring of torture, and the audience invaded the stage, breaking up their cabinet. This was considered to be capital fun, and at Huddersfield the same thing happened, though this time the police interfered.

This led to the Davenports cancelling any further engagements in England and going to Paris, where they operated for Napoleon III and the French Court, then to Prussia, Belgium, and Russia. In January 1867 they gave a seance in the Winter Palace at St Petersburg, for the Tsar. Like Home, the Davenports were confirmed in their social acceptability by the patronage of European royalty, and when they returned to England in April 1868, they received a rapturous welcome. At this date, Home's reputation was on the decline, and the Davenports could have taken over his role but they preferred to return to America.

There was a deal of animosity against them. The other mediums looked askance, considering them mere society entertainers, while the conjuring profession were reproducing their phenomena at the Egyptian Hall. The Davenports' phenomena were certainly less spiritualistic than those of Home. Those mediums who conceded that the Davenports were spiritualists, as the brothers themselves claimed, maintained that they were under the control of 'very low' spirits and that there was no uplift in the performances. In retrospect there does not seem much difference between the Davenports and his rivals Maskelyne and Houdini.

The Techniques of
Spiritualism

7. Seance Phenomena

On Tuesday, April 13th 1869, H. D. Jencken, the barrister husband of Kate Fox, attempted to bring the various phenomena of seances into some kind of order. He enumerated the following categories:

The movement and raising of ponderable bodies, including levitation of the medium.

The production of raps or knocks.

The uttering of words, sentences, sounding of music, singing, imitations of birds.

Playing on musical instruments, the drawing of flowers, figures, and writing by direct spiritual unseen agency.

The fire test.

Elongations of the medium's body.

Holding fluids in space without bottles or containers, the perfuming of water, the extraction of scent from flowers, or alcohol from spirits of wine.

The appearance of hands, arms, and spirit forms.

He appears to have omitted one important category: the sudden appearance of objects. The production of apports was one of the specialities of Mrs Guppy. At a seance on December 14th 1866, Mrs Guppy, then Miss Nichol, succeeded in having the table half-covered with flowers, including fifteen chrysanthemums, six anemones, four tulips, and half-a-dozen ferns. At a seance with the Spiritual Society of Florence in 1869, she was asked if spirits could distinguish colours. A noise was heard on the table, lights were put on, and there was a heap of coloured sugar plums. The lights were put out again, there was a rattling, and when the lights went up the plums were sorted into colours. Mrs Guppy repeated her success with the society, and produced a shower of fresh flowers, a large lump of ice a foot long and an inch and a half thick which hit the table so hard that it broke. It was put into a dish as it was melting. The room was warm, and the seance had been going for an hour when the ice appeared. Mr Guppy stated that the ice would have melted had the block been there all the time. At seances with Mr and Mrs Adolphus Trollope and Sir Augustus Paget, flowers appeared. Mr Trollope's hands and arms were found covered with jonquil flowers. Mr Guppy asserted that had the flowers been in the room all the time, their scent would have betrayed them. Mrs Guppy had been searched, and her clothing rigorously examined, the doors had been locked, and the windows were fastened.

At a seance in October 1868, the then Miss Nichol was asked by her sitters for fruit, and she obliged with a banana, two oranges, white and black grapes, filberts, three walnuts, a dozen damsons, a slice of candied pineapple, three figs, two apples, almonds, dates, pears, pomegranates, greengages, currants, lemon, and raisins. 'Why does not someone wish for vegetables, such as a potato or an onion?' asked Miss Nichol. As she was speaking, a potato and an onion fell into her lap.

The slice of candied pineapple would seem to imply that real pineapple was not available to the spirits. The selection includes the kinds of things that greengrocers would be stocking up for Christmas – the session was in October. There are no exotic items, nothing that the medium could not have got from a quality shop.

The investigators would seem to have pointedly neglected Mrs Guppy. No doubt they considered her phenomena to be too ludicrous to be worth spending time over. How were they produced? D. D. Home, who took time off from exhibiting phenomena far in advance of anything Mrs Guppy did to rap fraudulent mediums over the knuckles, suggested that apports were carried under the voluminous skirts of the mediums. Admittedly, in at least one of the instances above Mrs Guppy was searched, but as the search was carried out by Mrs Trollope, a staunch believer, this could have been perfunctory, for, as Frank Podmore wisely pointed out in 1897, 'The whole of our social structure is based on the assumption that normally constituted men and women will not cheat or lie without sufficient motive'.[1]

The central item on Mrs Guppy's agenda would have been

expected by the sitters, and little thought would have been given to the mechanism of the apport. As for the sceptical.

> When a person of nervous temperament, not strongly independent in thought and action, enters a spiritualistic circle, where he is constantly surrounded by confident believers, all eager to have him share their sacred visions and profound revelations, where the atmosphere is replete with miracles, and every chair and table may at any instant be transformed into a proof of the supernatural, is it strange that he soon becomes affected by the contagion of belief that surrounds him? He succumbs to its influence imperceptibly, and hesitatingly at first, and perhaps yet restorable to his former modes of thought by the fresh air of another and more steadfast mental intercourse, but more and more certainly and ardently convinced the longer he breathes the seance atmosphere.[2]

If the search of the medium's clothing had been proficient, what then? There were always opportunities for the medium to slip back to the cloakroom after she had been searched, for a call of nature, to fetch a handkerchief, to call on smelling salts if taps and rappings had particularly robbed her of nervous energy. Or the apports could have been brought into the seance room by a confederate, whom no one would have thought of searching. At certain seances put on for a rich patron or an influential observer *everyone* except the patron or the observer was a confederate. Where the circle joined hands to make certain that there was no fraud, it was common practice for three confederates to sit together. The one in the middle, of course, had both hands free to arrange almost any kind of phenomenon.

For the more spectacular and flashy displays of Mrs Guppy, a lot depended on the place where the seance was held. It did not have to be her own house; it could be at a confederate's. Apports could be arranged in secret compartments in the ceiling, and dropped on to the table by means of a primitive time mechanism or a crafty tug of an inconspicuous thread by a confederate. Where the apport was the principal *modus operandi* of the medium, it was probable that a trap would be made between the seance room and the room above, and a confederate could shower down whatever the medium requested. The prompting of Mrs Guppy – does no one want vegetables? – was a clear cue to the person above.

Some of the devices used in the production of Mr Jencken's first class of phenomena, the movement and raising of ponderable bodies, have been mentioned – the concealed rod up the sleeve to ease leverage of a table, the leather strap running up the sleeve to ease leverage of a table, the leather strap running up the sleeves and across the shoulders to do much the same thing, the split ring with a pin on the table. Wrote the Reverend Henry Douglas: 'We all saw the supper-table, on which there was a quantity of glass and china full of good things, rise to an angle of 45 degrees and then relapse into its normal position. Yet no damage was done; nothing fell off.' A fairly characteristic account. A similar thing happened at a seance given by Home, recorded by Lord Adare, where the table 'was repeatedly raised in the air to the height of 4 or 5 inches, Miss D—— R—— placing her hands between it and the floor; and it was also frequently inclined at such an angle that the vase must inevitably have fallen off under ordinary circumstances'.[3]

Many sitters were ignorant of the ingenuity that sometimes went into a medium's programme. If a table was to be tilted, the fact that items on the table did not fall off added to the effect. Granted that observers were more inclined to overestimate the angle than underestimate it, and granted that observers assumed that they knew the exact stage when an article began to fall off, there were ways of keeping the articles vertical with the table-top, including the use of magnets. The innocuous tipping table might well have a secret compartment containing an electro-magnet, and certainly intricate tables were constructed for the trade containing fairly sophisticated electrical equipment. These were used for table-rapping. The articles that did not fall off tables are never described in detail, but even china and glass could be doctored by inserting thin plates of metal for the electro-magnet to act upon.

The levitation of mediums was a more difficult problem. The most famous instance of this was accomplished by Home, who levitated at a house in Victoria in front of a goggling audience, floated out of one window and in at another. It happened after Home had been pontificating on the nature of justice:

'in human affairs let human justice prevail; but we cannot interfere; God's justice is so different from man's...'[4] He became both elevated and elongated and requested, 'Do not be afraid, and on no account leave your places'. He went out into the passage. One of the viewers said, 'Oh, good heavens! I know what he is going to do; it is too fearful'. Lord Adare asked what it was, but it was too horrible; then the spirit of Adah Menken said that Adare could be told (Adah Menken was the notorious bareback rider who caused a stir in an adaptation of Byron's *Mazeppa*, and was the mistress of Dumas, and, supposedly, of the poet Swinburne). Home was going out one window and in at their's. They heard the window thrown up, and Home appeared outside their window, standing upright. He opened the window and walked in. He laughed, and they asked him why he was laughing. He was wondering what a policeman would have done had one been passing and looking up.

Home then gave a repeat performance, passing out of the window almost horizontally and apparently rigid. It was dark, and Adare could not see if he was supporting himself at the balustrade. Afterwards there were other phenomena, jets of flames proceeding from Home's head, and a whistling and chirping sound as if from an invisible bird flying round the room, then the sound of a great wind rushing through the room. Home went into trance, and proclaimed that the sun was covered with beautiful vegetation and teeming with life. No, it was not, as the populace thought, hot, but cold.

The whole business is bogged down with errors and contradictions. In his account, Adare stated that it was all taking place on the third floor; later he said it was the first floor. The Master of Lindsay, one of the audience, estimated the height from the ground at eighty-five feet; in fact it was thirty-five to forty feet. There was also uncertainty as to where it all took place, either 5 Buckingham Place, or Ashley House, Victoria Street. Compared with this, the disagreement as to whether the outside ledge was four inches wide (Adare) or an inch and a half (Lindsay) was marginal. The outside world was, understandably, sceptical about these events. W. M. Thackeray asked why Home did not levitate in daylight? His 'admirers would then see his gracious countenance smiling benignantly upon their upturned faces'. The *Saturday Review*, considered Home 'a weak, credulous, half-educated, fanatical person, born, bred, and educated in wonderful stories, who has lived from his earliest years in an atmosphere and mirage of dreaming. The witnesses, few in number and almost entirely unknown, are much in the same condition'.

Were the three observers at Ashley House (majority opinion prefers this address) entirely unknown? One of them was all but unknown – Captain Charles Wynne, then a thirty-three-year-old serving officer at the Tower of London, a station notorious for tricks and japes of one kind or another. He later became a magistrate in Sligo, Ireland. The Master of Lindsay, later Lord Lindsay, was a young man of twenty-one living in the shadow of his formidable father, a savant, book-collector, and a prolific author, not to mention being a prodigious researcher (in 1848 he established his father's claim to the Crawford title, the premier earldom of Scotland). Educated at Eton and Trinity College, Cambridge, Lindsay went into the Grenadier Guards, wherein he was serving in December 1868, when the Home levitation took place. He was an avid believer in all the phenomena Home put out, frequently at Home's fire tests, and eight times holding red-hot coals without being burned.

Lord Adare was born in 1841. During his boyhood his father joined the Catholic Church. His mother remained Protestant, and Adare was sent for his education to Rome, forbidden to contact his mother. He subsequently went to Christ Church, Oxford, after which he entered the Army. In 1867 he went to Abyssinia to cover the war for the *Daily Telegraph,* returning in the winter, when he met Home. Home completely dominated him, reduced him to a state of nervous exhaustion, soothed and comforted him when the spirits were on the move. He pulled himself together sufficiently to cover the Franco-Prussian War for the *Telegraph,* and spent some time in France with Home and Lord Lindsay. He suceeded to the earldom in 1871, went into politics, and was Under-secretary for the Colonies 1885–7. He was a keen sportsman, and in the 'nineties was one of the leading yachtsmen of the day. His two years close association with Home do not fit in with any other part of his life.

Whatever the extent of Home's influence on these two young men, was it sufficient for them either to concoct this story for the added glorification of Home or to believe that the levitation actually took place? If the latter, was it a case of collective illusion – 'an agreement in the misinterpretation of sensory signs produced by a real external object'[5] or genuine collective hallucination; and if hallucination was it evoked by hypnosis? Neither of the men was a credulous fool, both were tolerably well-educated, and no one with their instruction would have believed for one moment that the sun was cold. Either they stood in such awe of Home that they voluntarily relinquished their reason or they were party to one of the biggest deceptions of Victorian spiritualism. Yet if the whole thing was one big stunt – and it is the kind of thing idle and bored army officers might have done – could the deception have been persisted with for so long? Admittedly the differences between the accounts by Lindsay and Adare could be the result of a modified failure to keep to the same spurious story, but they could also be the result of the gap in time between the events and their systematic recording. If it was all a hoax, would Lord Adare have played it up sufficiently to have written and had privately published his *Experiences in Spiritualism*?

Other levitations are recorded among the Stainton Moses circle, but the levitations of the minor mediums were very tawdry exhibitions indeed. Taking place at dark seances, there is strong evidence to suggest that all that happened was that the medium took off his shoes and waggled them about at a height to suggest that he had been levitated.

Strange sounds were often reported at seances. At a sitting with Stainton Moses on May 3rd 1874, there were 'new sounds, too, of a zither, five in all. They played over my head and round the circle. They were quite independent of the table. They were clear, very highly strung, and apparently graduated, giving one the idea of an instrument of five strings'.[6] The zither sounds reappeared on July 12th: 'The high noises were imitated exactly, and the runs executed with marvellous precision. Two instruments apparently were used, or rather imitated, one with three high strings, and another with seven lower ones. The little sounds of the smaller instrument were brought out most clearly, and then were followed by an elaborate run on the other instrument, as though the finger were drawn rapidly over the strings.'[7]

The most remarkable instances of music from invisible agencies occurred at the home of Dr Gully at Great Malvern, when three voices chanted a hymn, accompanied by music played on an accordion suspended in space eight or nine feet from the ground. Jencken mentions a case where a strain of solemn music – more than a strain (it lasted twenty minutes) – was heard in the room of a dying servant of his. A religious fanatic, Mr Glover believed that spiritualism was a device of the devil. He had made a close study of the coming of the Lord, which, he was convinced, was due the following August. Nevertheless, he had heard mysterious music; when the spirits were playing 'The Last Rose of Summer', he loftily considered that this was too trivial an air. The spirits, abashed, agreed, 'and immediately a most magnificent hymn tune, which he had never heard before, was played'.[8]

The two most prominent instruments at seances were probably the guitar and the accordion. The latter was one of Home's favourite props: his special instrument was ornately-decorated, with a very short keyboard. Its shape was dumpy and squat, more like a concertina than an accordion. Except when it was playing by itself away from everyone, he held it beneath a table, his hands away from the keys. Stage conjurors, the most damaging witnesses against seance tricks, explained how it could be done. The accordion was on a loop of catgut, by which means Home could turn the accordion round. There was also on the market a self-playing accordion.

The zither music heard at Stainton Moses' seances could have been produced quite easily. Musical-boxes had become extremely sophisticated, and were being made with a zither attachment, tissue paper in a metal holder that dropped on to the comb of a musical-box and modified the sound to give a very good impression of a zither. Small musical-boxes were strapped to the leg of the medium, and it is not necessary to stress again the difficulty of determining from where a sound is proceeding. Self-playing guitars were constructed by inserting into the body of the instrument a small musical-box. Guitars were also useful for concealing the medium's bric-à-brac, such as gauze or muslin, or small apports.

Spirit writing and drawing by 'direct spiritual unseen agency' will be dealt with elsewhere. And so we come to the fire test. 'I have frequently seen Home,' wrote Lord Lindsay, 'when in a trance, go to the fire and take out large red-hot coals, and carry them about in his hands without injury, when it scorched my face on raising my hand. Once I wished to see if they really would burn, and I said so, and touched a coal with the middle finger of my right hand, and I got a blister as large as a sixpence.'[9] A Mrs Honywood said that she had seen Home carrying one in a hand bell, then putting the coal on a piece of paper, which was not singed. Miss Douglass had seen Home holding a hot coal in his hand until the coal was black, then place it between his shirt and coat. She touched the coal; it scorched her at first, then immediately after felt as cold as marble. On March 17th 1869, Home took the chimney of a lamp, and thrust it into the fire. He clasped the chimney in both hands, took a match, asked a woman to touch the chimney with it, and the match burst into flame. He then took the chimney back to the fire, resting it on the upper bar of the grate. From a vase of flowers he selected a small fern-leaf, took the chimney from the fire, put the leaf inside the chimney, and replaced the chimney among the coals. After a few moments, Home took the chimney, and showed that the fern was apparently on fire, glowing red-hot, with each frond edged with gold. Home shook it out on to a lady's muslin dress, and the watchers expected it to crumble; but it was green, though dry and withered. Home then took a coal from the fire, and tossed it to one of the women, who caught it and threw it to Lord Lindsay, who put it back in the fire. Home then took a white flower, and waved it about in the flame of the lamp: the flower was unharmed. In trance, Home then said, 'The spirit now speaking through Dan, and that has enabled him to show you these curious fire-tests, in which he hopes you have all felt interested, is the spirit of an Asiatic fire-worshipper, who was anxious to come here tonight as he had heard of seances held here'.[10] This account was confirmed by the lady who had had the burning fern dropped on to her dress.

The seventh grouping that H. D. Jencken made of spiritualistic phenomena are a motley lot; it is doubtful whether 'holding fluids in space without bottles or containers' was more than a talking point, flung into the lists as a challenge to scientists. 'I will pass over the numerous phenomena of holding fluids in space, without vessels to contain them,' he grandly states, and these numerous phenomena are little evident in the literature of spiritualism.

The perfuming of water, the extraction of scent from flowers or of alcohol from spirits of wine seem to be pointless exercises, the first and last the kind of trick any trumpery conjuror could simulate. It is possible that by the second Jencken considered that the perfumes that pervaded seance rooms were extracted from real flowers. There are many instances of this phenomenon in the notebooks of Stainton Moses. On January 3rd 1874, for example, the seance room was showered with verbena in liquid form and musk in powder form. A Miss Birkett stated that on February 16th, liquid verbena was poured on one of the sitters, Dr Speer, as if from a watering-can.

Unquestionably some investigators were inclined to take everything at face value (with notable exceptions, such as Mrs Sidgwick), and were scandalised when doubts were expressed about the mediums' and sitters' reliability; that Moses was not above suspicion, despite his scholarly mien, is evident from the catch-phrase circulated about him, 'Where was Moses when the light went out?' Crookes took refuge in unambiguous self-assertion : 'I *know* the phenomena are true.'

Spirit lights were produced in great quantities, and phosphorised oil could be used to perfect these. Sir William Crookes testified that he had not been imposed upon by this means, and under test conditions, 'I have seen luminous points of light darting about and settling on the heads of different persons; I have had questions answered by the flashing of a bright light a desired number of times in front of my face. I have seen sparks of light rising from the table to the ceiling, and again falling upon the table, striking it with an audible sound'.[11] Typical spirit lights were recorded by Lord Adare: 'I saw the most beautiful little phosphorescent lights moving. I saw as many as three at a time; sometimes there were two together like eyes, sometimes two would come together, and then dart away from each other.'[12] Stainton Moses's lights were more spectacular, 'a cylinder of luminous substance, hard, and giving a golden light. It would be about four inches by three inches, and apparently circular at top and bottom. It was draped with something that Dr Speer felt, and said was coarse and rough'.[13] The light moved about the room in a slow and stately fashion; the intensity of the light did not fluctuate. Moses's control said that the light was fed from Moses's body, and next morning Moses felt cold, tired, and weak. At a seance the following day, there were 'great masses of floating light', and two months later light appeared in a flash like forked lightning, the reflection of which was seen in a looking-glass.

Certain of the descriptions of lights at seances bear a close resemblance to those observed in the days of mesmerism. Mrs Burns, the wife of an editor of a spiritualist newspaper, could see light issuing from various heads, flashes from brain to brain, and the wife of another spiritualist, the electrician Varley, saw light emitted from rock crystals and people. Lord Lindsay saw a crystal ball placed on Home's head flash coloured light following the order of the spectrum, succeeded by a wealth of pretty moving pictures. Other lights were flat and circular, somewhat larger than a half-crown, and appeared to drift in the manner of snow-flakes. When hands were held to catch them, they appeared to pass through the hands.

Phosphorescence was, and is, a mystery to the layman. The conjuring fraternity accused the spiritualists of importing glow-worms into their seances, but there was no need for this. Chlorophane, a variety of fluor-spar, becomes phosphorescent at hand heat, and phosphorus exposed to moist air in a dark room shines with a soft light. That phosphorus oil was used in seances is certain; when fraudulent mediums were caught, phosphorus oil was commonly found in their kit. The moving lights can be explained most easily by postulating optical tricks, though it is doubtful whether even the most benign of believers would have countenanced the introduction of a magic lantern into the seance room.

8. Materialisations

Although there was general agreement among keen spiritualists in the 1860s and 1870s that materialisations of spirits took place the theory was somewhat confused. Sometimes the spiritualists waded into a swamp of verbiage. For example, Miss Anna Blackwell: 'Matter is the ultimation of the Primordial Fluid, under the form of atoms, into the plane of Manifestation, or Corporeality. As the constituable element of Form, it exists in two states, which give rise to two realms, or modes, of Related Existence, viz, the 'Fluidic', 'Imponderable', or 'Etherealised' state, in which it exists in inter-stellar space and the 'Compact' or 'Ponderable' state, in which it exists at the surface of planets.'[1]

The popular consensus was that the spirits obtained their power from the mediums. Until the concept of ectoplasm was produced, how this was done was a mystery. Cromwell Varley, an ingenious electrician who rigged up gadgets to mediums to test that they did not break the circuit, tried to explain it metaphysically, arguing that thought was solid: 'I explain it in this way; all known powers have to be treated as solids, in regard to something; a man finds air not solid at all. He can move through it as though it did not exist.'[2] He produced a clever analogy: 'An iron wire is to an electrician simply a hole bored through a solid rock of air so that the electricity may pass freely.' It was perhaps presumptuous to associate air with thought, and Varley's logic was a little shaky, especially as he had been asked a question about spirit clothes, but by making the point that the air between the medium and the spirit was not necessarily a void it makes the contention that electricity, that magic word for Victorians, was the instrument of materialisation if not viable at least arguable.

The writers and journalists in spiritualist circles were always eager to speculate and testify. Mrs Hardinge had seen and felt a spirit hand. She maintained that spirits became visible by crystallising the magnetic and other emanations from these present around their own invisible spirit forms. A Mr Gannon asked her what was vital magnetism, and by what scientific tests had it been proved that people generated such a force. Mrs Hardinge, hoist by her own show of cleverness, took refuge in the time-honoured plea that science was not sufficiently advanced to answer the question fully, and she, implicitly, not at all.

The devotees of the seance could accept this, but they found it difficult to account for clothes. The mesmerists and magnetists had instilled into the layman the notion that certain objects, particularly dead bodies and magnets, threw off a glow, an aura, sparks, rays. The sitters could extend this to the notion that mediums threw off an aura which was capitalised by the spirits, or the aura was captured from the sitters. But this could not account for the spirit clothes. One explanation was that the apparent clothes were a sort of felt which the spirit built around itself, but the persistent found this hard to swallow, especially when the spirits were in period costume. Another theory was that the spirit acquired its clothes from particles of clothing material that they extracted from the sitters.

It could be that the body of the medium was *directly* supplying the material for building up the spirit. This was a useful hypothesis to apologists of the movement, as it would account for the innumerable cases where the spirit was grabbed and proved to be the medium herself: 'There being apparently no miracle in the shape of the creation of new matter, as materialised spirit hands, heads, and bodies grow heavier it follows that those of the medium grow lighter, until at last there may be no medium at all inside the sealed tapes, however securely they had been applied, and nothing but a medium in a state trance is then in the freed form.'[3]

The stages of materialisation varied. At a seance in February 1880, Kate Cook's spirit Lily 'grew up beside the sofa', short, white, indistinct, until she reached the height of Miss Cook, then put her left hand on Miss Cook's right shoulder, then held Miss Cook's right hand with both hands. A week later Lily 'appeared in the centre of the table, and spoke to us and kissed us all in turn. Her face was very small, and she was only formed to the waist, but her flesh was quite firm and warm. Whilst Lily was on the table in full sight of the sitters, I had my hand upon

Miss Cook's figure (for I kept pressing my hand up and down from her face to her knees to make sure it was not only a hand I held)'.[4] At this seance, Lily was asked for a piece of her dress or some hair. Mr Marryat-Lean handed her a knife, and she cut off a piece of dress; there would be no hair until next time. There was apparently no resemblance between the medium and the spirit, the former being slight and small, the spirit plump in face and figure.

A seance held in Newcastle-on-Tyne on Christmas Day 1879, reported by a stalwart of northern spiritualism, T. P. Barkas, was more like a cocktail party than an awesome supernatural experience. After three parts of an hour conversation and hymn singing the curtain opened, and a small female figure in white raiment and greyish-white shawl entered, shook hands with the sitters, embraced a lady, and stayed for fifteen minutes. She was succeeded by a woman of average height, very energetic and active, then a child-like form three and a half feet tall, with a piping voice. The culminating feat was a tall female spirit who pushed the medium into the room in a chair.

If the appearance of a succession of spirits created difficulties for those who believed that the spirit was constructed of divers elements from the medium, how was the simultaneous group of spirits to be accounted for? In her deposition to the committee of the Dialectical Society, an Honourable Mrs —— related: 'The most remarkable manifestations I have seen, were those of last Sunday evening at my house. We were seated in a partially darkened room. We first heard raps and then saw a human figure at the window. It entered and several other figures came trooping in after it. One of them waived [sic] its hands. The atmosphere became fearfully cold. A figure which I recognised as that of a deceased relative came behind my chair, leaned over me, and brushed my hair lightly with its hands.'[5]

Miss Anna Blackwell had an even more esoteric experience, being confronted by between eighteen and twenty male spirits dressed in white tunics, red belts, curious red hats with very broad brims embroidered in gold (though she considered that these might have been haloes), each carrying a stout crook. These spirits acted as though they had been halted on the march.

Some fully-materialised spirits were more exciting yet. 'Pocky', the Indian girl-spirit produced by Miss Wood, embraced one of the sitters, Mr Mould, a corn-merchant, repeatedly, and kissed the investigator Edmund Gurney two or three times through her drapery, paused to materialise her lips, then kissed him with uncovered lips. Mould remarked that when Pocky leaned over him to kiss Gurney, he felt no body, nothing but drapery. Asked whether her trunk had materialised, Pocky replied that it had not, only head, hands, and some kind of legs, with irregular feet. Stimulated by a variety of causes, the investigators brought Miss Wood and her friend Miss Fairlamb down to London and installed them in lodgings in Alexandra Square in April 1875, but away from the heady air of the north the phenomena were dismal; the spirit who emerged from a cabinet reminded Henry Sidgwick of nothing more than a girl on her knees.

Spirit hands were one of the easiest counterfeit phenomena. D. D. Home declared that the Emperor of Russia had seen hands and clutched them, whereupon they seemed to float away in thin air. Signor Damiani, as credulous a man as any trickster could hope to find, had frequently held disembodied hands. They were not so warm as human hands, but softer in texture; they would melt away and dissolve while he held them, They were generally beautiful in form with tapering fingers, and varied in colour and density from the white and opaque to the pink and transparent. Sir William Crookes described a hand coming down from the upper part of the room and hovering near him, taking a pencil from his hand and writing on paper. On one occasion, Dr Speer, Stainton Moses's disciple, encountered a hand in the middle of the table 'where no hand should be'.

Home's spirit hands seemed to be long kid gloves stuffed with some substance, and Browning thought that they were fixed to Home's feet. This was a device of some mediums, and in the dim light of the seance actual feet could simulate spirit hands, especially those of children or not quite materialised hands. Even when the adjacent sitters were keeping their feet on the medium's shoes this could be accomplished by the use of metal toe-caps on the medium's boots. The foot could therefore be withdrawn without detection. A dummy hand could also double for a spirit baby. This could be strapped to the medium's belt until needed, or to the leg a few inches above the ankle. When the seance lights 'accidentally' went out, the medium could thrust a stockinged foot into the dummy hand, and by resting the foot on the other knee, the spirit hand or spirit baby could peep over the table in an astounding manner. When the medium was a woman, the accomplishment of this feat was even easier, as the spirit hand could be concealed beneath the medium's skirts; at seances such as Mrs Guppy's where a table with a hole in the centre was one of the properties, it would be the simplest of accomplishments to thrust a foot covered with a dummy hand through the hole. Where there was no hole in the centre of the table it was possible to construct a sliding trap for the magical appearance of a hand 'where no hand should be'.

When the medium judged that the precautions to prevent fraud would be slack, it was easier to wear a black glove with the palm painted with luminous paint. Women could wear long dress gloves, men could use black cloth up to the elbow. If there were two confederates, one on either side of the medium, it would be laughably simple, but experienced mediums never had any difficulty in withdrawing one hand when both were initially held by adjacent sitters. A jerk when the medium went into 'trance' would immediately release one of the hands, and when the startled sitters recovered their composure and the hands they were meant to hold, they were really holding part of the same hand, leaving the free hand to do anything the medium thought fit.

With materialisations of the complete figure, much could be done with gauze and flimsy materials, the substitution of the medium for the spirit, or the assistance of an accomplice as the spirit. A seance described by Major-General J. N. H. Maclean with the medium Katie Cook produced almost inexplicable phenomena. Miss Cook sat a little in front of the others, then said, 'There is something gathering in a heap near me like coarse flannel, I cannot make out what it is, I have never had a similar experience before'. Maclean saw the heap rise up, and form itself into a figure covered by a plaid or shawl; a hand covered with the shawl was thrust out, and grasped the general's hand.

Against this evidence one must set the gigantic train of mediums exposed. 'I believe that the amount of imposture among *paid mediums* has been greatly overrated,'[7] declared Mrs de Morgan, but the scene depicted in *Mr Sludge the Medium* must have been played many many times:

Now, don't, sir! Don't expose me! Just this once!
This was the first and only time, I'll swear,—
Look at me, – see, I kneel, – the only time,
I swear, I ever cheated, – yes, by the soul
Of Her who hears – (your sainted mother, sir!)
All except this last accident, was truth—

Many of the exposures were sordid and squalid, taking place in scruffy parlours with cut-price mediums. Typical of these was at South Shields on August 24th 1889, when Joshua Ware achieved his ten minutes of glory. The medium was Mrs H. Davison. Another medium at the seance named Bowen was invited to go into the cabinet, probably to take in the spirit draperies. Bowen came out of the cabinet, followed by the spirit. Ware grabbed: 'To satisfy myself I *grabbed the spirit twice,* which proved to my satisfaction that it was quite solid, and none other than Mrs Davison herself. This, of course, caused an uproar, and Mr Davison, the husband of the medium, was much annoyed because the trick did not work well, and I came in for a good deal of abuse.'[8]

Frequently fraudulent mediums specialising in materialisations had associates among the sitters whose job it was to prevent any premature interference from the audience. At a seance with Florence Cook, one of the members of the audience was W. Volckman (who later married the celebrated Mrs Guppy after Mr Guppy had passed to the other side). After nine months trying, he managed to get into the seance by the presentation of jewellery to the medium. It was probably on the instigation of Mrs Guppy that Volckman was there. The seance was in December 1873; at the beginning of the year Mrs Guppy had had the idea of fixing Florence Cook by throwing vitriol in the spirit's face. However, it was not Volckman who grabbed at Miss Cook on this occasion. As the spirit form was seized, 'the figure appeared to lose its feet and legs and to elude the grasp, making for that purpose a movement somewhat similar to that of a seal in water'.[9] Spirit 'Katie' thus got away, and Miss Cook was found entranced, complete in black dress and boots, with a tape round her waist sealed with the signet ring of one of the sitters, the Earl of Caithness.

The spirit form 'Katie' would appear to have spent a fair part of her intermittent existence being sprung on by sceptics. 'Some months ago a Dialectical gentleman seized rudely on the spirit form of Katie, which struggled violently with him, scratching his face and pulling out his whiskers.'[10] Even more unfortunate was the spirit conjured up by Miss Showers. At one of her seances a lady 'drew aside the curtains, and exposed the un-spiritual form of Miss S standing on the chair; the "spirit-hands" at the same time struggling so convulsively to close the aperture that the head-gear fell off, and betrayed the somewhat voluminous chignon of Miss S herself. Thereupon ensued a row, it being declared that the medium was killed, though eventually order was restored by the rather incongruous process of a gentleman present singing a comic song.'[11]

If 'Katie' spent her time being sprung on at sittings, Miss Wood's 'Pocky' spent hers kissing gentlemen and being caught, when she proved to be Miss Wood on her knees partly undressed and covered with muslin; no matter that she 'protested that she was an unconscious instrument temporarily in the hands of an evil power'.[12] But probably neither Miss Wood nor the Miss Cooks, Florence and Kate, were as hard done by as Miss Showers, who was betrayed by one of her own kind.

The nomenclature of the spirits can lead to confusion. Just as Florence Cook had a spirit 'Katie' so Rosina Showers had a spirit 'Florence'. Miss Cook and Miss Showers did a double show, their spirits walking hand in hand and playing pretty tricks. The only snag was that the spirits 'precisely resembled' (Serjeant Cox's self-contradictory phrase) the mediums. Although Miss Showers could produce spirit voices above her head with her mouth full of water, although she could be taped down in a cabinet and yet cause spirit faces to appear at an aperture, although she could have a thread put through her ear (where her ear-ring had been) and yet the spirit had none, although she had a full complement of toes and yet the spirit had one large toe on each foot, she still admitted to another medium, Mrs Fay, that she was a fraud. Mrs Fay told William Crookes, and Crookes told his friends; the news eventually reached D. D. Home via Serjeant Cox, and as Home was then interested in exposing mediums he quoted Miss Showers' tricks in his book *Lights and Shadows of Spiritualism*.

A white band over the hair and around the chin altered the

appearance of the medium, and any sounds of motion in the cabinet would be concealed by exhortations to the audience to sing. The spectators would be sternly commanded not to peep inside the cabinet or grasp the form as this would kill the medium. As Serjeant Cox pointed out in his letter of March 8th 1876, 'This is an obvious contrivance to deter the onlookers from doing anything that might cause detection. It is not true. Several spirits have been grasped and no medium has died of it.' The medium goes in a dress that can be taken off swiftly, in two or three minutes. She wears two shifts, and carries a veil of thin material, hidden in her drawers. A pocket-handkerchief pinned round the head keeps back the hair. She keeps the two shifts on, and covers herself with the veil. The gown she spreads over pillows to simulate an entranced medium in the cabinet.

When an observer was permitted into the cabinet to inspect the sleeping medium, he or she was carefully vetted. If it were a friend, he or she would shrink from exposure, and the credulous would take the pillow bolstering up the gown as a body. If the texture felt strange, there were supernatural things going on, and who knows what effect the formation of a spirit body had had on the medium's physical structure? In no case was the visitor allowed to see the medium's face; this was invariably covered by a shawl.

Intellectuals anxious to believe but retaining their spirit of inquiry were constantly being let down: 'Every one who has had much experience in these perplexing investigations knows that what seems purposeless and stupid fraud often intrudes itself, after the most conclusive evidence of genuine phenomena has been obtained.'[13] The medium Haxby had impressed many critical observers, but to the watchful band who later formed the nucleus of the Society for Psychical Research his machinations were obvious. Henry Sidgwick assumed that the materialisation Haxby produced was simply the medium withdrawing gradually into his cabinet, having first fallen on his knees, and then slowly lowering his head. The difference between his two spirits Toby and Abdullah appeared to be that one was considerably more bent than the other, and without beard or head ornaments.

Materialisations did not immediately die away when the Society for Psychical Research came into being; but the scholarly treatment of materialisations so evident in the proceedings of the society was a salutary dash of cold water after the hysterical utterances of the spiritualist newspapers and the careless intellectual arrogance of the committed investigators such as Crookes ('Others – and I am glad to say they are very few – have gone so far as to question my veracity,'[14]). In 1882, for the very first time, the *Proceedings* of the Society for Psychical Research provided a balanced platform for qualified researchers.

The Society for Psychical Research encouraged accurate observation and cool objectivity. It had no axe to grind, unlike the editors of the spiritualist papers; the best of these was the *Spiritualist*, whose editor, W. H. Harrison, did include in his columns material prejudicial to spiritualism. Harrison did not sweep under the carpet the exposures of the fraudulent. *The Two Worlds*, the organ of provincial spiritualism, published in Manchester, was overloaded with damp editorial matter, *Medium and Daybreak* was edited by James Burns, a fervent and gullible enthusiast, *Borderland* was run by W. T. Stead, apostle of yellow journalism who veered more than once into mania, and who was drowned in the *Titanic* believing to the last that he would be miraculously saved – he was, he thought, the most important man alive.

None of these would have dreamed of studying the psychology of observation, the statistics of probability. If the Society for Psychical Research had done nothing other than draw attention to the possibilities of malobservation at seances its work would have been well done.

The word 'ectoplasm' was not known to the Victorians, and after it was coined by the French spiritualist Charles Richet it vied in favour with 'teleplasm' and 'ideoplasm'. Richet had thought up the term after a seance in 1903.

There are many descriptions in spiritualist literature of a misty vapour issuing from a medium which sometimes solidifies. When the medium Slade was in Australia in 1878 he produced a cloud-like whitish-grey vapour, 'Dr' Monck produced a white patch that turned into a cloudy pillar, and D. D. Home managed to extrude a variety of clouds that formed into hands. In 1885, Eglinton managed a dingy white-looking substance that swayed and throbbed. Madame d'Esperance, an almost forgotten medium born in 1849 and noted for her looks rather than her phenomena, described the production of ectoplasm as though fine threads were being drawn out of the pores of her skin and woven about her face and hands like a spider's web. The 'red, sticky matter' described by a Bournemouth medium, Vincent Turvey, was an unusual variation on the theme, and when Florence Cook was manifesting Katie King the latter 'was connected with the medium by cloudy, faintly luminous threads'.[15]

Ectoplasm is supposed to have exuded from any or all of the medium's orifices, and to have been responsive to light, when it would retract. 'Ectoplasm' was captured by an investigator early in this century; it burned to an ash, leaving a smell as of horn. Chemical analysis revealed the presence of salt and phosphate of calcium. It is perhaps unfortunate that modern chemists have not had the opportunity to try their skills on this mysterious substance.

9. Spirit Writing and Drawing

Automatic writing and drawing is no mystery to writers or artists; many authors, including Dickens, have related how they have been 'taken over' during the writing of a work, and many artists have told how they have progressed in almost a trance state from a fortuitous mark or a blob on the canvas to a finished work. Particularly in water-colour, the building-up from chance accidents was an acknowledged method of procedure in the nineteenth century, and many accomplished water-colour painters threw down a wash of colour, added a few dabs of pure colour, and waited to see what the result would suggest to them before determining the subject of the work.

The spiritualists did not discover anything new when they pursued automatic writing and drawing; the novelty was their attributing it to spirits.

There are two kinds of automatism, direct, and via a medium. The former was more sensational, and because of this the field was wide open for all kinds of tricks. The most popular mode of automatic writing direct from a spirit was on slates. There was also a type of automatic writing midway between the direct and the entranced: the planchette, a tripod device with a pencil as the third leg, with a platform on which the medium placed a finger or a hand, depending on his or her power or the freedom of movement of the castors.

Rarest of all was direct painting in oils or watercolours. In his statement to the Dialectical Society, Benjamin Coleman claimed to have a number of pieces in pencil and colours of birds and flowers done without any human agency; the time occupied in doing them varied from ten to fifteen seconds, and he had previously marked the papers to eliminate substitution. Clean pieces of paper and crayons were placed under a table-cloth, a scratching of the paper was heard, and after a few moments the crayons were heard to fall, and the work was done. Mr Borthwick confirmed this account, but added that there was water-colour as well, and when the paintings were produced they were still damp. It took the spirits between seven and nine seconds.

On December 5th 1867, Miss Nichol held a seance at which about two dozen people were present. On the table were two sheets of drawing paper, a lead pencil, a sable-hair brush, some water, and a tube of madder brown colour, some of which Miss Nichol squeezed into a saucer. The gas lights were put out, and the sheets of paper, which had accidentally been drenched with water, fluttered about the room. One was brought to Miss Georgina Houghton, laid between her hands, and she heard it being patted as if to dry it. Miss Houghton then held the paper up, heard the brush dipped into the saucer, and applied to the paper in rapid movements. When the lights were put on, there was a painting of a guardian angel, done on the side of the paper nearer to Miss Houghton. Although only one colour had been provided, the water-colour was done with two.

At a seance given by Mrs Guppy in March 1868, a message was given: 'You must undergo a process of purification before I can draw. I will draw the emblem of Spiritualism.' Miss Houghton and Mrs Guppy were drenched in perfume, requested to sing, and pen and ink were demanded. On a sheet of paper a drawing was done of a dove hovering over the world, holding in its claws an olive branch, and it was explained that this was the first of a series, though the second drawing had less relevance, being an illustration to a poem by Pope.

About this time Thomas Sherratt produced spirit writings, claiming that they had been done under full light at Mrs Marshall's in Bayswater. The paper had been placed under the table, the sitters could hear the pencil moving over the paper (assumption taking the place of observation), and the writings were completed. Sherratt mentioned, as though it had some special significance, that he had provided lithographic paper for the seance. According to Home, at a seance where Napoleon III was present a spirit hand wrote 'an autograph of the Emperor Napoleon I'.

Less impressive was spirit writing executed in the presence of James Edmunds, M.D., the most outspoken of the committee members of the Dialectical Society *Report on Spiritualism*. He had not been pleased by the arrangements; the medium, Mrs

Guppy, had delivered a lengthy address calculated to upset the ladies, the room was shuttered so that when the light was out there was complete darkness, and he himself was squashed into a corner. He contented himself with stopping Mrs Guppy's speech when he reckoned she had gone far enough in provoking hysteria.

The seance started off with unspectacular raps, and the gas was lighted to see if spirit drawings could be obtained. Edmunds asked that the paper should be initialled to prevent substitution; this was agreed upon, the paper was put in a portfolio with a pencil close by, the light turned off, 'and soon afterwards we heard the piece of paper being rustled about, precisely as if one of the Spiritualist party opposite to us were doing it, the only remarkable fact being the barefaced way in which the thing was being done'.[1] Lights went up, the paper was examined, but there were only a few meagre marks. This was declared a failure, and the spiritualists maintained that the spirits were sometimes captious. The lights were put off again, and a large basket of flowers and shrubs came down on the table, quite wet – one of Mrs Guppy's celebrated apports. From the positions in which the sitters were arranged, Edmunds concluded that they were simply taken off the sideboard and thrown over the audience by one of the spiritualists, though Mrs Guppy steadfastly maintained that they had come bodily through the wall or shutters.

Direct spirit writing was performed in the presence of Signor Damiani; he scoffed at the idea of a medium doing it with the toes. An anonymous lady giving evidence to the Dialectical Society committee stated that she placed a paper and pencil on a table, and that the spirits wrote out a complete programme of a concert. When a violin, flute, piccolo, and concertina were provided, the spirits condescended to carry out the programme.

A medium who found that he was inspired to paint under the influences of Ruysdael and Jan Steen attempted to produce spirit paintings while he himself was strapped in a chair. The lights were put out, and after a quarter of an hour they were put on again; two small pictures were discovered, painted in oils, one the size of a penny, the other slightly larger, depicting a stream dashing over rocks and a mountain lake in a sunset glow. As the medium had a knowledge of photography and therefore chemicals, he would have been able to produce instant pictures by the use of sulphocyanide of potassium or ferrocyanide of potassium. For more substantial spirit paintings in oils it would have been more convenient to substitute, by the simple method of laying a blank canvas over a prepared one, rubbed with poppy or linseed oil to simulate immediacy. A prepared canvas could also be coated with a mixture of water and zinc white which could be deftly removed with a cloth.

Spirit drawing and painting by a medium under spirit influence was almost an industry. The artistic results are what one might expect, and in a way mirror the work done by serious artists influenced by abstruse occult theories, such as the French symbolist painter Odilon Redon. A certain dexterity was wondered at: it seems to have been forgotten that instruction in drawing and water-colour painting during childhood was a rule rather than the exception for the middle classes, the section of society almost wholly responsible for the upsurge of spirit drawing. Mrs Mapes, the wife of an American chemist, painted flowers under spirit influence. 'Good artists in water-colours,' claimed Benjamin Coleman, 'declare they are both very perfect drawings and could not be copied in an ordinary way in less than two days.'[2]

More interesting was the symbolism contained in the spirit drawings and paintings, and the way enthusiasts interpreted it. The account of the spirit painter Camilla Toulmin (Mrs Newton Crosland) is typical of this: 'This first drawings were very crude indeed, like the uncertain tottering lines of a child, and also singularly resembling the designs of the very early Italian painters – heads of Christ, angels, and curious female figures seated within spheres and hearts; and always these drawings were accompanied with strange ornaments of spiral and shell forms, with dots and scroll-like ciphers, which I thought odd at the time, but only months afterwards, when accidentally referring to them, discovered to be the first undeveloped attempts at writing one of the spirit languages.'[3]

The paintings of Georgina Houghton included rows of circles with crosses, crescent moons, suns, hearts, and wings. The seven circles with crosses in one painting she interpreted as the seven days of creation, with a crucifixion symbol in each. A sun with a face represented 'the whole nature of the Divine Powers', and a winged heart with a cross above and below was mystically 'showing that the lowest as well as the highest organisation must be polarised to God by crucifixion or suffering'.[4] Miss Houghton was aware that the symbols could be differently interpreted; of one element in a picture of hers, 'to the externally minded it is a balloon, but to the internally minded it is a pair of lutes proceeding from a sphere of light and united by the martyr's palm'.[5]

The finding of significance in the accidental or the perfunctory was perhaps seen at its height in the 'sediment in water' exercise. Miss Houghton went to Edward T. Bennett of Betchworth for this ceremony, which involved collecting rain water in a large wash basin. The participants put their fingers on the side of the basin, one of them whisked the water round, and they watched how the sediment in the water formed. Instantly recognisable faces were constantly appearing. The less adventurous but more practical do it today with tea-leaves in a cup.

One of the oddest occurrences in spirit writing happened in the early spring of 1874, when Mr Watson came from Liverpool to Brighton to stay in the lodgings of the Jencken family. Mrs Jencken's baby was being nursed by a wet-nurse near the fire. The nurse suddenly said 'Baby has got a pencil in his hand!' Then, 'Baby is writing!' The message read: 'I love this little child. God bless him! Advise his father to go back to London on Monday by all means – Susan.' Susan was Mr Watson's dead wife. The nurse declared that she must give up her situation, but later withdrew her notice.

Writings with mediums frequently had no relevance at all to the medium. Signor Damiani reported a case in Sicily where 'a singularly illiterate person of the artisan class' wrote a two hundred line poem in the Sicilian dialect, and also communicated in German, French, Latin and English.

Automatic writers had to be on their guard against evil spirits taking an advantage over them, using them as a platform for blasphemy and irreligion. 'The writing should not be allowed to continue if flippant or irreligious sentences are given,'[6] said Mrs de Morgan severely; similarly, if objects of a frightful or grotesque nature appeared on the paper of drawing mediums the medium should desist. Miss Anna Blackwell's sister had problems, as she was receiving both good and bad messages, the authors of the bad messages striving to sign themselves Satan or Beelzebub. She spoke up against them, telling them that if they were permitted to come to her they ought not tell such outrageous lies. When she saw the capital S of Satan being formed, she would twist her hand. In response, the spirits turned over her table and broke it.

The results of what Myers termed unconscious cerebration baffled many spiritualists. Of spirit poems, Mrs de Morgan in *From Matter to Spirit* wrote: 'The verses written by the unseen power are often curious and quaint, sometimes ridiculous. But verses not of a low and mischievous character have been given to us as to many other experimenters. The best of these contained beautiful ideas connected with the happiness of a life among the blessed and good in the world of good spirits, very lovely descriptions of the scenery of that world or worlds, and much affectionate anticipation of reunion among friends and future progress in happiness together.'

Nevertheless, there were disconcerting features of spirit writing. The phraseology of messages purporting to come from specific spirits such as dead relatives worried Mrs de Morgan. "Clasp you in our arms", &c., was so wholly unlike any language used by my relations when with us, that it puzzled me.' And messages could distress. 'At length, written in the beloved name of a departed brother, came announcements of the approaching deaths of those dearest to myself, accompanied with the most painful details. . . .'[7] And although progressive medical men considered that automatic writing was occasionally therapeutic, there were cases when the spirits alias the secondary personality tormented the writer into committing dreadful acts – such as the woman who drowned her two children at the behest of the spirits.

The psychology of automatic writing is that it is an extension of the tricks of unconscious action, which in repressed and nervous individuals can result in bizarre modes of expression such as compulsions. A person can scribble the odd word or scratch out a sketch without being aware of it, though it is not likely that a long passage or a detailed drawing would be completed without the originator knowing something about it. The initial word completed, the conscious mind comes into play, and subsequent writing is conditioned by this. Anticipation can direct the course of a word and consequently the trend of a message.

If one uses a planchette, there are five interpretations that can be put upon the messages. They can be supplied by spirits, they can be supplied by other human minds, they can be supplied by a higher personal intelligence (the super-ego of the psycho-analysts), they can be supplied by the subconscious or a secondary personality, or they can be consciously written, the planchette serving no purpose at all, though there would be no evidence to viewers to indicate that the message was being written consciously. To fraudulent mediums a planchette was a useful property.

The experiment described in the *Proceedings* of the Society for Psychical Research of 1884 is singularly interesting, in that the man involved had an open mind, and although leaning towards scientific orthodoxy, he was prepared to revise his notions. The experiment was made in Easter 1883, four days in all spread over a fortnight.

The questioner asked 'What is it that now moves my pen?' Answer: 'Religion'. Question: 'What moves my pen to write that answer?' Answer: 'Conscience'. Question: 'What is religion?' Answer: 'Worship'. The narrator added that he did not *expect* these answers but once the word had begun he expected the rest of the word. 'Cons——' might have ended as consciousness, had he thought of that word. Although at first sight subsequent answers seemed to show an independent will and intelligence, the narrator concluded that it was all due to unconscious cerebration and expectancy. As he progressed, he found that the answers were coming in anagrams, frequently quite involved: iebiovogfwle = I go, vow belief; nebl6vbliyev86eearfee = believe by fear even 1866.

That there could be conflict during planchette writing is evident from the innumerable occasions when a blockage occurs, when two letters are repeated meaninglessly, or when a word-part that could form into a word with emotional charge ends in a meandering scrawl. The same phenomenon was noted when operating a ouija board.

Compared with automatic writing and drawing, slate writing was unutterably complex, and the investigations, analyses, and duplicities of slate writing stretch across Victorian spiritualism like a miasma. Esoteric attempts in the writing – drawing field, such as trying to get spirit writing in sealed tubes (it could be done by tricksters with sulphuric acid) or trying to get a typewriter to tap out a message without human agency (this was done by attaching invisible threads to the typewriter keys) were paralleled by devotees of slate writing.

The leading exponent of slate writing was William Eglinton; his leading critics were Mrs Sidgwick and Richard Hodgson. Hodgson had created a stir by his exposé of theosophy, and neither he nor Mrs Sidgwick was impressed by Eglinton, however much his disciples raved. Hodgson saw how Eglinton distracted his sitters by a variety of ploys, changing his hands because he was tired, aimless chat, dropping the slates. He was also a materialisation medium, and when he combined what was then elegantly termed psychography with materialisations there were endless opportunities for sharp practice.

Eglinton was visited at 12 Old Quebec Street by Mrs Burns, the wife of the editor of *Medium and Daybreak*. In their narration it is stated that the table was faced by a large looking-glass. Mrs Burns had brought her own slates, and these were used by Eglinton as well as his own. Her companion wrote the name of a spirit on a slate, but the messages from it were not so coherent as the messages from Eglinton's. Eglinton's hands were visible while the message was allegedly being written, and once when he withdrew one of his hands from the slate the noise stopped. The messages received were what one might expect. Mr Burns was an important man to roaming mediums. 'We hope you will accept our earnest sympathy with you and your good husband in the trials and difficulties besetting you through your efforts to promote the well-being of the cause in the manner best calculated from your point of view to do good.'

Two months earlier, Amy Fisher had had the same kind of experience at Old Quebec Street. She was particularly impressed because of half a dozen lines signed by her brother, *'a name quite unknown to the medium'*. She also had a bonus in the shape of spirit forms and a levitation – the medium rose so high that she had difficulty retaining her grip on his hand (and the odds are that she did not retain it, but did not like to say so). As the medium descended, she saw him lying in the air in a horizontal position.

In October 1884 a party of eight converged from Bath, London, Plymouth, and Dover for a seance. On this occasion it was a cabinet seance; Eglinton emerged briefly, then spirit lights flitted about, while one of the party passed out unconscious. C. W.

Dymond of Bath observed a light cloud behind the curtain of the cabinet, three feet from the floor, forming into a figure; it was a brunette woman in a white robe with a cowl over her head. She approached the woman who had just recovered from her stupor, then retired back to the cabinet, being replaced by a tall man with a beard, shrouded and hooded, who was recognised by one of the sitters as his dead brother. He was followed by a short, aged woman, who kissed one of the women at the seance. Then an Indian, greeted by one of the sitters who had been in India in the language, upon which the apparition salaamed twice; it was considered by those who knew their India that the Indian, apparently a tailor, had been a trifle forward in greeting the sitters before being greeted himself. Then a woman, not recognised; a short stout priest-like figure who elongated until his head reached the ceiling; another bewhiskered tall man who hit his head against the branches of the chandelier, and when asked for a sign by a woman who decided this was her dead husband brandished a chair in the air as this sign; and finally a small child, who was very dim.

Thus Eglinton in all his glory. But his appeal was not only to credulous visitors from the provinces; W. E. Gladstone was impressed by him, so much so that *Punch* mentioned it: 'Our Versatile Premier, not so called because he usually wears a bad hat, or at any event a worser tile than anybody else, attended a spirit-writing seance at Mr Eglinton's last week, and expressed his agreement with Hamlet to the effect that there is more in heaven and earth than is dreamt of in Brummagem philosophy . . .'

For all the tales of marvels that circulated in the eighteen-eighties around the figure of Eglinton, Mrs Sidgwick maintained that there was no clear case of him having done what he purported to have done. The only answer was a securely covered slate. This was supposedly done at a Hensleigh Wedgwood session, at which the slates were tied and sealed together, and had gummed paper added round the edges. However, Mrs Sidgwick was not satisfied that the gummed paper was the original gummed paper, and the messages obtained were of no greater validity than those obtained using ordinary slate-writing methods. An ingenious variation was thought up by F. W. Bentall in which the slate was covered by a sheet of glass, but this foxed the spirits who explained that the 'vital fluid' could not be retained in the confined space long enough to conjure up the power to write; so Bentall provided wire gauze instead of glass. Again the spirits failed to write. The spirits also failed to write when the Sidgwicks commissioned a capable conjuror, Angelo J. Lewis, to sit in on an Eglinton slate-writing session, but for Sidgwick himself they were very accommodating, seeking to impress the academic mind with five sentences in different modern languages ('obviously taken out of a conversation-book,' commented Sidgwick) and a phrase from the Greek New Testament.

Slate-writing presented psychical researchers with ample opportunities for accurate and precise observation in good conditions, not like materialisations where the strain of waiting for the unexpected was too much for unassisted human observation. It belongs to a select group of phenomena, along with having a knot appear in a continuous band, a message appear in a sealed tube, or the changing of chemical elements in a sealed tube, none of which was ever done to the satisfaction of objective investigators.

The concentration on slate-writing also had valuable side-effects. It enabled psychical research investigators to examine the critical faculties of investigators and producers of other supernormal phenomena. Stainton Moses was not a slate-writer, and his account of a seance with Eglinton on November 3rd 1886 is more interesting on account of the light it throws on Moses than on the phenomena produced by Eglinton. In the first place, Moses was predisposed to believe; he also had full confidence in the trustworthiness of his fellow sitters, especially his close friend, Dr Speer. To make it more convincing to his readers, he told how he had kept continuous watch on Dr Speer, invalidating his earlier statement that he had kept continuous watch on Eglinton.

During this seance, the slate answered an arithmetical problem (50 x 60) wrote the number of a blank cheque, told Moses that his control Imperator was there (everyone in spiritualism knew about Moses's controls and their names), and the psychic forces unleashed by Eglinton had a chain reaction, afflicting Moses with spasmodic jerks. The cleverest trick was writing under an inverted tumbler.

When the Society for Psychical Research calmly demolished Moses's account, explaining how the tricks could have been worked, there was a furore. This had a double effect. Previous sitters with Eglinton amplified their accounts, added magical details; others who had detected him in dubious practice and had kept quiet spoke out. One lady sent her account of her experiences to the society. She and Godfrey Webb went to Eglinton's house; she noticed the looking-glass. To Mrs Burns this was a tasteful piece of decor; to this lady it was a means of keeping Eglinton informed about everything that was happening. She sat between Eglinton and Webb, all holding hands, slate beneath the table, scratching sound, a few unsatisfactory words on the slate. While the writing was being done Eglinton's face was livid and contorted and trickling with sweat, and his breathing was hard. Realising that his sitters were hoping for something more conclusive, Eglinton said that the spirits were not willing and suggested talking for a while. He then asked the woman to think of somebody from whom she would like a message, the slates were put under the table with his left hand, but the words produced conveyed little. They should change places; this they did; they should change slates. While he was doing this, she distinctly saw him run his hand over a slate with the fist clenched.

For once in a way, this action did not go unchallenged. The woman asked to see the writing on the slate, but Eglinton replied, 'Oh, there is nothing'. The woman persisted, 'Yes, there is; please let me see it'.

He showed it to me, and I saw the beginning of a sentence. He then said, 'I was only scribbling.' But as he had no pencil in his hand, it must have been with a small pencil lead, which he placed in his closed hand (not his fingers), and which I could not see, as it was too small. He used the same kind of small lead for the slates (which he placed between the two slates before he locked them up). After this incident he became angry, and said, 'It is of no use to try, as you are incredulous and suspicious the spirit will not come,' and we then left him.[8]

Yet a hundred people testified their belief in Eglinton, whose seances 'conclusively establish the existence of some objective, intelligent force, capable of acting exernally to the medium, and in contravention of the recognised laws of matter'.[9] The President of the London Spiritualist Alliance said, 'It is to me wholly inconceivable that anyone can entertain doubt as to the genuineness of these phenomena'.[10]

The most damning indictment of Eglinton came from Professor H. Carvill Lewis. He went to see Eglinton alone, which Eglinton never liked. There were the usual preliminaries, but Carvill paid more attention than most of Eglinton's sitters, in particular observing that although he could see the thumb of Eglinton's right hand holding the slate beneath the table, the four fingers were invisible. However, he could see the wrist, and the tendons of the wrist. For three-quarters of an hour nothing happened. As with the woman who was suspicious, the medium thought that conversation would help; he claimed that he had converted a conjurer named Kellar to spiritualism, but unfortunately Carvill knew Kellar personally, and was aware that in America Kellar was offering £20 to anyone who could produce spiritualistic phenomena that he could not duplicate by conjuring.

It became increasingly obvious that unless Carvill gave the medium some rope, the session would be fruitless, so he looked away towards the window. He saw Eglinton look down intently towards his knees, and turning his head sharply Carvill caused Eglinton to bring the slate up with a rap against the table. Eglinton was confused, complained about the weight of the slate, and the heat of the room. Carvill suggested that they tried a slate of his own, and as Carvill was paying strict attention there were no results. Eglinton pointedly suggested that the spirits were not omniscient; could Carvill give some idea of the questions he was asking? There were three questions to which, firstly, a spirit would know the answer but Eglinton would not: 'Where is my wife?'; secondly a spirit would not know but Eglinton might: 'Define Idocrase' (a chemical combination); and finally both spirit and Eglinton would know: 'Multiply two by two.'

For the first question on a large slate of Eglinton's, Carvill deliberately let his attention slip, then turned back quickly, causing Eglinton to drop the slate question uppermost. The second question was one that a mineralogist could answer but not a layman. To give Eglinton ample scope, Carvill took up a book and began to read it. The spirits sprang into activity, Eglinton began to breathe heavily and loudly and move uneasily, and it seemed to Carvill that the medium was altering the position of the slate. Eglinton then left the room. The seance was resumed, the writing began, and Carvill saw the central tendon of the wrist, that corresponding to the middle finger, moving. Success attended this question. 'It consists of Silica, Albumina, and Lime.' Apparent success. But Eglinton had misread his dictionary – it should have read 'silica, *alumina*, and lime'. Carvill also noticed that the chalk used in the writing was worn down in an unconvincing manner, as though writing zigzags; the inference is clear. The sound of writing had nothing to do with the messages – they were either written already, or not yet written.

The third question Carvill offered in a sealed envelope, but Eglinton bowed out of this, proposing instead that they should use a fancy folding-slate, the one that Gladstone had used. Carvill wrote a series of numbers on different slips of paper, put them in a hat, selected one without looking at it, folded it in four, put it in the folding slate with a fragment of red chalk. The slate closed with a spring lock. Knowing that observation would preclude phenomena, Carvill began writing notes of the seance, listening to the various sounds such as paper rustling, slates opening, partially disguised by heavy breathing and spasmodic jerking. How would Eglinton close the slates, remembering that it had a spring lock? Eglinton gave a sudden and strong sneeze. He then said he felt the influence strongly, and asked Carvill to enquire for an answer. Carvill had no doubt the answer would be right, as Eglinton had opened the slates, unfolded the paper, read the paper, replaced the paper, and written the answer. Carvill paid his guinea, and left; Eglinton would have been wise to have refused the money. Subsequently, and after further sittings, Carvill approached a handwriting expert, F. G. Netherclift, who proclaimed that the spirit writing was Eglinton's own handwriting disguised.

One of Eglinton's sitters was S. J. Davey. At first he had been impressed by Eglinton's phenomena, and when the spirits told him he had developed his own powers in this direction he was inclined to believe them, a belief confirmed when writing appeared on his own slates. However, he soon discovered that practical jokers had been at work. Being in poor health, and Eglinton's *pneuma* having faded in his eyes, he set to, endeavouring to produce Eglinton's phenomena by honest-to-goodness conjuring. He became such an adept that he came out as an amateur medium, and became a valued guinea-pig for psychical research. Here was a man who could do most of what Eglinton could do, including the producing of writing in slates screwed together, a man who would describe both how he had done it and the means used to divert his sitters as he was doing it. The exposure of Eglinton gave additional proof of the inability of sitters to remember what they had seen. Vital facts were simply left out, and malobservation and obtusity ran rampant.

Slate-writing mediums used con-man psychology. For the 'domestic imbeciles' the most shallow and obvious tricks were enough to earn them their guineas – a few shakes and paroxysms as the slate was turned round so that the question could be seen either by looking down during the fit or by using the looking-glass. How was the writing done, even though the slate was now question side away from the table-flap, when the hand could be seen? But, in fact, only the thumb was seen. The chalk or writing implement was fastened to the middle finger with adhesive plaster. For the average sitter there would have been no need to use the refinements of the trade.

Perhaps the most ingenious of these was covering the slate with slate-coloured silk, held by pellets of wax at the corners, which could be removed to uncover a real message on the slate. A refinement of this was an endless roll of slate-coloured silk, with prepared messages on the unseen part; studs were provided to stop the silk going round too far. Great cabinet-making artistry could go into the making of a trick frame; on some of them there was a catch connected to a screw in one of the hinges. The screw jutted out slightly, but pressure on it would release the catch, and provided the framework came apart where the sitters were not expecting it (where it could be sealed with wax), there were no limits to variations that could be made on this theme.

Eglinton does not appear to have found it necessary to use a trick table, as he does not seem to have prevented sitters examining his. Tables were constructed with a trick top; the slate was put on top of the table, the sitters requested to keep their hands on it, the medium put his hands out of sight under the table, and writing appeared on the underside of the slate. The table had a secret sliding piece in it; the medium pushed it over, giving access to the bottom of the slate, on which he proceeded to write.

If the table had a heavy covering in velvet or damask or some similar material, then sitters should have examined not the table but the floor beneath it in case there was a trap-door to admit a small boy who could exchange slates, write answers to spoken questions, or assist in any legerdemain of the medium; the paroxysms and twitchings of the medium could cover an exchange of slates very effectively. The most impressive way to utilise a confederate was to give the aide the real slates while jerking and twitching, taking dummy slates in exchange; the associate would do the slate-writing, there would be further movements from the medium, and the real slates would be returned to him in place of the dummy slates. To the sitters it would appear that the slates never left the hands of the medium.

Suppose the medium crossed the room, and put the slates in a closed drawer. He would wait a while, the sound of writing would no doubt be heard, and the slates would be covered with writing when the drawer was unlocked and opened. The sitter had assumed that it was an ordinary drawer in an ordinary piece of furniture, but in fact the back of the drawer led not into the furniture but into an adjacent room, where an associate could do anything that was required in the way of slate-writing. Two shelves beneath the chair to contain substitute slates, a slit in the carpet leading to a cut-out in the floor to hold substitute slates — these were more tricks. If the medium was left alone with the slates, no matter how they were taped up, sealed with wax, screwed together with the screw-heads waxed, plastered over with adhesive paper, the medium would triumph. By carefully using a wedge and a piece of umbrella wire with a lead in the end the seeming impossibility of obtaining a message was overcome.

The audience too easily assumed that wax, adhesive paper, signed and countersigned, were sufficient to deter the fraudulent medium. Wax could be reapplied and seals counterfeited, paper could be steamed off and replaced. Ingenuity run crazy is the hallmark of one method of obtaining messages on a slate that really is hermetically sealed. A mixture of powdered chalk, water, glue, and iron filings, produced, apparently magically, a message. This was done by using a magnet on this mixture.

The seances followed a stereotyped pattern, and it was therefore possible to prepare the slates with prearranged answers to questions that would be asked. The simplest answer was 'Yes'.

If the sitters did not ask if the spirits were there, prompted or unprompted, the medium would. There were ambiguous answers that would apply to innumerable questions, and earnest sitters would always accept lengthy platitudes about the role of spiritualism in modern life, irrespective of the question asked.

Psychography in all its forms, spirit writing, spirit drawing, slate writing, was a modest and amusing Victorian entertainment, and it provided valuable evidence for pioneers.

10. Spirit Photography

Spirit photography is crucial in the history of spiritualism. If *one* photograph exists depicting a spirit, then the bizarre medley of manifestations that make up Victorian spiritualism must be re-evaluated in the knowledge that they may be true. Yet, despite the existence of thousands of so-called spirit photographs from the nineteenth century not one has succeeded in convincing the experts that it is what it purports to be.

It may be asked if these experts are any more qualified to judge than the host of reputable witnesses who have proclaimed the truth of spirit photographs, men like Conan Doyle or the naturalist A. R. Wallace, or a professional photographer, J. Traill Taylor, editor of the authoritative *British Journal of Photography*. The reader must judge. If spirit photography is true, Victorian spiritualism is all that it claimed to be. If it is not, we must again survey the credulity of those determined to believe in the reappearance of the dead.

Compared with today, the art of photography was crude, but it had made gigantic strides since the late 1830s when Daguerre and Talbot established it. To laymen it was more of a mystery then than it is now. The principal difference in basics was the use of a glass plate as a base for sensitive emulsions reacting to light, instead of a continuous roll of film. This plate did not react to red light, and could be freely handled in the dark-room. Prior to use, the plate was fitted into a container that excluded light and placed in the camera; the container was withdrawn, the photograph taken, and the container replaced. Both container and plate were whisked away into the dark-room, the container was removed, and the plate was placed in a bath of developer. When the image had appeared to the satisfaction of the photographer (in negative), it was fixed, and prints were made from the plate. At any point along the trail, the photographer could interfere with this process.

When no precautions were taken, then the photographer had a wide choice of mechanisms for making a spirit photograph, the most favoured being double exposures. The 'spirit' was photographed beforehand, and underexposed so that it would appear semi-transparent. But this was so obvious a trick that sitters frequently insisted on providing their own plates.

Photographic plates were sold in packets. It was therefore not possible for the medium to get hold of these beforehand to imprint on them the 'spirit'. Or was it? Some photographers had convenient arrangements with photographic suppliers so that the sitters would unwittingly buy a packet of prepared plates. More astute sitters purchased their plates at a distance; but these, the photographer might say, were not the right ones. Perhaps the sitter would go to such and such a photographic suppliers and obtain the right ones. So that there would be no mistake, the type would be written down.

The packet of plates could be replaced on the spot by sleight of hand; or the substitution could occur in the dark-room where the light was dim. If one plate was offered to the photographer, it was easier than a packet-full to switch, but the wary would frequently mark the plate. This would be countered by the photographer marking one of his own plates in the same way, for the devotees of spirit photographs were regulars and the photographer could easily retain a previous marked plate to examine the manner in which it had been marked. The most cautious of sitters would wish to mark the plate while in the camera; this difficulty could be met by a spirit photographer with a trick 'dark-slide' that already held the fake plate in a hidden partition. When the sitter's slide was put in the container this was secreted away, and the sitter would mark the fake plate unaware that this was not the plate he had seen put in the container.

If all else failed and the genuine plate was unavoidably put in the camera, then there would be an unfortunate accident. The plates would be underexposed or overexposed, or would be broken – in any event, they would be failures, necessitating fresh plates. If the sitter had brought extra plates for such contingencies then it is likely that they were in the dark-room, untenanted, or so the sitter assumed, though an accomplice could easily substitute prepared plates while the photographer and sitter were occupied in the studio.

Perhaps the most ingenious method was that used by the photographer Boursnell who painted a 'spirit' on a background with a substance such as quinine sulphite. This spirit could not be seen with the naked eye, but would be picked up by the camera. Other methods included ingenious trick cameras. Under the hood, the photographer could do all that he need do whilst preparing to take the photograph. By inserting a transparency in front of the plate he could get the same result as if he were using double exposure. Unlike materialisation seances, where the audience was unpredictable and could interfere, the photographic sitter was kept at a distance, immobile and looking appropriately solemn, while the precious seconds ticked away.

Spirit photography began in America in 1862. William A. Mumler, an engraver employed by a firm of Boston jewellers, was taking a self-portrait; the method he used was to focus on an empty chair, uncover the lens, and spring into position by the side of the chair. On this occasion Mumler found that on developing the photograph a young girl, whom he recognised as his cousin, twelve years dead, was sitting in the chair. She was clothed in a low necked short-sleeved dress, and below the waist the image faded away in a mist. The chair was distinctly seen through the body and arms, and so was the table on which one arm was resting.

Mumler published this photograph. It was the first spirit photograph, though Richard Boursnell was supposed to have had extras on photographs he took in 1851. He was begged to carry on, and take photographs of spiritualists with their accompanying dead friends, and although at first he appears to have been reluctant he eventually gave in, and set up in business as 'a medium for taking spirit photographs'. Either his technique improved or he became bolder, for his likenesses began to be clearer and less blurred, and in 1863 a spirit turned out to be a photograph of a living man, and furthermore a living man he had himself photographed a few weeks earlier.

At a seance held in 1856 by Thomas Slater, an optician in the Euston Road, with Lord Brougham and Robert Owen, the spirits rapped out that Slater would eventually take spirit photographs. In fact, the first Englishman to do so was Frederick Hudson.

On March 7th 1872, Georgina Houghton, a drawing and painting medium, went to the house of the celebrated Mrs Guppy. Mrs Guppy showed her some photographs that had been taken by Hudson. She and her husband had gone to Hudson's studio; while she was in a cabinet at the back of the studio, the camera had been trained on Mr Guppy. A wreath of flowers was placed by spirit hands on Mr Guppy's head, and when the photograph was developed a veiled figure could be seen behind him. Why not, suggested Mrs Guppy, go to Mr Hudson and see what he could produce for Miss Houghton?

They went over the same afternoon, and Miss Houghton was overjoyed by the results. There were accompanying figures on photographs of her, but so small and indistinct that only by using a magnifying glass could she determine that they were her mother and father; she could also see a dagger in the air, a hand, and various other items, which she interpreted symbolically. Hudson was anxious to get Miss Houghton as a full-time client, but the previous year an exhibition of her spirit drawings in Old Bond Street had crippled her financially, and she could see no way of financing sittings with Hudson. She did not reckon on the intense interest which her spirit photographs aroused when the word was dropped that Hudson was doing what Mumler had done in the United States, and certainly Mrs Guppy was not slow to be in on any new spirit manifestation. So Miss Houghton ordered from Hudson a large number of prints of the photographs taken of her, plus others that Hudson thought interesting, buying them wholesale, selling them retail.

It was arranged for Miss Houghton to go to Hudson's studio in Holloway, North London, every Thursday. On March 14th she and Mrs Guppy succeeded in enticing on to the sensitive plate a spirit rabbit (Hudson kept rabbits in a hutch in his garden). Hudson was so nervous 'that several times in the most critical moment the glass has slipped from his trembling fingers, and whatever might have been upon it has been utterly lost'. At this same sitting, a tall figure clad in white appeared on the plate, recognised by Miss Houghton as her mother, but Hudson coated this with varnish instead of collodion, and the plate was spoiled. It occurred to Miss Houghton that spirit photography, being different from ordinary photography, possibly needed extra chemicals added, and suggested to Hudson that perhaps a dash of varnish added to the collodion would improve matters, but in the meantime Mrs Guppy had evoked the spirit Katie, who instructed Hudson in a secret way to prepare the chemicals. But untoward influences were at work, and Miss Houghton took some frankincense to subsequent sittings which she burned in a large Javanese incense-burner.

Strange features were observed in the series of spirit photographs; in several of the photographs taken of Miss Houghton, she did not appear at all, her place being taken by spirit figures. Occasionally there would be symbolic additions, such as a rock in the right-hand side of the picture, and on one occasion the spirit extra had what seemed to be an arm about Miss Houghton's left shoulder. How could this be, when the two spirit hands were seen to be otherwise occupied? This was explained by another sitter, Mrs Tebb. It was not an arm at all, but a ray of coloured light passing from the spirit to the sitter, a spiritual link.

It was being noised about that Hudson was a fraud, and although in the earlier sittings Hudson had a free hand and no attempts were made to superintend his actions in the dark-room, Miss Houghton felt obliged to go with him into his dark-room to see what he was doing. Fraud, she proclaimed, was 'absolutely impossible'. Other inquirers were not so certain, and Mr Herne was openly accused of dressing up as a ghost. There was competition, too, from other photographers; photographs taken by John Jones of Enmore Park, an amateur, contained doubles, thought to be impossible to account for by the accidental shifting of the camera. Mrs Guppy was forbidden by her husband to go to any more sittings with Hudson.

Hudson was worried, and the demand for more stringent precautions against fraud resulted in no spirits appearing on his photographs. Miss Houghton received a spirit message via Mrs Guppy that she must not permit any more tests to be made, that she was the backbone of spirit photography, and that if Hudson was subjected to even the most amateurish of tests, she would not get any results for a month. Miss Houghton agreed, but not even she could deflect John Bruce Beattie, a celebrated Bristol photographer, who had carried out experiments in spirit photography, and who had visited Hudson in the guise of 'Mr Bruce'.

Beattie pointed out that the background not only appeared through Hudson's spirit figures, but through the images of the sitters themselves. Combined with twin outlines of the background, this could mean nothing other than that Hudson had been using double exposures. The most damning evidence was Hudson's attempts to remove the pattern of a carpet showing through a sitter's leg by retouching.

The photographers, unlike mediums with set pieces, had the advantage that the sitters were prepared for anything and that the most hazy of spirit faces would be instantly recognised. One of Hudson's keenest supporters was A. R. Wallace, and for him a mother's portrait was produced, 'not such a likeness as a portrait taken during life, but a somewhat pensive idealised likeness – yet still to me an unmistakeable likeness,' while as for his sister, there was 'something wrong about the mouth and chin. This may found to be due to the filling up of spots by the photographer'.[1] Some sitters had more than they bargained for. The Reverend Mr Barrett received a spirit companion 'of his other-half, the Bride awaiting him in the spirit-world; one all unknown to him, for he had passed on through life without any awakening of that sort of affection . . . he passed into the next life on the 24th of April of this year 1881, and I trust he may now be rejoicing in the happy union that was not vouchsafed to him on this earth'.[2]

The *annus mirabilis* of spirit photography was 1872. Hudson began operating in this year, and so did F. M. Parkes, experimenting with his friend Mr Reeves, proprietor of a dining-room near King's Cross. At first, the spirit appearances were restricted to unaccountable patches of light and irregular markings on the plate. It did not need a spirit to account for these; any amateur photographer who does his own developing and printing will be familiar with these phenomena, due to leakages of light during exposure or processing, uneven development, or careless handling of the chemicals. After three months, Parkes succeeded in obtaining a spirit extra for Drs Sexton and Clarke of Edinburgh. Stainton Moses gave Parkes his seal of approval, praising the enormous variety of the 'designs' (a curious word to use in this context): 'Out of 110 that lie before me now, commencing from April 1872, and with some intermissions extending down to present date (1875), there are not two that are alike – scarcely two that bear any similarity to each other. Each design is peculiar to itself, and bears upon the face of it marks of individuality.'[3]

Unlike some other spirit photographers, Parkes was reluctant to let outsiders examine his apparatus, and the odd effects on some of his plates he attributed to the eccentric habits of the spirits.

The most accomplished of the Victorian photographers of spirits was probably Buguet. He had built up a considerable reputation in France, and in June 1874 he came over to London, opening up studios at 33 Baker Street. His extras were not the anonymous spirits which could function as wife or daughter, or even husband and son, but the celebrated, such as Dickens and Charles the First. He created a great stir when the likeness of Stainton Moses appeared during a sitting with a Mr Gledstanes in Paris; Moses was at that time in a trance in London. When Buguet was arrested in April 1875 by the French police, Stainton Moses was indignant rather than numbed, even more so when Buguet confessed. 'The poor wretch,' declared Moses in *Human Nature,* 'was bribed by promises of immunity, and told his tale.' Buguet could hardly do otherwise, for the police had taken charge of the various props Buguet had used for the manufacture of his spirit photographs: cardboard figures and heads, and miscellaneous trappings. Buguet admitted that he had earlier used assistants, but the repetition of the same spirit faces was beginning to create suspicion, so he utilised cardboard figures instead; he also said that he had employed men to find out about the appearance of dead relatives of his clients.

'The case for psychic photography would be stronger without him', declared Conan Doyle in his history of spiritualism, but the discomfiture of the believers in spirit photography did not last for long. Led by Moses, they steadfastly maintained that it was a Roman Catholic plot instigated by the Jesuits, and ignored completely the evidence of the trial. The ambiguity of spirit photographs was graphically illustrated by Buguet himself in court. A figure had been recognised at different times as a sister, a mother, and a friend; another figure had been recognised as a dead friend, or alternatively a live father-in-law. And these were portraits, not the blurred it-may-be-this-it-may-be-that of Hudson. Once their ideas were fixed, said Buguet, nothing would change them; he only had to agree with what they said.

David Duguid stands somewhat apart from other spirit photographers. His extra figures have a bizarre quality, like badly cutout photographs clipped on anywhere, sometimes obliterating the sitter. He also operated without a sitter, leaving the camera for forty seconds with the cap off, then examining the plate with a magnifying glass to see what had transpired. His products fell somewhere between spirit photographs and the fashionable art photographs emulating paintings.

Spirit photography gave greater openings for fraud than any other aspect of Victorian spiritualism. But for the acrimony between rival spirit photographers, much of the fraud could have gone on longer. Spirit photography illustrates once again the credulity of the sitters, seeing in blotches of light the features of their loved ones, rationalising the appearance of a hand in the middle of the chest as clear evidence that the figure represented was a dead wife (who had broken her arm in five places). The photographers themselves were casual; it was so easy for them to fake spirit extras that they became slip-shod, and spirit photography contrasts sharply with areas where the mediums had to keep their wits about them, or be immediately exposed, such as slate-writing and materialisations.

The spirit photographers were also drawn into a false sense of security by the passiveness and eagerness to believe of sitters new to this branch of professional spiritualism. They felt they could provide anything and it would recognised. They failed to realise the strength of the spiritualist grape-vine, that photographs would be exchanged and discussed, that notes would be exchanged, that their methods would be analysed not only in the spiritualist journals but in the photographic magazines as well. While critical attention was focused by Mrs Sidgwick in 1891 in the *Proceedings* of the Society for Psychical Research, the edifice shuddered. But it did not fall, and the first two decades of the twentieth century sent an upsurge in spirit photography.

11. Clairvoyance

Mrs Sidgwick of the Society for Psychical Research provisionally defined clairvoyance 'as knowledge which would ordinarily be acquired through the senses, acquired supernormally without the use of the senses, and not by thought-transference from persons present'. However, clairvoyance in fact was an odds and ends corner, into which anything was thrown, from 'pure' clairvoyance such as crystal-gazing to platform clairvoyance subsisting on the clever employment of codes.

The crystal was only one of many objects used in acquiring knowledge through induced hallucinations. Water in bowls or translucent containers, mirrors of polished steel, liquid poured into the palm of the hand, a drop of blood or ink, the blade of a sword, a polished finger-nail – in fact any reflecting surface. Crystal-gazing in some form had been prevalent for upwards of three thousand years, and was of world-wide distribution. Known as scrying, peeping, viewing, speculating, or reading, it was, declared Andrew Lang, 'Perhaps the only 'occult' diversion which may be free from psychological or physical risk, and which it is easy not to mix with superstition'.

Scrying was regarded in the Middle Ages as heretical and the *specularii* were treated with scant ceremony, but like witchcraft, it never really died, and, like witchcraft, it enjoyed a revival towards the end of the nineteenth century. This resurgence was never so important as its principal supporters claimed.

The most voluble propagandist was Miss Goodrich-Freer, herself a crystal-gazer, and she analysed the mechanics of crystal-gazing with a good deal of acumen. Although many of the objects into which she gazed presented a circular surface, the images she saw were flat and in the objects rather than round the periphery. When she looked in a spoon (and she used that term rather than *at* a spoon) the images were distorted in the same manner as reflections would have been.

The images were in colour, though not naturalistic, and when the eyes became tired, the images would change from one colour to its complementary. Miss Goodrich-Freer professed not to know what the complementary colours of certain colours were.

Crystal-gazing was introduced to Mrs A. W. Verrall by Myers. She had no previous knowledge or interest in the subject. She used a number of objects – a cut crystal, a globular crystal, a glass paperweight, and a tumbler of water – and found no difference between them. She found crystal gazing extremely useful to recall things that she had forgotten to do, but on those occasions nothing appeared in the crystal, it merely serving as an exterior object to focus on. Her images built up from points of light in the crystal. Mrs Verrall discovered odd things about colour content; she once saw a flower in the crystal which she knew to be pink, though she could not see a colour, and once saw a black cat with a ribbon around its neck; the ribbon she knew to be red, though it did not appear so in the crystal, and no matter how she tried she could not bring out the red of the ribbon. The background of the crystal made no difference to the colour content of the hallucination.

A friend of the Countess of Radnor found that she had a talent for crystal-gazing. She first discovered this at a lunch where the topic was being discussed, and one of her companions said that a glass of water was just as good as a crystal. On looking into a glass, the woman saw a gold key that was so clear that she looked on the tablecloth for it. She purchased a crystal, and was rewarded with numbers of crystal visions, including writing. The writing came one letter at a time, each letter filling the crystal. The words were in reverse, so that the message was not clear until the end.

Although this particular crystal-gazer preferred to keep her name unknown, she achieved several interesting coups, the most impressive being recorded by Joseph Barnby, the composer. In 1889 he was invited to Longford Castle, the seat of Lord and Lady Radnor, where he was introduced to the crystal-gazer. She described in detail a room Barnby's wife had occupied in a hotel at Eastbourne, the dress his wife was wearing (a dress Barnby did not know she had with her), and his wife, tall, dark, slightly foreign in appearance, with rather 'an air'. Sixteen months later Barnby's wife and the crystal-gazer met each other in London, where the recognition was immediate.

'Miss Angus', the name by which the above crystal-gazer was referred to, did not profess to be able to tell the future, nor did the other 'respectable' crystal-gazers of the nineteenth century. The visions seen were arbitrary and fugitive, and the gazers did not know what they would be seeing when the mist cleared — whether it would be a geometric figure, a portion of a railway advertisement half-remembered from the previous day, or a meaningless tableau. Theoretically, crystal-gazing may be pure clairvoyance, but the results with few exceptions were not impressive.

Another form of pure clairvoyance was psychometry. This word was coined in 1854, and is defined as the alleged faculty of divining, from physical contact or proximity only, the qualities or properties of an object, or of persons or things that have been in contact with it. Postal phrenology forms a division of psychometry. Postal phrenology was practised on a considerable scale by Victorian spiritualists such as J. Burns, the Editor of *Medium and Daybreak.* For half a crown and on receipt of photographs, front and side, of the head, plus a little hair 'indicating organic quality', Burns would send back a reading. If the enquirer sent five shillings the reading would be extended. It need hardly be added that the readings were vague and favourable.

At least Burns had something to work on, unlike psychometrists who were given a name in a sealed envelope and invited to try their best on that. One step further was an object in a sealed envelope. 'A sensitive may pick up an object and as he or she does so a fact with regard to its previous history may rush into their minds with almost lightning speed,' even when the object was enclosed in an envelope. This was one of the talents of Mr Duguid, who had created a considerable stir as a painting medium, as a photographer of spirit forms, and as an adept in automatic writing.

In September 1885 the Spiritual Institution invited him to try his hand at instant psychometry, after a few speeches, biscuits, fruits, and glasses of lemonade. Upwards of a dozen envelopes were numbered, and handed round 'mostly to strangers'. Duguid did not know who received the envelopes. The fortunate dozen placed in the envelope a pencil, a coin, any other small item, or a written sentence. The envelopes were handed back to Duguid, and one by one he placed each envelope against his forehead.

Whether or not the object's previous history rushed into his mind with almost lightning speed is neither here nor there, but from the contact of the envelope with the medium's forehead (some psychometrists believed that here was the problematical third eye of legend), Duguid came up with a series of vivid portraits of the objects' owners. Reading between the lines it is evident that not all the owners were completely satisfied with the readings: 'Two gentlemen fancied that in their cases matter had been given more appropriate to others, while the conclusion of their reading had been given to someone else.'

Dr Stenson Hooker was a Harley Street physician, with interests in spirit auras and psychometry. Dr A. T. Schofield visited him, and handed him a gold pencil case from off his chain. Dr Hooker put the case to his forehead, told Schofield it was bought in Piccadilly and described the woman who gave it. Schofield made further investigations; he met a young psychometrist in Harley Street and gave her a stone to hold. It was, she said, a very very old stone, full of wickedness; she could hear savage shouts and yells, and was becoming hysterical. Schofield states that it was a stone thrown from the walls of Joshua's Jericho. To soothe her he took a cross from the chain of a young clergyman who was there; the cross, no doubt, would act as an antidote, but the cross was even worse, for the psychometrist sensed screaming and laughing and shouting. Angry and affronted, she asked Schofield why he gave her such terrible things? Schofield then discovered that the young clergyman had been for years a chaplain in a lunatic asylum.

Psychometry is practiced today in spiritualist circles with as much assurance and energy as it ever was, and it forms a useful pendant to the fortune-telling business. Is it telepathy, with the object being psychometrised acting as either a blind or a focus of attention, or are the psychometrists a good deal shrewder than their subjects, drawing data from their subjects as in fortune-telling or stage clairvoyance, and using knowledge of muscle-reading to see how close they are getting to the solution?

Even committed spiritualists did not wholly believe that there was a necessary spirit intervention between the psychometrist and the object, if only on the grounds that there was no time lapse between the object being handled and the psychometric reading. They felt that objects gave out an aura, that somehow both their physical make-up and their ethical overtones were made manifest. It is difficult to see how a name on a piece of paper placed in a sealed envelope could convey anything. If there is a time lapse between the receipt of the sealed envelope and the reading certain problems do vanish; there were many ways of reading sealed messages, from opening the envelopes and replacing the seal with another (favoured when the psycho-metrist – clairvoyant was familiar with the sitter and his seal), from extracting the sealed message through the top of the envelope where the flap comes over, to the sophisticated method of soaking the envelope in benzine so as to make it transparent.

Conventional clairvoyance lays itself open to even greater varieties of fraud.

The humdrum clairvoyance of the fortune-teller's booth can be extended. The first factor to be considered is the generality of the message; by being imprecise and enigmatic it can be interpreted as the subject sees fit. The second factor is the shrewdness of the operator. By the use of observation and a rough and ready applied psychology, the subject can leave the booth feeling that wonders have been unfolded. Anxiety will feed on any sort of comfort when backed by pseudo-science and the parlour occult.

Stage clairvoyance was frequently a studied and expert thing. Codes of great intricacy were used to inform the clairvoyant, blindfolded, with his back to the audience, of the objects being presented in the hall, of numbers on banknotes, of readings from a watch. The codes depended on practice, memory, and reliability, and were usually based on the initial letter of a sentence or on initial words which were used in lieu of numbers, the numbers being then equated with a significant series. These words were those which would naturally be used by the confederate, the in-between. He would harangue the clairvoyant so that the audience would think he was on their side, but there was a reason for this as we can see from the following, frequently-used, code:

1 is Say or Speak	7 is Please or Pray
2 is Be, Look or Let	8 is Are or Ain't
3 is Can or Can't	9 is Now
4 is Do or Don't	10 is Tell
5 is Will or Won't	0 is Hurry or Come
6 is What	

The early days of table-rapping

A seance in 1871
(Radio Times Hulton Picture Library)

Simulating levitation

The spirit hand above and left

Note the hands

D.D. Home with the cage invented by Crookes to test him

Home and his self-playing accordion

Florence Cook, 1874

The spirit 'Katie' 1874 – a striking resemblance?

Florence Cook in trance, plus 'spirit form', 1874

Mrs Tebb, Mrs Guppy (mediums) and Miss Houghton (dupe)

Spirit photographs by Hudson with Georgina Houghton as subject

Trick photography? *c.* 1860

Messrs. SLADE and LANCASTER,

In a Scene from the New Farce, "The Happy Medium;
No Spirits should be above Proof."

Cartoon at the time of the Slade *v.* Lankaster (misspelt) law suit

F.W.H. Myers (1843–1901)

Edmund Gurney (1847–1888)

Henry Sidgwick (1839–1900).
Founder member of the Society for
Psychical Research

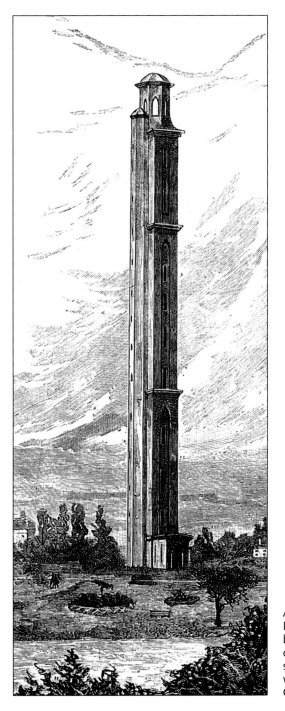

Arnewood Tower, Lymington, Hampshire, built in 1885 'to commemorate spiritualism'. The architect was under the 'control' of Christopher Wren

Samuel Carter Hall
(1800–1889)

PORTRAIT OF A MATERIALIZED SPIRIT.

"JOHN KING."

MEDIUM—CHARLES E. WILLIAMS.

After the seance, c. 1870

Thus, if the number 1234 is required, a likely rigmarole would be this: Say the number. Look at it. Can you see it? Do you know?

This system could be used in many ways. Numbers were equated with different items in a group – metals, gems, countries, materials, fabrics, etc. Suppose the clairvoyant had understood 'glove' through a system using the initial letters of a sentence, based on the following transposition used by the conjurer Robert Heller:

A is H   B is T   C is C   D is G   E is F   F is E   G is A
H is I   I is B   J is L   K is Pray   L is C   M is O   N is D
O is V   P is J   Q is W   R is M   S is N   T is P   U is Look
V is Y   W is R   X is See This   Y is Q   Z is Hurry Hurry up – repeat last letter.

The in-between would then transmit the fabric using the number code: The table of fabrics is as follows:

1 Silk = Say or Speak   5 Leather = Will or Won't
2 Wool = Be Look or Let   6 Kid = What
3 Cotton = Can or Can't   7 Buckskin = Please or Pray
4 Linen = Do or Don't   8 Lace = Are or Ain't

The colour of the gloves would follow, using the colour code:

1 is White   5 is Red
2 is Black   6 is Green
3 is Blue   7 is Yellow
4 is Brown   8 is Grey

With practice, this system of relaying information from the auditorium to the stage could be rapid and seemingly inconsequential.

With this system in mind it might be worth examining an episode recorded by the Society of Psychical Research during the celebrated Brighton clairvoyance experiments. The medium was G. A. Smith, who had ingratiated himself sufficiently with Gurney to become his secretary: Gurney had committed suicide, and Mrs Sidgwick had taken over.

The subject's eyes were apparently closed; Smith sat in front of him, facing him and holding up a card with its back to him. Mrs Sidgwick had made 'practically certain' that the subject could not see the face of the card. Numbers were being 'guessed' by the subject. They continued:

Smith: Now then, Mr W., here's another one.
Subject: Where?
Smith: Here it is. (Subject dropped off into deeper state of 'trance')
Subject: Twelve, isn't it?
Smith: Which figure looks the most distinct?
Subject: The two. I think.
Smith: Yes. Then look again at the other. Are you sure it is a one?
Subject: I can't see (pause). I think it is a three.
Smith: Well, then, what's the number?
Subject: Why, it's thirty-two!

This is characteristic dialogue, and although Smith was not using the Heller code, it could easily be a variant with 'Now' as three, and 'Here' as two, the rest of the dialogue being padding to impress the observers.

Clairvoyance need not necessarily be what it purports to be. Tricks could be used even when the confederate was nowhere near to the clairvoyant and not communicating with him by speech. Let us suppose that the clairvoyant is on the stage, sitting in a chair, blindfolded. The blindford is adjusted so that the man cannot see (though Mrs Sidgwick and her associates during experimental sessions found out how difficult it was completely to blindfold a man). A man holds up a note in the auditorium; the clairvoyant is asked to read out the number. He does so. How is it done?

The confederate is somewhere in the audience, probably near the back. He has with him a strong pair of binoculars, with which he can read the number on the note. He is not sitting in an ordinary seat, for he has, beneath his foot and covered by the carpet, a transmitting device. By tapping his foot he sends the clairvoyant the information he needs via a wire taken under the auditorium carpet, under the stage, and finishing beneath the clairvoyant's foot, when the message would emerge as a pulse.

At a less ingenious level, the clairvoyant used a trick chair, in which one of the uprights was a tube. The message would then be transmitted from below stage by voice from a person with a view of the auditorium or via a further confederate, communicating by an electrical transmitter as before or by using some other means.

There were a multitude of ways in which pseudo-clairvoyants acquired information, as the definition has it 'supernormally', from that in the session observed by Mrs Sidgwick where the clairvoyant, blindfolded, had a tiny area of vision near the floor so that the confederate could wag his big toe at him in code, through the obvious medley of nods and sighs of young lady mediums anxious to break into the larger fields, the skilful muscle-reading and applied psychology of the fair-booth operators, to the expert stage clairvoyant using all the modern techniques at his disposal.

Theatrical thought-reading and mock-clairvoyance does not, of course, invalidate clairvoyance, and during the mesmerism craze between 1830 and 1850 it was found that thought-transference between operator and mesmerised subject was commonplace. Twentieth-century investigations under test conditions undreamed of in the nineteenth century have confirmed the existence of telepathy, and although the dramatic feats of Victorian practitioners are rarely repeated today, the defiance of the laws of chance are just as significant when the variation is 3 per cent rather than 50 per cent.

The interest shown by the Society for Psychical Research in thought-transference encouraged its members to try for themselves. It was an area of investigation in which there were no strong feelings; spiritualists thought that the messages were passed from one to the other with the aid of spirits, non-spiritualists thought that only the sender and the receiver were responsible, and that they were exploiting a hitherto undiscovered sixth sense.

The amateurs used ordinary packs of playing-cards. In 1888 a woman made a series of experiments with her four-year-old daughter. The little girl drew a card out of the pack and looked at it, while the mother, with closed eyes, tried to guess what it was. The pack was an imperfect one, six cards missing. Fifty-two experiments were made; in fourteen of these no impression was received, and no guess hazarded. Of the remaining thirty-eight:

Suit only right	4
Picture only right	17
Suit and picture right but not number	10
Picture and number right but not suit	2
Suit, picture, and number right	5
Quite wrong	0

The probability is, of course, that less than one card would be guessed wholly right out of thirty-eight guesses.

Between November 1891 and October 1892 the Misses Despard and Campbell ran a series of experiments. Miss Campbell sat in an armchair with her back to a table, on which Miss Despard placed a pack of cards, drawing one out at random, which Miss Campbell tried to guess. The court cards had been removed. The first series was hopeless, so the ladies broke the pack down into four sequences of fourteen cards. The success rate was fifty per cent above chance. Results were more sensational using numbers written on paper in ink, but the series was so short (twenty-one trials, using numbers to twenty-one) that the five successes (par for the course is one) is statistically insignificant.

A series of experiments by Major Taylor of the Royal Military College, Sandhurst, anticipate ESP tests carried out today. Instead of playing cards, Major Taylor prepared geometric figures: a star, a diamond, a crescent, an arrowhead, a shamrock leaf, a Maltese cross. The results were slightly above average, but not significantly so. Between December 1886 and February 1887 three Kensington female art students and a male friend tried guessing the suits of cards. The results were carefully recorded; out of 921 guesses, 390 were correct, compared with the chance figure of 230. Miss Hopkinson of Woburn Place and some young lady friends also experimented with guessing the suits, and, if possible, the values of the cards. The series was extremely short (2,200 tests) by today's test standards. In Miss Hopkinson's tests, the 'suit right' successes are hardly above chance (571 against 2,200 – 26 per cent against 25 per cent), though the 'quite right' successes are well above chance (100 against 2,200; the chance would be 42).

One of the most extensive series of card-guessing experiments was carried out by Miss N. Robertson, who tried over 15,000 guesses. She claimed that her successes were double the chance figure. She tried several ways, from drawing out a card from the pack, face down, with her hand over the card, to putting the card in tin-foil and placing it in two envelopes (this was a failure). She achieved best results when a friend sat in another room and drew cards from the pack, when presumably some degree of telepathy was in operation.

The various percipients received their information as a spoken message, as a visual image at the back of the head, or as a hallucinatory replica of the anticipated card in space. Card-guessing is divided into two sharply differentiated groups: where an agent is used who sees the card and transmits its content telepathically, and where the percipient works alone. In the latter case, the analogy is with the abstruse kinds of psychometry rather than telepathy.

Spiritualists were indifferent to the cult of card-guessing, and they ignored those aspects of clairvoyance in which a spirit element was obviously missing. They were more attuned to the clairvoyance of Home, where simple telepathy could be construed as messages from the dead. In America, Home was staying with Ward Cheney of Connecticut; he stated that he was conscious of rustling of a silk dress, and of voices. A message came over to him, 'I am annoyed that a coffin should have been placed above mine,' followed by, 'What is more, Seth had no right to cut that tree down'. These messages had meanings to the audience, though the information about the coffin was not, ostensibly, known. At another seance, a Mrs Senior was told by her dead husband that she had forgotten to wind his watch up, and a Mrs Hemmings was informed that the night her father died she played whist with him. It needed no prompting for such straightforward telepathy to be assigned to messages from beyond the veil.

As awareness of telepathy grew from the accumulative evidence of amateur thought-reading sessions, as it was shown that people did not have to be particularly mediumistic to send or receive telepathic messages, so were spirit messages from the grave re-evaluated. Clairvoyance, the rag-bag of spiritualism, was not so phenomenal as was once supposed.

The Tearing of the Veil

12. Hallucinations

The Victorian period was not only a haunted age; it was also, in every sense of the word, a hallucinatory age, lending itself to every type of illusion, even at the level of bricks and mortar. The Victorian house, the Victorian street, encouraged illusion and hallucination, the Victorian theatre was a hotbed of optical tricks, only the kitchen escaped the obsession with the manufacture of articles which appeared to be something else: money-boxes disguised as books, substantial-looking doors that on examination was merely cunning paintwork, solid-looking chairs that were, in fact, featherlight, being manufactured from papier mâché.

Nineteenth-century man and woman were disposed to believe, not only theologically but in the day-to-day business of life, that things were not as they seemed. Their senses had a habit of letting them down, and they were mentally prepared for any odd happenings, fugitive visions, the unaccountable thing seen out of the corner of the eye, the strange sounds in the middle of the night, the tap on the shoulder that might be a visitation from another world.

To those who were convinced that the dead were continuously striving to get in touch with the living, this tap on the shoulder would have been particularly significant. Lewis Charles Powles, for instance, an associate of the Society for Psychical Research, described by a Mr Findlay to Lord Bute after the celebrated investigation into the Ballachin ghost: 'Mr Powles was I think the most nervous man I ever met. He seems to live in a world of influences, which are a perpetual source of annoyance to him. He can tell by instinct whether a room or house is haunted and his instinct is confirmed by his experiences. He sees nothing but is prepared by constitution to feel and hear.'

Everyone receives the type of hallucination he or she is equipped to receive, and this is conditioned by reading matter, the visual arts, physiological and psychological disposition, and the state of the subject's health. Dickens's *Christmas Carol* had a great formative effect on the ghost stereotype. The ghost of Marley is still the fashionable model for everyman. Miss Calmody-Hamlyn's experience in Bamburgh Castle in the eighteen-nineties tells us more about Miss Hamlyn than about ghosts: 'He came across the floor of the rooms about midnight, filmy grey, and he sounded to be clanking chains.'[1]

Those most fitted to the reception of visual hallucinations are those with defective vision. When this is coupled with a vivid imagination and that will to believe beloved of students of the occult, almost any stimulus can be transformed by the subject into a manifestation. Two of the principal crystal-gazers of the late Victorian period, Mrs Verrall, and Miss Goodrich-Freer, were short-sighted in one eye. By focusing each eye individually, the visions seem to move.

The process of transforming illusion into hallucination is governed and modified by psychological make-up and environment. The Victorians used mirrors massively as an item of decor, and theirs was the first age in which plate glass was used on a large scale. The mirror was a standard prop in stage optical tricks, and 'Pepper's Ghost', an enormous source of entertainment and wonderment to the theatregoer, was compounded of reflections and clever lighting. The *Cabaret du Néant*, invented in Paris and imported to Britain soon afterwards, centred on a man being transformed into a skeleton through the cunning use of plate glass. Mirrors, plate glass, and lighting, were also the sole elements in popular entertainments such as the three-headed woman and the talking head (a woman was screened up to her head by two mirrors which gave the two table legs the appearance of four).

Illusions were also fostered by the design of furnishings and fittings, by schemes of colouring, and by the configurations of wallpaper of the William Morris school. Heavy hanging draperies and curtains lent themselves to a subtle modulation, gas lighting was subject to breezes, draughts, and the vagaries of the power supply.

Even more, the eccentricities of Victorian central heating schemes created a series of hubble-bubble sounds that could be interpreted by the nervous in any way they fancied. The first high pressure system was invented by A. M. Perkins in 1845, and although modifications were made it rarely operated silently. The weird sounds heard during the Ballechin haunting were attributed by detached witnesses to this very cause: 'One theory is, that it was the hot water in the pipes getting cold, which, I am told, would make a loud throbbing noise.'[2]

An immense amount of publicity was given to this particular haunting in the late 'nineties, primarily because the ghost-hunters, by their persistence, had devalued the property (and property was ever sacred to the readers of *The Times*), but in less auspicious cases the throbbings and bangings of a hot-water system in labour gave rise to the most hair-raising speculation.

Antiquity is not vital to a haunted house. What for many years figured as the 'most haunted house in England', Borley Rectory, was not built until 1863. The houses of the Victorians were frequently quirkish in the extreme, and the extensive use of terra cotta, dark marble, and other exotic stone, combined with their tendencies towards meaningless steeples and gables, gave many of these houses a built-in sinister quality that they still retain.

It is not true, as is often said, that Victorian houses were not well built. But building features such as hollow walls could result in peculiar acoustic effects, which in themselves could create the reputation of a haunted house.

The 'classical' hauntings usually occurred in houses where there were large numbers of servants. The lower echelons of servants could be sharp and mischievous, and they knew the inner geography of the houses a good deal better than the owners. When the bangs and clankings of the hot water system had reduced guests to a state of hysteria, they were doubtless not slow in joining in the fun, adding distinctive touches of their own. At one haunting the mark of a boot was clearly seen on a door jamb, and it needed imaginative powers indeed to see in this the work of a ghost. Auditory hallucinations of the bang and clatter order must be treated with great circumspection.

What sort of people experienced hallucinations? Those who had a monetary interest in the efficacy of their hallucinations can be discarded, the crystal-gazers, and the fraudulent mediums; so can those who had a vested interest in the occult for the purpose of self-aggrandisement, for instance the Theosophists, and those who would see and hear anything if they gave their mind to it, that credulous and gaping mass categorised by Madame Blavatsky as 'domestic imbeciles'. An amusing instance of how far self-delusion can persist is given by D. D. Home. When an old lady sat down to dinner she tipped the table to get responses to her undeviating question 'Dear Charles, may I have fish today?' If the table tipped the appropriate number of times to indicate 'yes', she replied 'Thank you, dear Charles. I thought I might, for I felt a strong desire to have fish for dinner'. If the table tipped 'no' – 'Ah! I thought so, Charles! I felt one of my chills coming on, and fish is bad for me when I have my chills.'[3] Charles, incidentally, was her dead husband.

One must remember that the elements of a hallucination are pre-known. As William James wrote: 'Sensations, once experienced, modify the nervous organism, so that copies of them arise again in the mind after the original outward stimulus is gone. No mental copy, however, can arise in the mind, of any kind of sensation which has never been directly excited from without.'[4] He also states 'that whilst part of what we perceive comes through our senses from the object before us, another part, and it may be the larger part always comes out of our own mind'.[5]

A hallucination therefore is an amalgam of sensation and contemplation. One is predisposed to observe something that is familiar, though one is not aware of it. It is interesting to note that almost all the classic ghost appearances of the Victorian times are clothed in a manner of the period or of a stereotype of a preceding period. So-called Elizabethan ghosts are garbed according to nineteenth-century interpretation, as portrayed in contemporary illustrations to Shakespeare or in the steel engravings characteristic of history books.

Bizarre hallucinations there are, but these are frequently to be found in either an uncluttered mind – the mind of a child – or a mind in distress, or convulsed in creation (as in the macabre imaginings of Poe). The specific type of hallucinatory image does not tell us very much about the occult, but it does about the state of a percipient's mind.

It is not surprising that the greatest incidence of hallucinations occur in houses that are already reputed to be haunted. There was the anonymous Captain H., who in 1868 in a haunted house saw a lady in a blue dress, hair 'à Hogarth', soft stomacher, long train, very thin with sharp features, face very sad. In the same year a governess in that house, a Miss Oliver, observed at four in the afternoon a lady in blue appear from the mistress's bedroom, go along an upper hall towards the master's dressing room, dress rustling, feet bare. The governess saw the apparition's image reflected in a mirror and supposed it real, until she realised the awesome implications – what would a real unknown person be doing in a haunted house?

A possible explanation which few Victorians would have admitted is that the lady in blue really was a lady in blue, with an assignation with the master. An amusing instance of a pair of lovers being interpreted as ghosts occurs in Elinor Glyn's novel *The Visits of Elizabeth*. Elinor Glyn was well-acquainted with Lady Warwick's set-up at Easton Lodge, and there may be more than a tinge of autobiography in this extract:

> They asked me why I was so sleepy, and I said because I had not slept well the last night and that I was sure the house was haunted. And so they all screamed at me, 'Why?' and so I told them, what was really true, that in the night I heard a noise of stealthy footsteps, and as I was not frightened I determined to see what it was, so I got up – Agnes sleeps in the dressing-room, but, of course, *she* never wakes – I opened the door and peeped out into the corridor, There are only two rooms beyond mine towards the end, round the corner, and it is dimly lit all night. Well, I distinctly saw a very tall grey figure disappear round the bend of the hall! When I got thus far every one dropped their books and listened with rapt attention, and I could see them exchanging looks, so I am sure they know it is haunted and were trying to keep it from me. I asked Mrs Smith if she had seen or heard anything because she sleeps in one of those rooms. She looked perfectly green but she said she had not heard a sound, and had slept like a top, and that I must have dreamt it.

With this in mind, one is inclined to seek a more mundane explanation in, for example, Miss M.B.'s narrative of July 1st 1883, that she awoke at two a.m., saw a woman silently moving towards closed doors whereupon she disappeared.

That many instances of hallucinations by the insane have infiltrated into the world of the spiritualistic and occult is not surprising, as they commonly have an air of bizarrerie that relieves the humdrum processions of shrouded and draped ghosts. That spiritualism was not only a haven to the neurotic but also the psychotic was appreciated at the time. Spiritualism was a useful safety valve for mild forms of insanity, especially those involving delusional states, and was an area in which delusions could be freely expressed with the certainty that they would be sympathetically appreciated.

That the hallucinations of the insane can be compared with the occult phenomena reported by spiritualists is evident. The Reverend Mr Walford became insane enough to be locked away, but he recovered and recounted his experiences. His hallucinations began when his brother was ill, and he was praying. 'When at prayer, something would pull at my back, blow in my face, as if in derision, and hovering around my mouth, try to snatch the words from my lips. At night when in bed, I felt something press upon my chest, and awake in great trepidation in the middle of the night, when I sometimes heard music at a distance.'[6]

Dr Forbes Winslow wrote that 'a lady informed me that her insanity commenced by her morbid fancy suggesting to her mind a number of lewd images ... everything she saw, and heard, appeared to be associated with physically impure notions'.[7] Such phenomena were commonplace in spiritualist circles, and at times they were given utterance. 'I have seen a medium, at other times calm and respectable, suddenly under some mysterious influence or control, break out into a tirade of the most horrible blasphemous and obscene language, which drove all the sitters from the table, to which no persuasion would ever afterwards induce them to return.'[8] So wrote an anonymous member of the Society for Psychical Research. The same impulses could motivate automatic writing; the member of the SPR was himself the victim here. 'At last – I shall never forget it – the pencil settled down to steady writing, and there came the most filthy, foul, vile, language such as the mind could never have imagined.'

Hallucinations of inanimate objects are quite as common as those of beings of one sort or another. Haloes are a particularly popular item, and when transformed into auras they have the effect of giving the percipients a certain cachet. Dr Forbes

Winslow is very severe on such phenomena: 'Photopsia, or the appearance of luminous phenomena, objects in a state of ignition, or surrounded by a phosphorescent halo, are common incipient symptoms of acute disease of the brain.'[9] This view was not shared by spiritualists: 'One evening, while at prayer, I saw a circle descend slowly on my head, and afterwards told my wife that I was the anointed of the Lord.'[10]

Even members of the Society for Psychical Research could be in peril of photopsia. The Reverend Charles J. M. Shaw was 'in the habit of seeing figures outlined in light against a dark background. These he told me he could see at will. He seems to have little critical instinct, and a thorough belief in the supernatural'.[11]

Animal hallucinations figure considerably in annals of the occult, and with the exception of horses and dogs, which are inclined to behave in a predictable manner, there must be some doubt as to whether or not they are real. Smaller creatures have a way of behaving in an arbitrary manner, and it is no surprise that they turn up at suitable psychological moments. In witchcraft, the convenient appearance of a real black cat was proof positive that it was the witch's familiar or the witch herself.

West Drayton Church near Uxbridge is said to be haunted by a large black bird. In 1749, knockings were heard in the vaults of the Paget and de Burgh families, a large black bird appeared, it was attacked by the bellringers, who hurt it, and it disappeared. In 1869, two ladies, no doubt aware of the legend, were arranging flowers on the altar when a bird perched on a pew, and in 1883 Mrs de Burgh, the wife of a former vicar, heard fluttering in the chancel.

Unquestionably many churches are invaded occasionally by birds, but a mystique associated with West Drayton Church has led to the casual appearance of a bird being interpreted in cosmic terms. The bird is searched for, and expected; in ninety-nine times out of a hundred it is not there; when it is seen, it strikes awe into the watchers, and when the mind is strung up to expect something any sound can be made into a fluttering in the chancel. No ornithologist would dispute that successive generations of birds can attach themselves to one site.

Something similar can operate in the case of death omens. The White Birds of Salisbury Plain are said to appear when a Bishop of Salisbury is dying. In 1885, Miss Moberly, the daughter of the bishop, saw one rising from the Palace garden when her father was near death; on August 16th 1911, Miss Edith Oliver, returning from taking choir boys on a treat, saw them. The bishop died unexpectedly. No account is kept of the birds that were seen when the bishop did not die.

The death omen of the Wardours of Arundel is two white owls on a roof. When a Wardour was dying no doubt the owls were eagerly searched for, and when none was found it would be easy enough to interpret anonymous white splodges as the death omen. Naturally there are death omens which cannot be assigned to real creatures making an apposite appearance. The Oxenhams of South Dawton see a white-breasted bird by a sick person's bed, which vanishes, and this must be ascribed to pure hallucination.

Writers on the subject, who tend to be gently cynical about death omens, are not too sure about that wide-spread phenomenon known as the spectral hound. This varies from county to county. There is the Black Shuck of East Anglia, with one eye like a lantern, which howls as it runs, the Padfoot of the north of England, saucer-eyed, with backward-turning feet, a trick shared by the Shriker of Lancashire, a large shaggy animal which can go either forward or backward on paws which make a splashing sound. There is the Black Dog of Lyme Regis, and innumerable headless hounds, especially in the north-west of England. In 1825, a headless hound placed its paws on the shoulders of a tradesman named Drabble outside Manchester Cathedral. But the best setting for a headless hound is unquestionably Swaledale, and that part of Swaledale known as Corpse Way, which led over a humpback bridge to Ivelet. Before 1580 when a local church was built, bearers had to travel twelve miles on foot with a coffin. They stopped at the Punch Bowl Inn, leaving the coffin in a barn. It is evident that the combination of macabre circumstances and strong drink created the ideal situation for the appearance of a headless hound.

13. Collective Hallucinations

'Collective hallucinations,' wrote G. F. Stout, 'though their existence is guaranteed by the Psychical Research Society, are of rare occurrence, and stand much in need of explanation.'[1] The Society was certainly happier about them than were psychologists and physiologists, and it had three possible theories. Either transference from one percipient to another came through the senses, or through telepathy, or else the hallucinations were of supernatural origin. In the *Census of Hallucinations* there were ninety-five instances of collective visual hallucination against 992 instances of unshared. There were thirty-four cases of collective auditory hallucinations, of which five occurred to people in different rooms.

A few words need to be said about this *Census*. Although many of the collators were men of probity, the field-workers were recruited on an *ad hoc* basis, and their reports were governed by a number of arbitrary factors. Timidity encouraged many of the census-takers to flinch asking the awkward questions, laziness meant that many of the answers were reported in a botched fashion. A grab-all-opportunities enthusiasm on the part of the instigators of the *Report* meant that there was little statistical consistency in the samples, and the fact that there were eager census-takers in Brazil resulted in lop-sided geographical coverage. The actual figures, therefore, serve as a guide, but can in no way be looked upon as authoritative. The chief value of the *Census* lies in the written statements made by the percipients.

There is no novelty at all about shared illusions, the financial future of a conjuror being dependant on them, and many of the so-called collective hallucinations were unquestionably similar illusions.

A fruitful source of collective hallucinations that the *Census* did not draw on was the spiritualist seance. When the politician and journalist Labouchère was at a seance, a piano is reported to have passed through the wall. Labouchère asked how it was that the other people had seen it but not him, and he was told that he was not sufficiently sympathetic. Similarly meetings of black magic enthusiasts encouraged collective illusions, such as those who operated in Dublin in the 'nineties, 'a whole colony of them of the most iniquitous kind. They are great mesmerists and blackguards, but picturesque in their hideous costumes of black cloth which covers all but their eyes'.[2]

Collective hysteria especially in closed communities such as convents, hospitals, prisons, and asylums, frequently resulted in collective hallucination, particularly amongst the women. As Benjamin C. Brodie noted, the primary factors in hysteria were 'fear, suggestion, and unconscious simulation'. In his notebook for the date February 3rd 1871, Dr Crichton-Browne commented that two of his patients independently and without communication with each other developed the delusion that the earth was 'of soft and spongy consistency like jelly or *blanc-mange*, and that by the exercise of a little force they will be able to sink down into it and end their sorrows. They both allege that they find the hard stone floor of the lobby spongy under their feet'.[3] One of them tried jumping from the top of steps to effect this purpose. During the witchcraft scares of the later middle ages and after, collective hysteria followed by collective hallucination contrived to put to death many innocent women.

Many of the higher-powered mediums had a centre-piece during their sessions, shaping a seance like a theatrical performance. One of D. D. Home's set pieces was the handling of red-hot coals in front of an audience. One such performance was noted on May 9th 1871 by Professor William Crookes: 'After stirring the hot coal about with his hand, took out a red-hot piece nearly as big as an orange, and putting it on his right hand, covered it over with his left hand, so as to almost completely enclose it, and then blew into the small furnace thus extemporised until the lump of charcoal was nearly white-hot, and then drew my attention to the lambent flame which was flickering over the coal.'[4]

Crookes confirmed this in a letter to Mrs Honywood. Home 'delicately pulled the lumps of hot coal off, one at a time with his right hand, and touched one which was bright red'. Home's demonstration of his powers was reported by Mrs William Tebb to one of the most astute of psychical investigators, Frank Podmore. Home 'put his hands over a flame . . . held the flame close to his eyes . . .'[5]

There were no fire tricks when the conditions were 'too positive', when there were uninvited witnesses, and where the witnesses had too little faith. It would be a clever conjuring trick to produce not only a glowing coal (which conjurors' suppliers would easily do) but flames and heat. Home's fire trick might well be a classic example of expectation heightening the sensibilities and producing an hallucination. The trick was not a one-off; percipients were aware of previous viewers' experiences, and this combined with the awe in which Home was held – and it must be remembered that Home was never caught out during his long career as a professional medium – made it difficult for the believers *not* to appreciate the phenomena Home was gently urging on them, the flames, the heat, the combustibility of coal. The first of all ingredients for collective hallucination is sympathy, and Home achieved this by the simple method of excluding the unsympathetic from his circles.

In 1887 a full-scale investigation into spiritualism was launched in America. The Seybert Commission was perhaps the most objective investigation of the phenomena during the nineteenth century, and the British equivalent, the report by the Dialectical Society, compared ill with it. One of the Commission's members was Dr H. H. Furness of the University of Pennsylvania:

Again and again, men have led round the circles the materialised spirits of their wives, and introduced them to each visitor in turn; fathers have taken round their daughters, and I have seen widows sob in the arms of their dead husbands. Testimony such as this staggers me. Have I been smitten with colour-blindness? Before me, as far as I can detect, stands the very medium herself, in shape, size, form and feature true to a line, and yet, one after another, honest men and women at my side, within ten minutes of each other, assert that she is the absolute counterpart of their nearest and dearest friends, nay that she *is* that friend.

This was affirmed by Frank Podmore in *Telepathic Hallucinations*. 'It seems difficult to place any limit on the untrustworthiness of human testimony, especially in cases where the emotions are involved, or where there is occasion for edification.'

The most succinct appraisal is that of T. H. Huxley: 'The rule of common sense is *prima facie* to trust a witness in all matters in which neither his self-interest, his passions, his prejudices, nor that love of the marvellous which is inherent to a greater or less degree in mankind, are strongly concerned; and, when they are involved, to require corroborative evidence in exact proportion to the contravention of probability by the thing testified.'[6]

The seance situation illustrates how easily the credulous mind interprets an event or an object when it is craftily guided. The cases mentioned in the *Census of Hallucinations* are of a different order; some of them are evidently telepathic (a word coined about the period of the *Census*), some prompted by suggestion.

In 1884, Mrs Greiffenberg and Mrs Erni-Greiffenberg, were at lunch. One of them suddenly looked beneath the table, the other enquired if she had dropped anything, receiving the answer, 'No, but I wonder how that cat can have got into the room?' Beneath the table was a large white Angora cat. The women got up, opened the door, and the cat circled the table and went out, down a passage where it turned, faced them, and dissolved away like a mist. The same cat reappeared the following year. It dissolved away at the door to the cellar. Both women testified to the appearance, describing it as 'uncanny and gruesome'.

Is self-interest involved in the propagation of this story? Or were the percipients victims of what medical writers scathingly called religious insanity, and even if they had seen nothing, thought it worth while in the cause of the occult to pretend to the compilers of the census that they had? Where there was money and a career in the supernatural at stake, there were many whose scruples about the truth were overcome, and the train of 'investigators' and 'mediums' who vamped up their material was depressingly large. Some of the revelations of sharp practice on the parts of allegedly scrupulous men and women have only recently been published, and had the collectors of information been aware of this, no doubt they would have subjected their cases to a greater scrutiny. One bad egg in a clutch makes the rest suspect, and significant case-histories, without cautious treatment, become aimless anecdotage.

The collective hallucination reported by Mrs Charlotte Goodhall has the advantage that her account was scrutinised, and she herself was interviewed, by Frank Podmore who was certainly no fool.

In 1873 or 1874 – Mrs Goodhall was writing in 1890 – she and her daughter were driving in a low pony carriage on the northern outskirts of London. Mrs Goodhall suddenly 'saw a figure, dressed in black from head to foot, advancing; it appeared to glide along'. She said to her daughter, 'Oh, do look at that strange figure!' The figure passed to the left of the carriage on the grass within two yards, and as it did so it turned its face their way 'and of all the fiendish faces it was the most horrible you can imagine; its garments seemed to train behind it'. Her daughter looked back at it. The figure watched them go, then disappeared.

Podmore visited the Goodhalls in 1892, ascertaining that the hallucination had been seen in all but full daylight (though the original statement reported that it was a summer evening), that Mrs Goodhall had had two or three auditory hallucinations, and that Miss Goodhall was still unmarried. Miss Goodhall recalled that the face was coarse and had a large mouth, that the figure looked like a man in women's dress. If it had been a real figure it could not have disappeared, as the distance to the hedge was too great.

The Society for Psychical Research was not too happy about this case, stating 'we require clearer cases to prove the fact of collective hallucination'.[7] Distances are difficult to judge from a moving vehicle, and the Goodhalls did not return to ascertain whether there was a gap in the hedge through which the figure can have darted.

An interesting case from 1879 was investigated by Myers in 1891. A wife was awoken suddenly, saw at the end of the bed a white form 'without features visible', and sat up in bed. Her husband also awoke. 'What is that?' asked his wife. He saw 'indistinctly a white figure, unrecognisable, which at once vanished'. The husband got out of bed, made sure that there was no moonlight effect as the shutters were closed and no white garment to create a stimulus. The same kind of fleeting experience occurred to two young women, guests of the Archbishop of York; one of them saw 'a white figure fly through the room from the door to the window' as they lay in bed. The other heard 'an angel singing'. The white figure was interpreted as an angel, no doubt because of the status of their host.

Collective hallucinations prompted some very fancy theorising. F. W. H. Myers suggested this: 'When two or three persons see what seems to be the same phantom in the same place and at the same time, does that mean that that special part of space is somehow modified? or does it mean that a mental impression, conveyed by the distant agent – the phantom-begetter – to one of the percipients is reflected telepathically from that percipient's mind to the minds of the other – as it were secondary – percipients?'[8]

Myers preferred the former theory, but it would seem to most objective observers that a modification of space, if that means anything at all, is an unnecessary complication. A point which Myers pursues at great length has more appeal; it may be 'that the continuous dream-life which we must suppose to run concurrently with our waking life is potent enough to effect from time to time enough of dissociation to enable some element of the personality to be perceived at a distance from the organism'.[9]

The idle phantasies of imaginative young girls in strange environments, a starting-up from sleep and the mixing of dream images with dimly picked-out shapes and reflections, worry about a dying person and an interior image projected – such hallucinations have little of the occult about them. Yet there are some that puzzle, conforming to no easy category. In 1882, a Major W. of Conon Bridge, Ross-shire had a strange shared experience:

'It was the month of August; rather a dark night, and very still; the hour, midnight; when before retiring for the night, as is often my custom, to the front door to look at the weather. When standing for a moment on the step I saw, coming round a turn in the drive, a large close carriage and pair of horses, with two men on the box. It passed the front of the house, and was going at a rapid rate towards a path which leads to a stream, running, at that point, between rather steep banks. There is no carriage-road on that side of the house, and I shouted to the driver to stop, as, if he went on, he must undoubtedly come to grief. The carriage stopped abruptly when it came to the running water, turned, and, in doing so, drove over the lawn. I got up to it; and by this time my son had joined me with a lantern. Neither of the men on the box had spoken, and there was no sound from the inside of the carriage. My son looked in, and all he could discern was a stiff-looking figure sitting up in a corner, and draped, apparently, from head to foot in white. The absolute silence of the men outside was mysterious, and the white figure inside, apparently of a female, not being alarmed or showing any signs of life, was strange. Men, carriage, and horses were unknown to me, although I knew the country so well. The carriage continued its way across the lawn, turning up a road which led past the stables, and so into the drive again and away. We could see no traces of it the next morning – no marks of wheels or horses' feet on the soft grass or gravel road; and we never again heard of the carriage or its occupants, though I caused careful inquiries to be made the following day. I may mention that my wife and daughter also saw the carriage, being attracted to the window by my shout. This happened on the 23rd of August 1878.'[10]

Frank Podmore visited the house in 1884, being sufficiently intrigued to make the long trip to Scotland. Major W. impressed him. Podmore saw where the carriage was supposed to have turned, finding barely enough room for a carriage to go let alone manoeuvre, noting that the grass was soft and sappy. The house itself was in a peculiar situation, on a peninsula, three miles from its neck, very desolate, no villages or hamlets. The corroboration of the major's wife he also noted. Perhaps the whole family was crazed and that was why they were living in isolation; there is no mention of servants – pity, as they were an observant breed; or maybe the carriage had some legitimate journey, though it would need a wayward driver to mistake the route in such an isolated part of the world, and in any event even the most churlish of drivers encountering the major and ploughing up his lawn would have made some pretence at civility. But, of course, the lawn was not ploughed up.

14. The Haunted Situation

Just as it takes two to make a quarrel, so does it need two to make a haunting – a haunter and a haunted. To make a plausible haunting, it needs three at least; no haunting is worth a scrap of paper that has only one haunted. A haunting also needs a suitable locale, an old place where something strange *may* have happened, a newer place where something strange *did* happen, or an eerie place where something *could* happen, such as a church-yard.

Critical students of phantasms considered that 'the first crude hypothesis, that 'ghosts' are the spirits of deceased persons, actually walking this earth in quasi-material form, and holding familiar intercourse with their survivors, is probably held now [1889] by few if any of the intelligent students of the evidence amassed by the Society [for Psychical Research]'.[1] Frank Podmore suggested that their appearance could arise from a reflection of a deceased person's 'uneasy dreams' or the 'fragmentary thoughts of a decaying personality'.[2] Recurring hauntings could be explained by the idea that the initial percipient had somehow projected his or her experiences into the mind of subsequent observers. It was also possible that in rural districts the locals' instinctive and irrational belief in a haunting could communicate itself to out-siders, projecting an indeterminate aura of fear and trepidation. This could lead to the newcomers seeing *something,* the precise details of which varied according to the personality of the percipient.

A general rule of the thumb for owners of allegedly haunted houses would be this : if you have doors sealed up or mysterious rooms bricked off, leave them that way. Whether it was incautious of Daniel Adye, owner of Markyate Cell, near Dunstable, to have a bricked-up doorway in the chimney cleared, is one thing; it was certainly expensive, as the locals refused to do it and Adye had to import workman from London, who found a hitherto unknown staircase, and an empty room with a strong oak door. The house was said to be haunted by the wicked Lady Ferrers, a noble lady who got her kicks by turning highwaywoman, and who bothered those who came later with groans and sighs and by hanging from a branch of a tree (she demoralised a parish tea party early in this century by her appearance).

Preferably the scene should be like the one that greeted William Reid, a London professional man, who departed to rural Warwickshire – the great iron gate with rusty hinges, the neglected lawn, the overgrown gardens with limp dejected flowers, the muddy pools of water, the grimy windows broken. Reid encountered two pretty girls in red damask gowns, high-heeled boots, and long gold ear-rings – ghosts, of course. Then there is Creslowe, near Aylesbury, with its gables, ornamented chimneys, square tower with rectagonal turret, mullioned windows, and a crypt, haunted in the 1850s by Rosamond Clifford of a soft light tread and rustling silk gown. When we read of a church in Essex, 'a picturesque old edifice, well mantled in ivy, and half-concealed on two sides by cypress and the dismal yew, stands in the park, about a quarter of a mile from the hall,'[3] we can pretty well guess that we are being prepared for a haunting – in this particular case by a headless woman.

The irksome thing about ghosts is that they are unpredictable: 'He comes when it suits his own purpose, not yours; and he has never shown any willingness to subject himself to experiment. He simply presents himself; if you believe in him, well and good; if not, it is impossible for him to produce credentials.'[4] But they are less unpredictable if the environment is right for them. An environment can produce the phenomena, even when there is no ghost, as witness the strange case of 50 Berkeley Square, which enjoyed a vogue as the most haunted house in London up to the time it was taken over by the book-dealer Maggs as a storage place.

Intimations that 50 Berkeley Square was not as other houses seem to have been whispered about 1840. Strange sounds were reported, boxes banged about, bells rung, windows flung open; one night, it is said, all the windows were smashed. It had one special room, and it was believed that once every six months a weird man came to the house, locked the two servants in the basement, and went to *the* room. It was said that a young maid-servant had been bold enough to penetrate into this secret room, and had gone mad on account of what she had seen. A young man who was determined to solve the mystery was said to have been found dead inside a locked room.

It was good copy for the sensational magazines, for although the reporters could not get in to number fifty, they could obtain access to number forty-nine, so they could say, 'The very party-walls of the house, when touched, are found saturated with electric horror'.[5] During the 1880 season, a ball was held at forty-nine, and the guests shuddered and shivered their way through the evening, speculating about the nameless horrors next door.

That there was something odd about number fifty was certain; that there was anything supernatural was not. The house had been taken many years before the walls were saturated with electric horror by a Mr Myers, intending to live their with his wife. He made every preparation, ordered furniture, carpets, china, everything, but shortly before the wedding his fiancée jilted him and married another man. This upset Myers's reason; all was left as it was, the furniture anywhere, the carpets still un-rolled. For upwards of twenty years he did not leave the house, though his sister paid him an occasional visit. 'During the day Mr Myers (whose presence in the house was not believed in by the neighbours) remained quiescent, but at night-time he would flit about, rambling from room to room, producing in his nocturnal progress the weird sounds which occasioned so much gossip.'[6]

Eventually Myers died, leaving all to his sister, who sent a house agent to see if the house could be renovated sufficiently for the remainder of the lease. He found everything mouldering and in decay. Two old maid-servants were in the house, and they laughed when he asked them if they had ever heard or seen any ghosts. So does one of the most celebrated of hauntings drift into history.

Why did ghosts appear at all? This was a question posed (and answered) in a spirit poem given through J. S. Schutt.

> Why do we come, from Realms of Light,
> Into the earth's dark shadowy night,
> Where dwell dire want and pain?

Why do we leave our homes on high,
On thought's swift pinions cleave the sky,
   To visit Earth again?

If the ghosts were vestiges of a decaying personality – thought complex, then clearly they had little choice. Popular ghost stories had persuaded general opinion that they came back for a purpose, to disclose to relatives the existence of a deed or a cache of gold, or to reveal a dire deed. Frank Podmore, when the results of the Society for Psychical Research's researches into ghosts began to roll in, was not so sure: 'his connection with skeletons and tragedies is obscure and uncertain. He is, in fact, usually a fugitive and irrelevant phantom phantasm. He flits as idly across the scene as the figure cast by a magic lantern, and he possesses, apparently, as little purpose, volition, or intelligence.'[7]

An interesting case turned up in 1885. In November of that year a nursemaid was going along a passage at eight in the evening when she saw a figure in light grey; the nursemaid put out a hand to touch her, but the figure avoided it. The nursemaid saw the figure the following March; the figure appeared to be taller than a man. She also saw a ghostly male figure, heard footsteps, scuffling sounds, and the noise of something heavy being dragged downstairs. The butler confirmed the sounds – like barrels rolling and planks of wood being stacked – and in March he saw the figure, too, all except the head, which appeared like a black mist. The figure touched him with a cold hand. The following day he told the master, who did not seem surprised. The master decided to hold a seance, and imported a table-turning medium; they learned that the ghost was anxious to tell them about a box of jewels that had been buried in the cellar.

The butler was left out of the seance, but later he was rung for, and told that the ghost would appear at eleven with precise details of the location of the jewels; the presence of the butler was required. The butler, a delicate man of about thirty, was not too sanguine about this. The gas was put down low, and the door opened; at eleven the ghost entered. The figure was not clear, and the medium asked her to appear more distinct, a request granted. The ghost was dressed in a shiny kind of Japanese silk, with a flower design; her feet were in a dark cloud, and she threw up her hands, clutching at her hair. Her face was long and haggard-looking, and she had a long thin nose. Her hair was torn, and hung over her shoulders almost to her waist; her eyes were cast upwards, and looked like balls of fire. The butler was requested to follow her, and she led the way to the cellar, a journey interrupted by a flash, as though someone had switched on and off an electric light. The table was taken down to the cellar, and by tilting it the sitters found that the ghost wanted them to start digging. So the butler and another man began to dig. They got up the flagstones, found that the soil had apparently never been disturbed; they then found a hole, but there was nothing there. They summoned up the ghost again, who was agitated, and reported that she had forgotten where exactly she had buried the jewels, an operation she had performed with the help of a maid. The butler was convinced that there were jewels there, that eventually someone would find them, and then the ghost would rest.

Frank Podmore went to investigate this strange episode; he commented that the butler seemed to realise the dramatic possibilities. The owner, who had not seen the apparition at all, remained cool about the whole exercise, though his wife confirmed the butler's account. Podmore wrote that the appearance of a phantasm on several distinct occasions for a period of minutes to three persons simultaneously was a phenomenon perhaps without parallel in the Society's records. Possibly unique also was the appearance at a predicted time. Unknown to the inhabitants of the house, the property had enjoyed the reputation of being haunted for twenty years or so, and had been known colloquially as the 'Haunted House'.

Another haunted house, infested by heavy steps round the drawing-room table, mysterious bell-ringings and hammerings on the door, and a female ghost heavily draped in black from head to foot, was rented by an associate of the Society for Psychical Research. There had also been strange voices, saying 'Oh, do forgive me!' three times, sobs and moans, heavy boxes thrown about. A clergyman had performed the ceremony of exorcism without much success. The house was occupied by the investigator between August 1888 and September 1889, and he and his wife heard nothing and saw nothing. Nor did his visitors, twenty-five different men and fourteen different women. A zinc pail was heard to drop in the kitchen, and the bells rang again.

If ever there was a house to be haunted this was it. Unknown to the various occupiers, there had been a suicide there in 1879, when the owner, a woman of forty-two, had hanged herself by a skipping-rope from a peg behind a bedroom door. And suicides were a group with a higher ratio of posthumous return than others.

15. The Haunters

The psychologist Jastrow wrote: 'We are creatures of the average; we are adjusted for the most probable event; our organism has acquired the habits impressed upon it by the most frequent experiences'. Certainly the Victorians were protected from the improbable; The mass of the people had to be content with an interpretation of events out of the ordinary offered by journalists or graphic artists. The mass communication medium of the artist was the steel engraving, and his work had to go through another sieve, that of the journeyman engraver, before it reached his public. When Roger Fenton took photographs of the progress of the Crimean War a new spectrum was opened, but these photographs were only seen by a few before a way was found to print photographs on to newsprint.

The great Victorian reporters, such as Sala and Dickens, too, were interpretative. The result was that the Victorians rarely got their information raw. Their range of precise data was limited to what they personally could see and hear. When the supernatural intruded into their own lives they were at a loss to know what to do about it, as they had been conditioned to a stereotyped supernatural, and this bewilderment is reflected in their accounts of ghosts and hauntings. They are torn between relating what they saw and trying to adapt it to the formula; being subjective phenomena, the latter was very easy to do. Yet by and large they were scrupulous, and the communication business being naïve – until the arrival of Stead and yellow journalism – they were not egged on to make more of the phenomena they had witnessed in the interests of increased newspaper circulation.

In the 1880s, modern journalism was born, and in the more sensational papers and periodicals fact was turned into a kind of fiction. In a series entitled 'True Ghost Stories' that ran in the 1890s in *Pearson's Magazine*, the distinction between fact and fiction was obliterated completely, and, as photographs were by then being printed in mass circulation weeklies, pictures of haunted houses were published alongside romantic accounts of hauntings, utter bosh full of high-flown and implausible dialogue. The tendency to write up the supernatural infected percipients who half a century earlier would have described what they had seen or heard in a sober manner befitting their non-professional status.

Thus the chief warder of Newgate Gaol, haunted by the ghost of the Reading baby-farmer, Amelia Dyer who was executed in June 1896. He was describing her as a prisoner: 'It wasn't that she was a troublesome prisoner, she was too submissive and oily for words. But her eyes were always watching me, and her hands folded on her black dress. . . . Those glittering eyes of hers instilled into me a strange feeling of disquiet and foreboding . . .' One is aware of the sharp journalist helping Scott over the difficult words, producing a sensational account and not just the unvarnished truth.

There is no obvious pattern of nineteenth-century hauntings, but unquestionably hauntings that came later in the century were conditioned by earlier ones. In the 1870s and 1880s hauntings were, to use a contemporary phrase, all the go; accounts of the earlier ones were haphazard and indiscriminate, but as hauntings became more common they were shaped into a literary form and the details were influenced by ghost stories written to entertain. Earlier writers, such as Mrs Crowe in her *The Night Side of Nature*, aware that they were on to a very good thing, could intermingle fact and fiction knowing that the readers had nothing to compare the book with.

Comment has already been made about the high proportion of phantasms resulting from suicide, although why this should be, apart from the natural horror surrounding suicide, is not clear.

When Sarah Fletcher, aged twenty-nine, of Clifton Hampden, heard that her husband had bigamously married an heiress, she hanged herself. The house was turned into a school, and on June 7th 1864 she was seen by the Reverend Edward Crake. She was dressed in a long silk cloak, with a purple-red ribbon in her auburn hair. When a journalist jumped from a window of a house in Belsize Grove, London, and killed himself, the house retained an aura, especially in the bathroom, users of which felt, according to W. T. Stead, an 'evil presence bending over them'.

It is strange that suicide claimed so many of the psychical researchers, possibly aware of the posthumous repercussions.

Probably the most practical way to judge ghosts is by their capacity to frighten; in his researches on ghosts, Podmore made the point that the sheeted horrors of Victorian fiction were largely lacking in coherent and corroborated accounts, that the ghosts reported to him and his colleagues were for the most part ephemeral, inconsistent, and a little wistful, that impressions were so momentary that even the most level-headed of percipients found it difficult to convert their vision into communication. Apparitions assumed different shapes at different times, and a ghost described by one as being in a greyish or mauve dress was to others dressed in lilac, white, red, slate coloured silk with red cloak, with hair fair, dark, brown or brownish. And this was only a short time after the occurrences took place, between 1885 and 1887. Who could tell what the percipients would say five years on?

It may be argued that ability to perceive ghosts was evidence of a pathological state of mind, that the more extreme phantoms merely recorded an advanced psychotic state, that the fact that different percipients saw what should have been the same ghost in irreconcilable terms only indicated that some brains were more disturbed than others. In one haunted house there appeared to different people a dark swarthy-looking man with black whiskers dressed as a merchant sailor, a man with an evil face in a white working suit, and a devilish face with hands but no body. A tall slender woman was metamorphosed at a different time into a short woman, and the dress colour was altered from black to green. The ghost could even change its sex, from a clerical gentleman to a woman, and another haunting created a little girl in white with long fair hair, a man in hunting pink, and a tall lady with a child in arms. The most diverse collection, perhaps, of phantoms congregating in one house included an old man, a large white 'waddlewayed' dog, a white figure, a stout middle-aged woman with large flapping frills and a baby, and a shower of blood. With this in mind, what is one to make of the tradition 'that the hallucinatory figure necessarily bears some resemblance to the person by whose agency it is, on the hypothesis, produced?'[1]

We see this most clearly in classical ghost stories: the suicide who returns, the murdered man or woman, the ghost who strives to furnish successors with details of a lost will, jewels, deeds, or wicked people – Lady Ferrers, Dick Turpin – who plague the spots where they once operated. It is understandable that when a haunting persisted there was a strenuous effort to attribute it to a past murder, or if not a murder a macabre circumstance. In Birmingham there was a ghost that appeared as two dense clouds or forms of steam, along with fearful noises, shrieks and sobs. A gas fitter at this haunting saw a spectral figure no less than nine times, on one occasion accompanied by a dog. 'Its features were never apparent. There were neither eyes, nose, mouth, nor ears to the spectral head; but long hair and an oval wholly unformed face.'[2] It was considered locally that the apparition arose because about 1829 the owner of the house supplied bodies for dissection.

In several recorded cases, a murdered man is said to have betrayed his displeasure in more subtle ways than in appearing as a ghost. In July 1823, William Wood, a manufacturer, was returning to Manchester when he was set upon by three footpads. There was a fight, Wood's skull was crushed and thrust into a hole. One of the men was hanged at Chester in 1824, but this was not revenge enough for Wood. No grass would grow on the spot where his head was thrust, and when the hollow was filled with stones in 1859, the stones were scattered around the depression. In 1874, a stone was put up to mark this curiosity. A similar case occurred during that same decade. John Newton alias Davies was taxed with highway robbery with violence, and, protesting his innocence to the last, he was executed in 1821 in the middle of a suitably dramatic thunderstorm. He swore no grass would grow on his grave. In 1852 the Reverend R. Mostyn Price commented that thirty years had passed away and grass had still not grown where Newton was buried. An effort was made to remedy this by returfing, but in 1886 there was still a bare patch.

Not surprisingly, murders with religious implications were linked with supernatural phenomena. In 1641, a Roman Catholic priest was captured by a mob led by a Puritan clergyman, put on trial and executed, his head being placed on the tower of Manchester Church, whence it was rescued and taken to Wardley Hall where, with extraordinary lack of taste, it was displayed at the top of the staircase. Attempts to bury it failed, nor would the head allow itself to be thrown into a pond. The obduracy of the head established its former owner as a martyr, and in 1861 pilgrims came to visit it.

Certain individuals were seemingly able to perpetuate their grievances from beyond the grave. Sir George Blount of Kinlet, in Shropshire, died in 1581; his anger at the marriage of his daughter Dorothy left an abiding memory, and when his ghost appeared suddenly by a pool in his grounds it was assumed that he was still incensed; this was confirmed when a spectral coach and four raced into the Hall and across the dining room. Much to the relief of the locals, the house was pulled down in 1720, leaving the wine cellar.

A band of clergymen believed that they had trapped his turbulent spirit in a glass bottle seven or eight inches high containing a liquid. To assuage any remaining elements of Sir George's personality, the bottle was kept under his monument in the church. It was unfortunate that no one had ever taken the trouble to have the liquid analysed, for when the church was restored between 1890 and 1893 the bottle disappeared. The disappearance may have been a merciful release for those who believed in the hypothesis of a bottled ghost, for malicious rumours had it that the bottle really contained photographic liquid left accidentally by the aunt of a parishioner.

A neat trick of fate is exemplified when ghosts who pestered the living were themselves set upon by other ghosts. This apparently occurred to the highwayman Dick Turpin, seen at Trap's Hill near Loughton regularly about three times a year. As he was riding along an old woman was seen to jump up behind him on his horse, the supposed ghost of a woman who had been tortured by fire to reveal where money was hidden.

Accidents, coincidences, hoaxes – how many 'reliable' ghost stories may be laid at their doors? Delusion, personal aggrandisement, insanity – how many more? Many owners were anxious to keep their ghosts to themselves for fear of having their property devalued. Others did not have to bother with paltry financial considerations, and were proud to have a ghost as a status symbol. The 'Yellow Boy' that haunted the novelist Lord Lytton's estate at Knebworth complemented Lytton's interest in the occult. Lord Lytton was never tired of telling the story of Lord Castlereagh's visit to Knebworth during his father's time. Castlereagh came

down in the morning looking worn and pale, and told his host
how he was awoken from a deep sleep to see a quaintly dressed
boy with long yellow hair sitting by the fire. The boy drew his
fingers across his throat three times, and vanished. In 1822, in
a fit of insanity, Lord Castlereagh cut his own throat with a
penknife.

Castlereagh had not been told of the 'Yellow Boy', whose
appearance foretold death for the percipient. But visitors in the
novelist's reign of tenure assuredly were. An artist visited
Knebworth, and Lord Lytton hoped that he would not mind
being put in the haunted room. The artist smiled feebly, and
thus encouraged Lord Lytton proceeded to scare the life out of
him with the story of Castlereagh. On reaching his room, the
artist began to undress. 'But a cloud of fear surrounded him,
and the sight of his white face in the mirror, seen in the dimly-
lighted huge room, gave him a shock. The room was panelled
in dark oak, the furniture funereal. The wardrobe, huge in
dimensions, was like an inverted hearse.'[3]

The terrified man longed to open the wardrobe, but could not
bring himself to. When something blew out the candle, he kept
his clothes on and waited for the dawn. He eventually told his
experiences to the painter E. M. Ward, who was due to visit
Knebworth. Remembering the wardrobe, Ward opened it: 'Judge
of my horror when on opening the door something flew out and
fell on the floor with a crash. It proved to be a bath.' A further
shock was in store for him; in the looking-glass he saw above
his own face another, long, narrow, white, with gleaming eyes.
It was Lord Lytton, intent on making the artist's visit a memorably
frightening one. If he did see anything else, E. M. Ward did
not tell his wife; but he, too, committed suicide.

Other locales, such as lonely moors, old battlefields, prehistoric
burial grounds, can stimulate the imaginative into terror. They
have appropriate sounds, and these noises frequently give names
to the locality; the most graphic is perhaps the 'Shrieking Pits'
in Norfolk, with prehistoric background, and a white figure
(mist?) and agonised cries (bird noises?): 'Talking about
things uncanny, Webster [a friend of Arnold Bennett] said that
the weirdest thing of all was the vibrating cry of the snipe on
the moors at night – a cry which you hear, faint and wavering,
in the distance, and which the next second has shot past your

ears in the darkness. . . . There is nothing more horribly scaring, and the awfulness of it cannot be conceived by those who have not heard it. He described it effectively as "the *last cry on earth*".[4]

Old battlefields are celebrated for the way in which, at set times of the year, the battles are refought by those dead for centuries. The battlefields of Britain, particularly those of the Civil War, are conveniently situated in areas where natural sounds could be converted easily into ghostly sounds, a misinterpretation leading to aural hallucinations, leading to visual hallucinations, similar in construction to the odd natural noises in old houses that are expanded into fully-fledged supernatural phenomena. Where there is expectation there is a built-in error.

Yet honest, sober men and women, going about their every-day business in neutral surroundings have been confronted with ghosts. A London solicitor, a widower with a cat, was reading *The Pickwick Papers* when a woman in mourning appeared and backed through a wall. 'I was surprised but not startled', he related. 'I had only drunk tea and eaten a moderate meal. I was, furthermore, reading a book tending to laughter and not to depression.'[5] A rural Catholic priest heard a confession in a cottage, and then read a paper. He looked up; the opposite wall had gone, and he could see a sick man. He said that he was greatly astonished, but not frightened. C. Happerfield had promised a friend to look after his widow after his death. He did so for a while, but money ran short, and he despatched the widow·to a grandson in Gloucestershire. The dead man's ghost appeared, sorrowful and troubled. 'I felt no fear', said Happerfield, 'but surprise and astonishment kept me silent . . . I am not a nervous man, nor am I superstitious. At the time my friend came to me I was wide awake, collected, and calm'.[6] We know nothing about these narrators, there was no confirmation, but their quiet laconic air commands a certain respect. Of Sir Risdon Bennett, we do know quite a lot. An old-style physician, he was made President of the Royal College of Physicians in 1876, whereupon he took a house in Cavendish Square. It was there he revealed to Francis Galton, the specialist in heredity and founder of the science of eugenics, that he had seen a ghost whilst writing in his study. There was a knock on his study door, and a man entered in medieval costume, 'perfectly distinct in every particular, buttons and all, who after a brief time faded and disappeared'.[7] Galton urged Bennett to publish this, as it would become a classical example of a vision in a sane person; Bennett did so after a time, but then in a specialist medical journal and over initials. Sir James Crichton-Browne, a sardonic debunker of ghosts and a critical member of the party that investigated the Ballechin haunting, declared that Bennett was the last man in the world one would have expected to have such an experience, a calm, austere, rigorous man.

It might be supposed that only the over-imaginative and nervous could be taken in by simple objects appearing in another light, window curtains flapping in the breeze, a half-caught reflection in a mirror, that their attitude is at one with that of the Reverend J. M. Shaw of the Society for Psychical Research ('. . . he went down the avenue in order that he might see the apparition of the nun. He went predisposed to see and he did see what he described as "something" ').[8] But a combination of events could produce an image that would cause the most objective to catch breath.

Those cases where the apparitions are hideous apparently eliminate illusion, for which lack of detail is the first requisite; on the other hand, there is more evidence for a mind in some kind of disorder. Theoretically, it might be that ghosts should be hideous rather than not; one 'sensitive' put it this way: the ghost is a duplicate of the dead person, and as the corpse decays, so does the ghost. Phantasms of suicides were traditionally expected to be sad and woebegotten, those of murderers evil and violent.

A characteristic specimen of the two combined comes from 1852, when a man renting part of a house (at a low rental because of strange noises) went up to his bedroom, and as he opened the door of the passage leading to his room he was unable to see because of the bright light. There were no lights on in the house. After a time the man became accustomed to the glare, and saw about thirty-five feet away an old man in a figured dressing-gown. The face was 'most hideous', and stuck in the percipient's memory. The man's first impression was that he had had a hallucination (he had been reading Brewster's *Natural Magic* and knew the symptoms), but he decided to trace the matter through, and an old lawyer told him that the owner's grandfather had strangled his wife and committed suicide. Further research told him that the date was September 22nd some year in the eighteenth century. It was September 22nd when he saw the ghost. Precisely a year later a guest at the house came down to breakfast angry and fuming about the cryings, groanings and oaths, he had heard from the room where the murderer had committed suicide. Other occupants of the house complained about footsteps that had followed them down the passage where the old man had been seen.

A spectacularly frightening ghost was recorded by W. T. Stead. A man named Foster had been riding along when his horse began to show symptoms of distress – nostrils distorted, perspiration, tremblings. Foster looked at the hedge closely to see if he could detect what was upsetting the horse:

There in the moonlight, bending limp and apparently lifeless over the hedge, was the body of a tall man. With arms outstretched, the figure seemed touching the ground with its fingers, the legs being on the other side of the hedge. What was his horror to see the body move! Slowly, mechanically, the long arms were outstretched, uplifted; the body swayed, up, up; and there in the bright moonlight was the man's face. How ghastly it looked! The glassy eyes were staring at the young man, whose blood seemed chilling in his veins. Motionless, upright as an elm, with outstretched arms, stood the gaunt sceptre. Its throat was cut.'

A rather similar, and better authenticated case – and with W. T. Stead drumming up excitement in the above episode, one could hardly have a worse – was reported by Mrs Sidgwick, a case she considered quite unique: a persistent multiple apparition seen by three women simultaneously. She speculated that it suggested a borderland between illusion and hallucination.

One night in the 1870s, two sisters and a maid went to evening service in the village church. There was moonlight combined with thick fog. As they returned, they heard a man whistling; they then heard his footsteps, and saw him. He passed them. Another man appeared, but one of the sisters did not see him, and the request 'Let that man pass' mystified her. He appeared to disappear into the non-perceiving sister's dress. The three women were suddenly in the middle of a mass of people, misty, moving purposelessly, disappearing when they encountered the bodies of any of the women or when they passed over or along two strips of grass alongside the pathway. Some seemed to rise out of the grass. They were short and dwarf-like, the women dressed in high bonnets, big shawls, with large flounces on their dresses (probably of the crinoline period of the 1850s). There was agreement between the three percipients; if one saw a man all saw a man, if one saw a woman all saw a woman. They all appeared to be walking on the ground. Two of the men, not together, had sparks round their faces.

There was one man who was twice as tall as any of the others. The other apparitions were disappearing into the hedges and into the grass, but this tall figure kept to the carriageway, never changing his step nor swerving. The women reached the gate of their house; they were relieved when the man did not turn with them but kept on up the road, and as they watched him go he was the only one they could see. The apparitions had been with them for about two hundred yards. The maid and the younger sister were crying aloud, terrified by the experience.

Mrs Sidgwick was inclined to believe that the single tall figure was real, his soundless quality relying on the mundane effect of goloshes, and the rest of the gathering a collective hallucination sparked off by moonlight penetrating fog, producing the kind of wraith which motorists observe when driving through patchy fog.

It might be supposed that the maid and the younger sister, aged sixteen, were silly girls, and their common terror was crossing backwards and forwards between them, confirming and augmenting it; but the elder sister seems to have been level-headed, and although frightened, she kept her wits about her. As she was the leading character, as she was aware of the others' terror, had the effect been moonlight and fog it is reasonable to suppose that she would have interpreted the unusual visual phenomena as being that and nothing more. One suspects that Mrs Sidgwick had spent so much time at bogus seances in the service of truth that she was pre-disposed against all supra-mundane phenomena.

The enigma of these malevolent appearances appealed to devotees of diabolism, and if their existence can be explained in terms of morbid pathology they also slot in with occultists' theories of elementals. This was occasionally recognized by the percipients, and there is an amusing instance of a lady who went to see MacGregor Mathers, one of the leaders of the occult revival of the nineteenth century. She asked Mathers for 'help against phantoms who have the appearance of decayed corpses, and try to get into bed with her at night'. Mathers commented, 'Very bad taste on both sides'.[10]

It is evident that the hideousness of the more extreme apparitions was almost totally subjective, that the mind instinctively equated hideousness with the initial unnaturalness of the occurrence. It was an expression of shock and indignation, 'hideous' used as a multi-purpose adjective demonstrating disapproval at the bad taste of the hereafter. But there is a residue of data where total subjectivity is ruled out, as in the case of a woman who at a concert in London in the early 1830s had been terrified by an apparition of someone she knew lying naked at her feet, with the face partly covered by a cloth mantle. She was taken ill at the concert, and had to be taken home, where she told her friends what she had seen. They reassured her, but on the following day she received news that the person whose apparition she saw had been drowned that very night by the upsetting of his boat, and the body was discovered entangled in a boat-cloak.

Clearly some of the accounts of frightening phenomena were influenced by popular fiction and sensational journalism. This is especially evident in accounts of supernatural sounds. A house in Enfield Chase was permeated by odd noises, described by Mr T. Westwood as 'sounds of shuddering horror, faint but audible'. 'Shuddering horror' is a patent piece of journalistic hocus-pocus.

Hideous apparitions, hideous noises – even furniture could strike dread into the hearts of the impressionable. Miss Goodrich-Freer, self-styled seer and crystal-gazer extraordinary, was called to investigate a house recently built that the owner thought had its evil side. With uncanny prescience, Miss Goodrich-Freer found the eerie room and the eerie cause of the distress: a wooden bedstead, 'an ugly unsanitary anachronism, a splendid text for a suggestion. Its origin was obscure, vague, easily represented as mysterious'. With admirable decision, Miss

Goodrich-Freer turned on the owner: 'Clear out this room, clean it, whitewash it, put back all else, but *burn that bedstead!*'[11]

Victorian writers on the supernatural in general and on ghosts in particular were beset by the need to make their accounts meaningful. If accounts of ghosts were incoherent and inconclusive, there would be an effort, sometimes conscious sometimes unconscious, to pull them into some sort of shape, to use a formula. Writers could even sketch in the predominant emotion to be aroused before the set of objects, the situation, or the chain of events, were mentioned, as in the introduction to W. T. Stead's *Real Ghost Stories*. Stead requested: 'That the narratives printed in these pages had better not be read by any one of tender years, of morbid excitability, or of excessively nervous temperament'.

The ease of the operation, the ridiculously simple formula needed, meant that mediocre writers were able to produce the requisite emotion with considerable success.

Lets us first see how a 'real' writer, Tennyson, evokes horror:

I hate the dreadful hollow behind the little wood,
Its lips in the field above are dabbled with blood-red heath,
The red-ribb'd ledges drip with a silent horror of blood,
And Echo there, whatever is ask'd her, answers 'Death.'[12]

Then to hack ghost fiction, *The Haunted Grange*, serialised in 1889: 'The night is bitterly cold, a driving wind is whirling round and round the ruined gables, and whistling in long and mournful cadence through the avenue of leafless trees which leads up to the desolate old pile. Ruin, everywhere ruin!' leading up to 'mysterious voices, whisperings ... unaccountable lights, and even in the dim gloamings of twilight, a shadowy form, as of a woman with dripping garments and streaming hair ...'[13]

Quite naturally, this humourless, intense tone was adopted by writers who were recounting supposedly supernatural occurrences which turned out to be explicable in matter-of-fact terms. Sir Francis Burnand, editor of *Punch* for forty-four years, itself a matter for awe, was staying in the haunted room at a house called Theobalds. He was awoken by a mysterious scratching or tapping at the window, 'and following the example of Hamlet in calling the good supernatural to his aid against the evil [he] made, boldly but shivering, for the window. Scratch, scratch, scratch. Hold! If it should be a rat! Impossible, no rat ever born would climb up a wall and sit on a narrow window-sill scratching at the glass...'[14] Burnand went through the possibilities: a bird, a woodpecker in error, an owl, a bat? 'Heavens! what was to be the next act in this tragic drama?' He opened the shutters, the blind moved. There was 'no pale vampire-like face peering in through the window panes.' The hasp of the window was unlocked; he must close the window, but the sash resisted him:' *The lower part of the frame was struggling upwards.* Then he saw ... '*Something that had penetrated under the frame forcing its way in between the sash and the ledge*! ... It was the thin end of a branch of a tree.'

Certainly many writers found a good deal of humour in the supernatural. There is the case of the haunting which proved to be a sleep-walking butler laying out a dinner for six on his employer's bed. Or the laconic cameo in *The Diary of a Nobody:* 'More table-turning in the evening. Carrie said last night was in a measure successful, and they ought to sit again. Cummings came in, and seemed interested. I had the gas lighted in the drawing-room, got the steps, and repaired the cornice, which has been a bit of an eyesore to me. In a fit of unthinkingness – if I may use such an expression – I gave the floor over the parlour, where the séance was taking place, two loud raps with the hammer. I felt sorry afterwards, for it was the sort of ridiculous, foolhardy thing that Gowing or Lupin would have done.'

Yet no matter how many humorists scoff at ghosts, many would agree with Johnson: 'All argument is against it, but all feeling is for it.' In fact seventeen per cent of the population, according to Geoffrey Gorer (*Exploring English Character*), believe in ghosts, with twenty-three per cent uncertain. And although the archives of ghostology are not bursting with accounts of ghost-spottings, forty-two per cent of a sample of 4,983 reported that they had seen ghosts.

16. Poltergeists

The phenomenon of the poltergeist is of considerable antiquity, and belief in it cuts across accepted tenets. Those who refuse to believe in apparitions will accept the poltergeist if it is relabelled telekinetic force, those who believe in apparitions will not take kindly to the poltergeist as it is a brash intruder and cannot be tamed for the purpose of a seance. Although the word was anglicized quite early in the nineteenth century, it only became acceptable considerably later, and it does not appear in the annals of the spiritualist movement.

A case has been cited as early as 856 AD, there was the notorious Cock Lane poltergeist of 1762, an outbreak of mysterious bell-ringing in a Russian monastery in 1753, stone-throwing in Saxony in 1750, while the roll-calls of modern poltergeists usually starts with the Bealings Bells of 1834.

Strictly speaking, a poltergeist is a noisy spirit, but later definitions take as much account of phenomena such as objects flung across a room. The Bealings Bells case is a classic example of pure poltergeist. This means that there were unexplained noises, that they were recorded enthusiastically and unobjectively, that observation was slack, amateurish, and arbitrary, and that the noises evoked mystic awe about the parish pumps of England. It was written up in 1841 by the owner of the property, a Major Moor, FRS. The bells in question were the old household bells, a row of nine; two or three used to ring without reason, sometimes the whole row. The wires of the bells had been cut. Lieutenant Rivers, an official of Greenwich Hospital, was invited by Major Moor to investigate, and at one time there were thirty-seven watchers, day and night.

They did not see anything to account for the incidents, nor could they make anything of the dents on the walls and ceilings caused by violent supernormal blows. The claim that when the bells began ringing there were no wires would seem to be contradicted by the fact that a bellhanger and his assistant came to cut every wire. The phenomena persisted from February 2nd to March 27th of 1834.

The ringing of bells presupposes that there were bells in the house to ring. Most poltergeist phenomena have more inexplicable noises. In 1835, Captain Molesworth rented a house two miles from Edinburgh. He was troubled by the sound of invisible feet, knockings, scratchings, and rustlings. The owner was a man named Webster, and he investigated his property thoroughly; the house was cordoned off by sherriffs' officers, he had the floorboards lifted up, and bored holes in the walls. Suspicion fastened on a young girl, Jane, aged eleven or twelve, who always seemed to be near the disturbances, a sickly child who later died. To make certain that she was not responsible, she was trussed up in a bag.

The presence of a young girl, usually near the age of puberty, proved to be a common factor in poltergeist phenomena. When in December 1838, there was suddenly a flurry of sticks, pebbles, clods, flying about the yard of a farmhouse at Baldarroch, in Aberdeenshire, the fact that there were two servant girls around whom the events revolved impressed the hundreds of observers. The phenomena moved to the interior of the farmhouse, and spoons, knives, plates, rolling-pins, flat-irons and mustard pots were thrown around.

The farmer, thoroughly unnerved by these happenings, decided to consult someone better versed in the supernatural, and called in a conjuror, Willie Foreman, who speedily put an end to the trouble: the two servant girls admitted that they were responsible and were sent to prison.

In 1835 a nursemaid at Willington Mill, in Northumberland, told her mistress that she lived in dread and alarm. She had been hearing the sound of a dull, heavy tread on the floor above, knowing that the room above was unoccupied. The other occupants of the house were soon involved; they heard ten to twelve obtuse deadened beats as of a mallet on a block of wood, a rap on a cradle leg as if with a steel implement, the sound of a clock being wound up. In 1836, they heard voices: the word 'Chuck' twice from the foot of the bed, the sound of a child suckling. In 1840, they heard phrases, 'Never mind', and 'Come and get', and a bat was felt on a pillow, along with the sound of a shoe dragging over boards.

As was often the case, where inexplicable noises were heard the most ordinary sounds were subsequently invested with dire import. The sound of a clock being wound up could easily be the sound of a clock with escapement trouble. The mysterious voices could have been real voices.

There is a family resemblance about poltergeist phenomena, and whereas descriptions of apparitions vary enormously from place to place, and from class to class, the noises produced by poltergeists are recorded by the auditors in very similar ways. The locales usually lack the aristocratic distinction of those favoured by the true phantom. Perhaps typical was the building visited by poltergeists in 1894. This was a barrack hospital left over from the late eighteenth century, converted to a comb factory, and later used as dwellings. The sounds were like the butt of a gun hit against the floor, a rumbling like a cannon-ball, and a dragging noise as if heavy furniture was being pushed around. The occupant of one of the dwellings (the building had made two cottages) 'had had some few Borderland experiences'[1] and naturally associated the sounds with the chequered history of the old barrack block.

Poltergeist phenomena occurred contemporaneously at Ballechin House. There were loud noises, reported Father Hayden, S. J., 'like continuous explosion of petards', along with a sound as if a large animal was throwing itself against the bottom of the bedroom door outside. Despite the wild yarns of nuns in the garden, Myers wrote to Sir Oliver Lodge in April 1897, that 'knocks on the wall, a sewing noise, and a droning and a wailing are all we have heard'.

A precise and graphic description of this type of haunting was tendered by an associate of the Society for Psychical Research who occupied a suspect house between August 1888 and September 1889. He wrote up his experiences in the form of a diary: 'December 9th, 1888 – On this Sunday evening occurred the most really unaccountable noise of any yet noticed. I was in the house alone, writing at my desk. Time, 3.30. Suddenly I heard a noise which seemed to come from the hall, outside my room door. I can only compare the sound to that which would be made if half a brick were tied to a piece of string and jerked about over the linoleum – as one might jerk a reel to make a kitten playful.'[2]

Such belligerent but pointless exhibitions of occult force could not be reconciled with any of the tenets of spiritualism, though they did do something to confirm anti-spiritualist clergy in their view that spiritualistic phenomena were directed by Satan. Perhaps it was only a question of degree. Perhaps these thunderous knockings could be made into a pattern just as the gentle raps had been done. No one tried. The raps were friendly, the more boisterous noises were not; the raps were friendly even when they were not saying anything, when they were just a background noise as exemplified in *The Haunted Grange:* 'Often they would sit far into the night, discoursing in low tones of subjects which in some eyes would have condemned them both to the stake; and if evidence were needed of their dark and dangerous communion with the invisible world, the never silent, rap, tap, tap which sounded on panels, floor and door, and the patter of unseen footsteps, which kept time to their discourse, would have been evidence sufficient.'

It was believed by many that poltergeists who created untimely havoc were those same spirits that made a mockery of serious seances. 'These may be intermediate beings of mixed nature, not deliberately evil nor steadily benevolent – capricious, uncertain, and only able to get at crude and imperfect *rapport* with humanity.'[3] They were the sprites, the imps, the hobgoblins of traditional folk-lore.

The theosophists could explain the phenomena: they were caused by elementals. However, the nineteenth century was geared to, and conditioned by, the belief that hauntings were caused by the spirits of the dead. Mischievousness and saucy behaviour were a display of bad form when so many worthy people were endeavouring to establish a link between the here and the hereafter. It was immaterial whether this unsociable activity took the form of loud and uncouth noises, 'disgusting scratches' (from Major Moor of Bealings Bells fame), misleading and offensive messages in the seance room, or mere childish frivolity, as at a 1868 seance with D. D. Home, where 'all of a sudden the gas went out and the room was in darkness; the gas was not turned off, but went out. They all declared that no one was near the burner'.[4] It need hardly be added that the frisky but not actively hostile spirit was a godsend to mediums when a session was going wrong or where he or she wanted a point of drama to heighten proceedings.

Certainly one can understand the reluctance of spiritualism to take cognisance of poltergeists; not only did they present a threat to the notion that spirits were anxious to communicate with the living, that the dead still possessed many of the attributes of the living, but also poltergeists were in the mainstream of the super-natural while Victorian seance effluvia were not. The dyspeptic and unpredictable poltergeist harked back to the days of pre-Christian Rome and Greece, what Aldous Huxley called the squeak and gibber period, when ghosts were thin, shadowy, hardly personal beings, and the dead survived, if they survived at all, as mere shadows.

The presence of poltergeists was partial confirmation of the belief that if the dead appeared to the living they were but vestiges, wisps of memory, what in more recent times has been called a psychic factor, which allied to a material brain makes a personality, but by itself is no more personal than matter. A theory that was totally unacceptable to all kinds and conditions of spiritualists with 'their up-to-date version of the Red Indian's Happy Hunting Ground, a superior and slightly less material repetition of the present world'.[5] The poltergeists can be interpreted as raw psychic power not amenable to argument.

Only in the 1880s were poltergeists subject to serious investigation, and a report of a mysterious sequence of events in Worksop brought Frank Podmore of the SPR to look into the matter. Podmore did what is now common practice, but was then exceedingly rare; he interrogated the seven principal witnesses separately, and took signed statements from the more important. This encouraged the witnesses to view the occurrences individually and not as a group, and it persuaded them that it was not a lark. For hoaxers, the heavy treatment was a steam-hammer to crush a nut, and when confronted by serious, almost scholarly, investigation, practical tricksters retired abashed or involved themselves in such uncomfortable contradiction that their *bona fides* were immediately questionable.

The house where the disturbances happened had been built about seven years before, and was occupied by a small horse-dealer, Joe White, who had been there three years. There was nothing especially interesting about the house, nothing was known of the earlier occupants, and the land itself had been waste land without sinister connotations. The whole house was hung with bacon, and everything was filthy.

About the 20th or 21st February 1883 Mrs White was washing up the tea-things when the table tilted, the candle overturned, and the wash-tub only saved by Mrs White hanging on to it. A few days later, White being away, Mrs White allowed a girl, Eliza, the child of an imbecile mother, to come and share her bed at night. On the night of March 1st, Eliza and Mrs White were alone in the kitchen. Suddenly, various things that had been in the kitchen – a corkscrew, clothes-pegs, a salt-cellar – tumbled down the kitchen stairs, step by step. Could it have been the prank of White's brother, Tom, a bright youth of between eighteen and twenty? He denied it. At least twenty minutes after he retired, hot coals were thrown down the stairs. The following night, there was the sound of someone coming down the passage between White's house and the one adjacent, and stopping outside the door. White was at home that evening; he told the girl Eliza to open the door, but she was too frightened. More things came down the stairs, pieces of carpet, knives, forks, and as fast as the girl picked them up, more objects came. White went up to see his brother, and while he was away one of the mantelpiece ornaments 'flew' into the corner of the room. It 'appeared' there, though neither of the women saw it move. Aroused by their screams, White returned. His candle went out, and in the dark he was struck on the forehead. The candle was retrieved from the floor and lit, and another ornament left the mantelpiece and fell into a corner. It was replaced, but did the same again, and was broken. White considered all this with foreboding, thinking that it presaged badly for a child of his who was ill.

The children of the house were gathered together, a doctor and a policeman were summoned, all in a crescendo of activity, things flying around, a glass jar travelling from a cupboard into the yard, a chest of drawers set on end and smashed. The company including the policeman saw a cream jug fly four feet in the air and smash on the floor. The doctor was there also when a basin ascended to near the ceiling, then dropped, and smashed. The disturbances finished at two in the morning, beginning again the following morning, when a nearly empty port bottle leaped from a table four feet into the air and splashed into a bucket of milk. The locals were turning up, avid for anything novel. One of them was there when an American clock which had not struck for eighteen months made its bid for glory, struck, and fell off the wall on to the floor. Plates, a cream-jug, and other items, flew up in the air and smashed on the floor, and a Salvation Army girl came, a brief visit as a candlestick flew and fell behind her, and she left hurriedly.

Other things happened at intervals. Medicine bottles fell, a lamp-glass fell, and by four in the afternoon, White had had enough. He had fastened responsibility for the events on Eliza, and told Eliza she must go. So Eliza went, and everything returned to normal. It was a short-lived poltergeist attack, but unquestionably spectacular.

The locals considered that Eliza had been made a scape-goat and that White himself was responsible. White was a shady character, and the idea was put out that he was anxious to buy the house and wanted it on the cheap. Otherwise there was no gain; he estimated the damage at £9. Although White was the centre of suspicion, no one argued that he had thrown the articles. The clock had moved horizontally from its nail (still intact on the wall) and cleared a bed immediately beneath it; the smaller items had been wafted, rather than thrown.

If it was a conspiracy, then the policeman would hardly be involved. But he was at the house when things were on the move. Podmore pointed out certain differences in the witnesses' statements, though they do not amount to much, and if anything eliminate the idea that it was all a conspiracy with a prepared story. Podmore was also supercilious about the people themselves, commenting that as they were ill-educated they could not be expected to present their accounts with the precision an investigator would like. On reading the individual reports, however, it would seem that these inferior people could describe what they had done, seen, and heard, with considerably more accuracy than their betters, and White's comment about the girl Eliza to a neighbour, a Methodist coal-miner has a ring of truth: 'It doesn't matter a damn where that lass goes, there's something smashes.'

Nevertheless, Podmore brought up an important point. Five

weeks went by before the occurrences were investigated, during which the matter was the reverse of *sub judice*. Podmore's colleagues in the Society for Psychical Research learned their lesson speedily, and when the next poltergeist performed, in the November of that same year at Wem in Shropshire, they were only a week behind.

Wood's Farm was a secluded farm about ten miles from Shrewsbury. One afternoon the servants were in the kitchen preparing tea when the saucepan in which eggs were boiling 'jumped' from the fire, coincident with tea things being thrown from the table, and hot cinders flying from the grate, firing clothes in a basket. On the table was a lighted paraffin lamp with a globe; the globe was lifted off the lamp, and thrown across the room. A mat under the lamp was set on fire. By this time everyone in the house was advised of these happenings, and a neighbour was summoned, a Mr Lea who immediately assumed that a Satanic agency was at work, and who when approaching the house thought the place on fire, such was the light in the interior. The occupant began to take things to safety as the disturbance continued, and he was taking down a barometer from the wall when something struck him on the leg, a loaf of bread hit him in the back, and a volume of *Pilgrim's Progress* dived through a window accompanied by a large ornamental shell. In another room in the house a sewing-machine was thrown about, and fire jumped from the grate, slightly burning a baby in the arms of a nursemaid, who, panic-stricken, rushed out to a neighbour's. As she went, her clothes caught fire and had to be torn from her body. At the neighbour's house, the nursemaid was beset by further disturbances.

The police were called in, and as it seemed to them that the leaping of the coals was the main item, they had the coals taken into the open in case there was some explosive material in them. There was not. The farmer's wife wholeheartedly believed in the supernatural cause of the occurrence, a servant girl was excited and fascinated, and the nursemaid, around whom the events revolved, seemed nonplussed by it all. A sour note comes from a farm hand, who considered that the two girls had concocted the whole thing, a line taken in the newspaper report.

Unlike the manifestations at Worksop, at Wood's Farm there was danger to at least one person, the baby, who was set on fire several times. It was perhaps ominous that the nursemaid, Emma Davies, was always the first to discover this, and once she was seen shaking the child's pinafore, though the farmer's wife had told her that this was dangerous. Even more significant was the sound of a match being struck, and when the farmer's wife entered the room she caught the odour of brimstone, and a used match was found near the baby's head. It was found that the baby's clothing was very little singed when the flames were put out, and an experiment was tried. A piece of the baby's hat was cut off, dipped in paraffin, and lit; when the flame was extinguished, the material presented a similar appearance to that charred apparently by spontaneous combustion.

Although witnesses swore that Emma was not invariably about when the articles were flying around, she was obviously a menace at the farm, and was sent home, five miles away, where happenings continued, buttressed by rumour and anticipation. The country way of washing was to dry the wet clothes on a hedge, and when Emma was hanging them observers saw the washing jump into the road. Emma had a more sensible explanation; she and her sister put the washing on the hedge, went indoors, came outside again, finding the linen on the ground and seeing two small boys running away.

The police were called to Emma's home, and a police-constable witnessed a fender moving from the fireplace to the centre of the room. A cushion at the back of the chair on which Emma was sitting flew across the room, the stitches in her apron were undone, and the buttons on her dress were wrenched off. Emma became a nine days wonder, and up to twenty people were watching her at one time, including the village schoolmistress, an hysterical spinster of about forty, who swore that Emma's boots fled off her feet and, when replaced, did it again.

Not surprisingly, all this put Emma into a nervous state, and eight days after the first phenomena she was taken to a doctor's and kept there, watched over by the housekeeper, a shrewd and observant woman of about thirty. She and the doctor were inclined to suspect fraud, exhibitionism being a known state though not yet so labelled. At the farm most of the watchers had been at least half-credulous. The doctor and the housekeeper watched. A piece of bread jumped across a room, a pair of slippers appeared on a sofa when they had been on the rug, and on one occasion, when Emma screamed, the housekeeper turned round and a bucket descended. A knife was thrown across a room, a servant seeing it in motion. The housekeeper said that she had never seen Emma throw these objects, though on all occasions Emma *could* have done.

Yet surely all speculation stopped when the housekeeper, unobserved, saw Emma holding a piece of brick in her hand, scream to attract the attention of the servant, twist her wrist and hurl the brick so that the servant would see just the missile in motion? The investigator sent down by the Society for Psychical Research, Frank Hughes, was inclined to prejudge against the supernatural, but he was not certain that all was trickery, plumping for a combination of genuine poltergeist phenomena and trickery. The circumstances surrounding the burning baby would indicate that Emma was psychotic rather than neurotic. Hughes thought her precocious, but whether her 'confession' was another way of dramatising herself, and possibly benefiting her pocket at the expense of the daily newspapers, it is impossible to say.

At Bramford, near Ipswich, a conglomeration of raps, noises and furniture upheavals occurred towards the end of 1887. They centred around Ellen Parker, a girl of eleven. She then went to stay with an aunt in Stowmarket. One night there was a rapping on the house door, but no one was there; the rapping was repeated in the house, followed by loud noises that terrified the aunt. The uncle saw a clothes chest jumping about the floor (later he admitted that he only saw it move once, and then only a few inches, though he stoutly claimed that it had been jumping when he was out of the room). From then, it was only a short step to the uncle sensing that everything was alive.

Investigators went to both Bramford and Stowmarket. At Bramford a policeman had been set to watch the cottage when the occurrences started, and he saw Ellen producing the mysterious noises and tapping the window when she thought she was unobserved. Her younger brother, Cornelius, aged ten, admitted that he had assisted in the matter.

The events drew the neighbours like wasps to a honey-pot. One of them pretended he was taken in, and, lulled into a sense of security, the children made their play, the boy throwing a glove and a baby's bib while his arm was concealed behind his mother, hurling a poker across the room while the neighbour averted his attention, and rolling a kettle across the floor. The girl kicked off her boot, screamed, and said that the spirits had taken it.

Living in the house was a moribund old lady, and the children had been amusing themselves by throwing things at her. To avoid punishment they said that the spirits had done it. From there there was no turning back, and they piled on the tricks, impressing not only the family but many outsiders. Ellen was a hysterical girl, given to fits.

So many of the cases reported from this period break down under examination, and but for the odd inexplicable incident the entire outbreak of disturbances might well be put down to mischievous neurotic young people out to get a bit of fun out of their elders. It happened in the seance room, too. At one session spiritualists waited with bated breath for tables to perform at the bidding of two 'psychic' youngsters. The table moved all right, but it was clear to even the most bigoted of spiritualists that the children were happily rocking the table backwards and forwards without pretence that it was being done by the spirits.

A case that stood up stronger to outside observers was the Durweston case of December 1894. Durweston was a small village about three miles from Blandford, and the disturbances happened in one of a pair of cottages somewhat isolated from the rest of the houses. The occupant was a widow, Mrs Best, a quiet, inoffensive woman with respectable Nonconformist beliefs, well-liked by the other villagers. She was puzzled by strange knocks and scratchings all over the house, which increased in loudness until the occupant of the adjacent cottage heard them as well. The noise rose to a crescendo, until it was likened to sledge-hammer blows, and this was followed by stones through the window, smashing panes, then returning.

The man who lived in the cottage next to the Best's home was gamekeeper to the owner of the property, Viscount Portman. One day he was told by Mrs Best that one of two orphan girls boarded on her by rich patrons had seen a boot come out of the garden and strike the back door, leaving a muddy mark. No doubt the gamekeeper was prepared to disregard the fantasies of a thirteen-year old girl, but when he went into the Best house, objects began to hit the window on the outside, beads, a toy whistle. The door was open, and a quantity of small shells floated in at intervals from half to one minute. They came very slowly, and if they struck the man he did not feel them. Other articles began to move, a pencil, a hasp, and a boot moved slowly into the house, gliding a foot from the floor, the same boot that the girl had described hitting the door. Mrs Best threw the boot out, and the gamekeeper, with a touch of bravado, put his foot on it and defied anything to move the boot. Nothing happened. He stepped off the boot, and it rose up behind him and knocked his hat off. No doubt impressed by her neighbour's courage, Mrs Best and the orphan children moved into his cottage.

When the local intellectuals – the vicar and the schoolmaster – heard of these strange events they decided to pay a visit. The phenomena now took the form of vibrations and rappings in the gamekeeper's house, and while Mrs Best and the children were in bed, one bed with the children at the foot, scratchings in the wall and in the mattress. It was decided to find out the reason for this very suspect phenomena by communicating with the spirits via a slate. They asked the slate where it should be placed, suggesting a site and waiting for disagreement or confirmation by a reply in taps; the auditors were not certain what 'yes' was, but 'no' was decidedly one tap. Eventually all except Mrs Best and the children left the room and the lights were put out; when four raps were heard the message would be written. The men waited at the bottom of the stairs, with the bedroom door open; they could hear Mrs Best groaning and the scratching of a pencil. The woman called out 'Come!' There were scratches on the slate, but nothing more, but on the second attempt there were a series of whorls 'such as no child could produce', third attempt, two letters, fourth 'Mony', the fifth 'Garden'.

During this time the vicar was steadily getting nearer to the bedroom door, until he was close enough to hear Mrs Best breathing; he was positive that he would have detected the slightest movement, and was impressed by Mrs Best's inability to write, though one of the girls could (and 'Mony' is a typical child's misspelling).

The children were moved to another house in the village, and finally separated, though Annie, the elder child, the one who could write, still had disturbances about her: noises on the outside of the house, a large stone flung on the roof of the porch, snowdrops dug up and thrown about. A lady official concerned with the boarding out of orphan children took Annie to London, where no disturbances occurred, and the girl was examined by a doctor, a step long overdue, where it was found that she had pronounced consumptive tendencies, was extremely hysterical, and had had hallucinations of an animal with a green head and green eyes pulling her doll to pieces.

As was so often the case, it all finally hangs on the characters of the witnesses and the participants. The investigators could not put the case down categorically to the supernatural, though they considered that Mrs Best should have been above suspicion. The vicar declared that she had perhaps the highest character of anyone in the village, and was aghast at the thought of connivance on her part. This, clearly, may reflect only on his own credulity.

Other cases investigated during this poltergeist season of the 'nineties confirmed that the phenomena were compounded of trickery, expectation and hallucination, executed for mischief, a certain local fame and, occasionally, money. One case investigated by General Pitt-Rivers was a collaborative effort, and no doubt the initiator of this particular charade was disconcerted when the general invited the police to take action, stating that he and his wife would give evidence of fraud.

When taxed by outsiders, the children responsible for the events confessed quickly enough, and in several cases other children in the house helped with the disturbances. The children were more lively and inventive than their elders gave them credit for, and, it would seem, considerably more imaginative, even more intelligent, than the classic dupes – vicar and policeman – who stumbled through rustic poltergeist phenomena. The hiding of the skeleton of a cat in a 'secret' cupboard predictably created consternation, and it must have been highly enjoyable for children to throw stones and break windows, tear up snowdrops, toss cats into fires, knowing that they would not be punished. Almost certainly the children would have desisted earlier but for the local interest aroused. The servants also played their parts. It is perhaps not surprising that they should have scratched and tapped and knocked and hid things if their betters could be thrown into panic.

The Victorian poltergeist was a scapegoat. Widely reported and skilfully investigated, the almost total absence of the supernatural makes one wonder about the credibility of more traditional hauntings. It has a lot in common with seance materialisation. It was a set piece, suited to scrutiny, unlike the aimless arbitrary spectral appearances, the grey ladies of this or that great castle, the phantasmagorical nuns in shaded walks, Dick Turpin suddenly appearing in the middle of nowhere.

17. The Walking Dead

The walking dead are different from apparitions and spectres in several ways. They are assumed to be solid, and they are assumed to hold menace for the living. Apparitions are potents, and their presence means something. The walking dead have no message for the percipients, except 'Beware!'

The most familiar of the categories that make up the walking dead is the vampire, although its origin lies in Eastern and Central Europe and there is no evidence to indicate that its presence was ever encountered in Britain. Only slightly less familiar is the werewolf, but the emphasis here is on transmutation; the werewolf was commonly held to be one of the guises of a witch or warlock, and only a few held the view that the werewolf was a dead person come to life.

Both vampire and werewolf are symbols of easy horror, and their numerous appearances in the literature of the nineteenth century were a sure indication that readers loved to be frightened and that the writers had found an agreeable formula. The forms the vampire took were varied and miscellaneous, ranging from the creation of E. F. Benson of a horrible creature tangled in a rotting shroud covered with foul mould, through the early work of Algernon Blackwood, to entities more akin to the world of science fiction. Their existence was also diversely explained. Smyth Upton was an obscure writer whose novel *The Last of the Vampires* was published in Weston-super-Mare in 1845. The hero of this novel became a vampire because he sold his soul to the devil.

Most of the writers failed to make vampires anything other than humorous, pantomime creatures with as much capacity for rousing horror as Mother Goose. *The Vampyre,* 'by the wife of a Medical Man', published in 1858, has more of the quality of a genuine vampire than that of Smyth Upton, but she is hardly more frightening: 'They fly – they bite – they suck my blood –

I die. That hideous "Vampyre"! Its eyes pierce me thro' – They are red – they are bloodshot. Tear it from my pillow, I dare not lie down. It bites – I die! Give me brandy – brandy – more brandy.' On the stage, the vampire's appearance in burlesque had the audience in howls of laughter, and not until the publication of Bram Stoker's *Dracula* in 1897 did the vampire become an agent of menace.

But perhaps the laughter and merriment was a trifle too energetic, a way of avoiding something genuinely frightening, as a vampire surely is. Originally it was the soul of a dead man which leaves the corpse at night to suck the blood of living persons. When a vampire's grave is opened, the body is rosy and fresh from its nightly intake. To put a stop to its antics, a stake is driven through the body, or the head is chopped off, or its heart torn out, or the grave soused with boiling water and vinegar. A variation of the traditional vampire is the living man who assumes some other form, sometimes insignificant like a piece of straw, to feed off the blood of other men.

Vampirism was especially prevalent in Hungary between 1730 and 1735, and Calmet's *Dissertation on the Vampires of Hungary* published in England in 1750 had caused a considerable stir. What had caused the panic was the discovery in exhumed coffins of marks of blood on the shroud and on the face and hands, and, from the twisted and contorted configurations of the corpses, all the indications of ghastly struggles. Incorrect conclusions were drawn from these phenomena. Quite simply, these unfortunate people had been buried alive. As the years went by – although witches and warlocks were more likely to be vampires anyway, in addition to dead people who had been jumped over by cats while lying before burial – it was considered that those most likely to become vampires were those who had been buried alive. This was put explicitly by Franz Hartmann in *Magic: White and Black:* 'Personal consciousness returns, and it finds itself alive in the grave, where it may pass a second time through the pangs of death, or by sending out its astral form in search of sustenance from the living, it may become a vampire, and prolong for a while its horrible existence,' and only slightly less so by Z. T. Pierast: 'As long as the astral form is not entirely liberated from the body there is a liability that it may be forced by magnetic attraction to re-enter it. Sometimes it will be only half-way out when the corpse, which presents the appearance of death, is buried. In such cases the terrified astral soul re-enters its casket, and then one of two things happen: the person buried either writhes in agony of suffocation, or, if he has been grossly material, becomes a vampire.'

Dread of vampires can be seen as a handy synonym for dread of being buried alive. Throughout the nineteenth century, this was not only a real fear, but a justified fear, and for those in most terror there was no alleviation until cremation was introduced at Woking on March 26th 1885. In the 1880s, those who opted for cremation were more concerned with not being prematurely buried than with theology or hygiene.

Premature burial had been warned against by many prior to the nineteenth century. In a treatise *The Uncertainty of the Signs of Death, and the Danger of Precipitate Interments* published in 1746, a surgeon, M. Cooper, wrote: 'Though death at some time or other is the necessary and unavoidable portion of human nature, yet it is not always certain that persons taken for dead are really and irretrievably deprived of life, since it is evident from experience that many apparently dead have afterwards proved themselves alive by rising from their shrouds, their coffins, and even from their graves.' Cooper went on to the specific. Many people had narrowly escaped being buried alive; obviously many more had not.

As the nineteenth century proceeded, the dangers of premature burial were increased. In the poorer parts of the great cities, the doctors were hard-pressed to keep control, and when the deceased had been ill or had been manifestly dying they were quite happy to issue death certificates on the application of a relative without having seen the corpse. Despite the Acts concerning metropolitan burials passed between 1850 and 1867, all was haphazard and chaotic. The leading medical journal of the day was especially lyrical on the topic of premature burial:

> Truly there is something about the very notion of such a
> fate calculated to make one shudder, and to send a cold
> stream down one's spine.... The last footfall departs from
> the solitary churchyard, leaving the entranced sleeper behind
> in his hideous shell soon to awaken to consciousness and
> to a benumbed half-suffocated existence for a few minutes;

or else, more horrible still, there he lies beneath the ground conscious of what has been and still is, until, by some fearful agonised struggle of the inner man at the weird phantasmagoria which has passed across his mental vision, he awakes to a bodily vivication as desperate in its torment for a brief period as has been that of his physical activity. But it is soon past. There is scarcely room to turn over in the wooden chamber; and what can avail a few shrieks and struggles of a half-stifled, cramped-up man![1]

Those most in danger of being buried alive were those who had been in an extended state of trance for several days. During the flood of speculation in the 1880s, doctors received many letters from people who had narrowly avoided being buried alive. One old man, now aged eighty-four, had had a traumatic experience when he was twenty-four. He heard an undertaker say, 'Would anyone like to see the corpse before I screw him down?' To his surprise, the undertaker was referring to him. Another man in a condition then known as 'cold abstraction' was about to be screwed down. He was aware of all that was happening about him, but could not communicate with those about him, but at last the doctor noticed that the 'corpse' was breaking out in a sweat and rescued him. When the trance extended to several months, as it did in the case of a Stevensworth girl in 1896 who had been in a coma for nearly three hundred days, there was a strong tendency for doctors to lose patience and cut their losses.

The newspapers of the period reported many convincing cases of premature burial. In France in 1873, a young woman died during confinement; because of the intense summer heat she was buried in six hours. Her mother wished to have the daughter's remains moved to her native town, Marseilles: 'When the vault was opened a horrible sight presented itself. The corpse lay in the middle of the vault, with dishevelled hair and the linen torn to pieces. It evidently had been gnawed in her agony by the unfortunate victim.'[2] About the same time, a similar thing occurred in Naples. When the grave was being opened for the reception of another body, 'it was found that the clothes which covered the unfortunate woman were torn to pieces, and that she had even broken her limbs in attempting to extricate herself from the living tomb'.[3] The doctor who had pronounced death was sentenced to three months imprisonment for his hasty diagnosis.

Not surprisingly, many people guarded against these eventualities. The novelist Wilkie Collins always left a letter on his dressing-table adjuring anyone finding him dead to call a doctor and make certain, Harriet Martineau left her doctor ten pounds to see that her head was amputated before burial, the actress Ada Cavendish willed that her jugular vein be cut before interment, and the journalist Edmund Yates did likewise, providing twenty guineas as a fee for the officiating surgeon. Lady Burton provided for her heart to be pierced with a needle, while Meyerbeer arranged to have bells tied to his extremities when he was dead.

Franz Hartmann collected seven hundred cases of burial alive and narrow squeaks, and in 1889 the *Undertakers' Journal* stated unequivocally: 'It has been proved beyond all contradiction that there are more burials alive than is generally supposed. Stories of these cases are numerous.' By 1896, there were nearly two hundred books on premature burial. It was small wonder that people who had been buried alive were believed by the superstitious to return as vampires to revenge themselves on the living, or, as Hartmann maintained, to sustain themselves.

It is perhaps surprising that writers on ghosts and hauntings have neglected premature burial as a cause for such hauntings, especially when they occur in or near a churchyard. The widely-held notion of an astral form that leaves the body on death would hold up if it could be ascertained that ghosts and hauntings arise from a terrible happening that disturbs the natural order of things: a sudden unexpected death such as murder, a crime against nature such as suicide, or a ghastly accident such as burial alive. It is reasonable for hauntings to occur in places where tragedy has stalked.

Beyond the Veil

18. The Moment of Truth

> Through mist that hides the Light of God, I see
> A shapeless form: Death comes and beckons me:
> But gives me glimpses of the summer land:
> And, with commingled joy and dread, I hear
> The far-off whispers of a white-robed band.

This was the attitude of the typical spiritualist. Or at least, when not personally faced with death. More truly, this was the armchair attitude, mused over by the philosophically inclined after a good evening with a happy medium. To continue with the same poem:

> Why shrink from Death? Come when He will or may,
> The night he brings will bring the risen day.
> His call, his touch, I neither seek nor shun;
> His power is ended when his work is done.
> My Shield of Faith no cloud of Death can dim:
> Death cannot conquer me! I conquer him![1]

But even the above writer, S. C. Hall, had occasional doubts. 'If the Soul, on its departure from the body, its sometime tabernacle – the house in which it has dwelt – loses all consciousness of a past, what can be its future?'[2] And this was the crux of it. The decomposition of the body could be accepted, but how could the putrefaction and gradual disappearance of the organ of consciousness, the brain, be reconciled with the existence of a something that retained consciousness? Without consciousness of the past, an individual soul might just as well not exist. A fresh dilemma arose on the introduction of cremation in 1885; the body did not gradually decay, and possibly give up its soul in a slow manner, but was speedily reduced to a handful of ashes. Most spiritualists believed that there was no time lag between death and the emergence of the soul, which was imagined as a duplicate of the body. When theosophy used the term 'astral body' it was appropriated by the spiritualist movement. Similarly, the transition from life to death envisaged by spiritualists has been taken over by orthodox Christians, even those who have not consciously rejected the hypothesis of the Day of Judgment. Mrs Cora Tappin's trance addresses enjoyed a great vogue during the Victorian heyday of spiritualism. Allegedly speaking through her was the American Judge Edmunds, an ardent devotee of the cause. His description of the transitional state between life and death is typical:

My body sank into a sweet repose, over which my spirit, already freed, stood and looked upon it as you would stand and look upon a worn-out garment. I was not conscious of the loss of one instant of time; my mind did not slumber. I was not aware even for one brief interval of the loss of control of any faculty. I knew I was about to die. I knew also every instant of time that my spirit was gradually losing control of the physical body. I re-entered the tenement at intervals to look around, as you might a house you were about to leave, to see how the loved ones were getting on that were watching beside me.[3]

Victorians had no idea how common these out-of-the-body experiences were, and there are a formidable number of cases of people who have been given up for dead who have subsequently related experiences identical to that of Judge Edmunds'. Lord Geddes, a physician and professor of anatomy, related his out-of-the-body experience in 1937. He was aware that he was suffering from acute gastroenteritis, and it was odds-on that he was going to die. He reviewed his financial situation, and as he did so he became aware that *his* consciousness was separating from another consciousness which was also him. Afterwards he classified them A personality and B personality. The B personality belonged to the body, and the A personality could track with interest its gradual disintegration as the illness became worse. Gradually Geddes could see not only his body and the bed it lay in, but the house, and outside the house; in fact anywhere he cared to focus his attention. He also became aware of seeing 'things' (his quotes) not only in the ordinary three-dimensional world, but in a fourth or more.

It is perhaps not surprising that there is a paucity of such accounts in the nineteenth century. When men were dying, they were dying; there were no medical devices to wrench them back. Yet it did not need the imminence of death to convince great minds of the isolation of the spirit from the body, or that consciousness was indivisible. In the Gifford Lectures of 1901–1902, William James told of his experiences under the influence of nitrous oxide. He came to the conclusion 'that our normal waking consciousness, rational consciousness as we call it, is but one special type of consciousness, whilst all about it, parted from it by the filmiest of screens, there lie potential forms of consciousness entirely different'.

Have these statements any importance? Do they merely arise from unique psychological states, the mind bending under unusual stresses? Have the percipients been kidded into a cosmic exaltation – Geddes by his near scrape or William James by an excess of laughing gas? On another occasion, Tennyson was in raptures over the *disappearance* of personality, not its perpetuation, maintaining that the whole was more glorious than the part, that if his individuality was lost in a universal pool he would be quite contented. And it must be remembered that mystical states akin to the above have been produced to order by the intake of mind-bending drugs, such as mescalin and lsd. It may be that mystical experiences have a built-in incommunicability; as Myers put it, 'Any attempt to deal with these spiritual phenomena as *realities* – as phenomena capable of correlation with the material phenomena which we know – does at once and inevitably demonstrate the uselessness for such a purpose of ordinary metaphysical terminology.'[4]

The out-of-the-body experiences were known during the Victorian period as 'travelling clairvoyance'. Myers did not care for this phrase, preferring 'psychical excursion'. Whether or not psychical excursions are part and parcel of the business of dying – and the very ease with which mystical experiences can be evoked by drugs makes this a distinct possibility – these hypothetical phenomena would key in more with modern views on the role of the brain than with those of the nineteenth century, and with modern physics and metaphysics. The twentieth-century notion that the brain is a device for keeping information *out* rather than in, the astonishing realm of advanced physics in which sub-matter may vanish and reappear, exist without weight or mass, and travel backwards in time, the possibility that there do exist universes interpenetrating with our own and maybe containing their own forms of awareness – when one considers all these then the hypothesis that the personality can release itself from thrall to a few pounds of grey substance encased in a web of membrane is small beer.

In the context of out-of-the-body experiences it might be interesting to remember the extraordinary number of cases where dying people have appeared to relatives and friends. Extraordinary, yes, if these excursions are seen as astounding exemptions from natural law, but on the other hand, if the soul leaves the body at the time of death as described by Judge Edmunds and Lord Geddes in such similar terms, *if this procedure is customary*, then the number is extraordinarily low.

Can these excursions be authenticated?

Yes, on two grounds: if the person experiencing the hallucination has told someone else before the information of death has formally arrived by post or messenger, if the person has recorded the hallucination in a diary or letter before the information has been formally received.

The accounts of · Victorian veridical hallucinations, though they span forty years, have a certain similarity. The cases below are placed in chronological order:

1845: Mrs Sewell was in Bangalore, and one night was awoken by a feeling that something was not quite right. She saw her sister-in-law in her nightdress at the foot of the bed, with her hair falling loosely around her. One lock of hair had been cut off at the temple. The apparition gazed steadily at Mrs Sewell, then gradually faded away. In due course a letter arrived, informing Mrs Sewell of her sister-in-law's death in transit from South Africa to England. In the letter was enclosed a lock of the woman's hair. Confirmation of the hallucination was given both by Mrs Sewell's daughter and son. Was Mrs Sewell subject to hallucinations? There was an occasion twelve years later, when a flame-like light at the end of her bed encouraged her to think that something had happened to a near relative. A relative had had a miscarriage, it afterwards transpired.

1855: Mr Heather was a farmer and miller. He was building a house and a yard for pigs on a slope. His son was in full view of the buildings, and Mr Heather shouted to him: 'Jack, just see what your Uncle Ned is doing in the pigsty.' Jack a young man of twenty-four, knew that Uncle Ned was seriously ill and could not be in the pigsty, but his father swore that he saw him enter the sty, and would not be dissuaded until a search had been made. In two hours a messenger brought news that Uncle Ned had died.

1864: Mrs Clerke lived in Barbados. Her black nurse was pushing Mrs Clerke's daughter in a perambulator. Mrs Clerke went into the house, and the black nurse asked who the gentleman was who had been speaking to her employer. Mrs Clerke was indignant; there had been no gentleman, but the nurse was insistent. He was tall and very pale, and Mrs Clerke had been rude not to have spoken to him. On being requested, Mrs Clerke noted down the day, and later she received news of her brother's death in Tobago on the same day as the nurse had seen the apparition. Mrs Clerke was living in Upper Norwood when she recounted her tale in 1885. She said that the black woman had *no object* in telling her. Similarly Mrs Clerke had no object in making the story up; if anything, it told against her. Her servant, an uneducated native, had clairvoyant gifts that she herself lacked.

1872: An interesting American case occurred in which a death apparition was seen by three different people in three different places. The dead woman had died of smallpox in Boston and appeared to Mrs Coote one morning between five and six, dressed in a long nightdress, bending over her bed. The figure touched Mrs Coote, though her husband, asleep beside her, heard and felt nothing. The apparition also appeared to an aunt in the form of a bright light in the corner that developed into the figure of her neice with such sharpness that the aunt could discern the detail of the needlework on the nightdress. It was also found out later that the apparition had also made itself known to Mr Coote's half-sister. Mr Coote was positive that there had been no collusion in the matter.

1885: This is a particularly interesting case, as no emotional attachments were involved. Alfred Bard was a gardener, and his path home took him through Hinxton Churchyard, Saffron Walden. In the churchyard was the mausoleum of the de Fréville family, and leaning on the rails surrounding the vault was Mrs de Fréville, dressed in a coal-scuttle bonnet, black crêpe jacket, and black dress; Bard was not surprised, for the woman was morbid about tombs. The gardener, who knew Mrs de Fréville well, having once been employed by her, assumed that the mason from Cambridge was in the mausoleum doing something and the woman was waiting for him to emerge. Bard walked carefully around the mausoleum to see if the gate was open, while Mrs de Fréville watched him. He could not see the gate, as Mrs de Fréville blocked his view. He stumbled on the grass, and looked at his feet; when he looked up, the woman was gone. Assuming that she had entered the vault, he went up to it, but it was locked up and there was no key in the lock. Puzzled, he remained there for some time, certain that Mrs de Fréville could not have left the churchyard without being seen, and between nine and ten he went home, and told his wife.

The following day, news reached Hinxton that Mrs de Fréville had died in London. The Vicar of Hinxton had heard of Mr Bard's experience, and interviewed him. Bard was a man of integrity, and the vicar was satisfied that he had seen exactly what he had purported to have seen. The vicar was positive that the woman's death could not have been known in Hinxton before May 9th, whereas the gardener had seen the apparition on the 8th; Mrs de Fréville was found dead at 7.30 on the evening of the 8th.

From this mixed bag of hallucinatory experiences certain similarities peep out. It would appear that every one validates the proposition of William James. Each hallucination is 'as good, and true a sensation as if there were a real object there' despite the fact that the percipients differ widely in education and social standing.

The most obvious conclusion to draw from these cases is that telepathy was in operation, but are there grounds for assuming that telepathy, the communication of mind to mind without using any of the senses, is any the less *outré* than the withdrawal of the personality from its corporeal housing? The credence given to telepathy is encouraging to the belief that past opinions of the role of the brain are antique, and no more valid than another obsolete theory connected with the cranium, phrenology.

If the personality dissociates itself from the body at the time of death, what then? What are the 'glimpses of the summer land' promised by S. C. Hall at the opening of this chapter?

The Victorians did not go for a disembodied intelligence. In a sense, spiritualism is materialism turned upside down. They opted for a simulacrum of the human body, which *seemed* to occupy space; if they did understand the concept of a plurality of worlds and interpenetrating space, they wanted no part of it. They were concerned with the everyday space of Queen Victoria's England. Assuming that a personality could not exist without a body, and aware that the dead one was not much use now, they evoked an idealised version of that one; as Judge Edmunds put it, 'To my utter amazement I beheld my form renewed utterly as the form of youth and strength.'[5] This bypassed certain obvious difficulties, where the dead person was old, crippled or wracked with disease. They were also aware that the everyday space of Queen Victoria's England was no place for these recreated souls, but were at a loss to know where to set them. Favourite was a never-never-land on one of the planets – Jupiter and Venus were both candidates, far enough away to be unknown, near enough to be cosy – but when the theosophists came along with their concept of an astral plane, this seemed more suitable still. By giving an abstract a name, it was rendered companionable.

Victorian visions of the after-life varied widely. In 1863 Mrs de Morgan visited the hereafter in trance.

Mrs de Morgan was in a garden full of flowers. There was a group of eight-year-old children hanging garlands over a lamb. They told Mrs de Morgan that she saw them as they were then, implying that people perceptibly age in the spirit world. The style of architecture appears to be a mixture of Taj Mahal and mock-Byzantine. She saw a church of emeralds, with illuminated steeple, an inlaid pavement in rich colours, predominantly purple (purple and green!) while the ends of the pews were arched in the Gothic style and made of precious stones. The windows were of purple and gold, and in the centre of each was a jewel as big as a dinner-plate. The people in this fantasy wore loose robes of purple, the children wore white, with wreaths on their heads. They climbed a tower, and now they had wings, and fluttered off. The vision dissolved to be replaced by a tableau of Christ in glory in a church more than a mile across.[6]

Not all spirits were so fortunate. Suicides lived in 'gloomy workhouses, and dull miserable stone-yards, with many disgusting accompaniments.' Even those who lived in what might be termed not the New Jerusalem but the New Bayswater had their ups and downs; in particular, there was the tedium of eternity, which could lead to discontent. This was the lot of those who had led idle, dissolute lives, and only those who had learned content 'amidst life's hardest lessons' were free to enjoy the aeons opening up to them. The relationship of the sexes was elegaically glided over – God permitted union but He did not compel it. There were also occupations and amusements in heaven suited to every spirit taste, though some of them must have been tiresome. One cannot relish being in close proximity to the clique arrayed in garments of white with crowns of gold on their heads 'and each held a book and a stringed instrument. On the latter they with one accord performed, accompanying the music with their voices ... some were formed into groups, whence they sang and read together from the word of God; some were dictating spiritual exercises and lessons, while others were instructing little children in the way and work of God. Every individual was beautiful – not one deformity of face or form was distinguishable of all the myriads that here convened together.'[7]

It would not be too much to say that mediums' descriptions of the hereafter are not only insipid, but juvenile, and an interesting parallel can be made with the death of a child in Mrs Henry Wood's *East Lynne*, with the child's forecast of the future life. As the novel appeared only two years before Mrs de Morgan's outpourings, it is more than possible that this description ('I wonder how it will be ... There will be the beautiful city, with its gates of pearl, and its shining precious stones, and its streets of gold ...') subconsciously influenced Mrs de Morgan in her choice of superlatives.

The selection of the planets as a *mise en scène* appears more inapt now than it did then. Venus was believed to have an atmosphere resembling that of the earth, and authoritative-seeming drawings of Mars by Beer and Madler and Dawes led to the construction of a fully-worked out map of Mars, with south polar ice, north polar ice, and continents, islands, and oceans (predictably named after the men who dreamed up these quaint drawings). As for Uranus, anything might happen there, though the astronomers did draw the line at Jupiter as a planet supporting earth-like creatures; nineteenth-century astronomers were well aware that the atmospheric pressure ruled out any hope of quasi-human life.

About 1897, a constructor's clerk from Paddington, an abstemious, devout man, had proof positive that Mars had already been booked by mortals of another order. A 'lady resident' in Mars by the name of Silver Pearl came to him in trance and gossiped 'pleasantly and glibly' concerning Saturn and Jupiter, and of her life on Mars, where mammoths were the beasts of burden, where the farmyard animals included one-horned cattle, sheeps, and goats, where the inhabitants were all clairvoyant and could fly (but not far), and could glide over water. Silver Pearl pointed out to the clerk that the general terrestial opinion that Edison had discovered wonderful things was erroneous — emissaries from Mars had visited him. The Martians were great in invention; they had ships with side-fins, submarines, and were able to transmit pictures in colour by telegraph. Each Martian worked two hours and three minutes a day, vice was virtually unknown (there was but one prison on the face of Mars), and if one wanted to marry one had to take a personality test, a test performed by spirits.

Yet at least these bizarre reflections, concocted from neuroses and early science fiction, have a certain distinction, and do not lean too heavily on the Bible. The descriptions of the hereafter by the New Bayswater school are clearly keyed in to *Revelations,* Chapter 21 ('the foundations of the wall were garnished with all manner of precious stones ... the twelve gates *were* twelve pearls ... the street of the city *was* pure gold, as it were transparent glass').

Revelations not only supplied a set of pretty pictures for the Victorians to revamp, but also gave the dimensions of the New Jerusalem: 'and he measured the city with the reed, twelve thousand furlongs.' Captain J. D. Sharkley, a measurer of vessels, took this literally. Would the New Jerusalem accommodate the hosts of mankind? He worked it out that there would be 7,920,000 feet cubed, which he made 497,793,088,000,000,000,000 cubic feet. Half of this would be devoted to the throne and the court of heaven, the rest was living space. Captain Sharkley was generous; everyone would have at his disposal a hundred rooms sixteen feet square, and the New Jerusalem on these terms could cope with up to 2,970,000,000 every hundred years. In

1889 when these ingenious calculations were made no doubt the situation seemed promising, though those who had read, listened to, and were taken in by, travelling mediums with their prognostications of the hereafter must have considered the paradise postulated by Captain Sharkley a trifle austere and notably lacking in home comforts.

Now for the disembodied conception of survival after death. Professor H. H. Price postulates a kind of dream-world, and goes further; 'The point of life in this present world, we might say, is to provide us with a stock of memories out of which an image world may be constructed when we are dead.'[8] The ordinary dream provides a good stepping-off point. Dream-images are in a space of their own, and have spatial relationships with other dream images. They do not conflict with other dreamers' images. Such an afterlife would be psychological rather than physical, but the fact that we are oriented to the physical does not mean that the physical is any the more *real,* and in such an afterlife the psychological might well seem to be physical. Such a life might well be as vivid, unexpected, arbitrary, as the one here, and may contain a persistent image of our own body. A private and subjective existence, perhaps, but telepathy may provide a link between the various subjective existences, and we are speaking of subjective from the here and now position: *in situ* subject and object lose their distinction. Price additionally postulates a possible 'common image world' for disembodied intelligencies.

It is not nineteenth-century spiritualism that one goes to for any exploration of these tantalising possibilities, but to the poets, the artists, the thinkers, those who could discern that

> the veil
> Is rending, and the Voices of the day
> Are heard across the Voices of the dark.[9]

The spiritualists thought they had the whole matter sewn up. They were the goodies, for ever proclaiming

> I've a beautiful home on the other shore,
> A home on the golden strand.[10]

They need make no effort. Smug and complacent, they waited for their call into the summer land, where there were no irregularities, no division.

19. Family Reunion

For partisans of the theory that the dead merely shed their body, retaining all their attributes including their personality, there were a number of problems to face. These included the relationship of the sexes in the hereafter. One of those who faced up to this was William H. Holcombe, MD whose *The Sexes: Here and Hereafter* was published in 1869. 'A woman who closes her eyes in this world and opens them in another,' he wrote, 'has lost nothing of her feminine character. She is not a man, nor an hermaphrodite, nor a nondescript, nor a spiritual vapour floating in the mystic ether or universal thought. She is a living, breathing, sensitive woman; and, if regenerate, she has every womanly quality intensified for a higher and better life. Woman is woman still. Every muscle there, as here, is a feminine muscle; every bone is a female bone. From her delicate and *spirituelle* features beam forth the softness and beauty of the feminine soul, and on the elliptical curves of her graceful form accumulates, as in this world, the charm and magnetism of life.'

This was exactly what the spiritualists wanted to hear. The manner in which Holcombe contemptuously dismissed the notion of the disembodied intelligence was music to the ears of grass root enthusiasts, as was the promise of *la dolce vita*. Assurance was wanted, and few were so explicit as Dr Holcombe, who hammered at this point time after time. 'The spiritual body is ethereal, beautiful, incorruptible, immortal. But it is not the less a body, compounded of organs and tissues, and possessed of sensibilities and functions corresponding to those of the natural body.' This, maintained Holcombe, was the 'common perception of mankind, undarkened by metaphysical speculations'. His blatant creed of wish-fulfilment can only be compared with the religious sentiments of society preachers who told their audiences what they wanted to believe, who were therapeutic rather than theological, and whose main aim was not to perpetuate a religious dogma but to alleviate anxiety. Dean F. W. Farrar, author of *Eric or Little by Little,* assured his congregation and readers that there was no hell; the fashionable society photographer Julia Margaret Cameron wrote to him on December 18th, 1877, from Ceylon: 'My dear Canon Farrar; I seem to draw a new breath! to live a new life! to have heard the best tidings of comfort to all men that I have *ever yet heard* during the sixty-two years of my life . . .'

So echoed was the message of Dr Holcombe. Man and woman not only did not die; nor did they persist in fragmentary form; the next life was like this, only better. Holcombe's credo was – as Myers wrote in respect of himself – 'far from that lofty resignation which subordinates all thoughts of a personal future to the welfare of the Universe as a whole'. What Schopenhauer described as the 'passionate affirmation of the will to live' was diluted into a weak but frothy solution by Holcombe and his like.

Not that Holcombe was unaware of the problems. By being direct about the emergence of the new woman in the hereafter, Holcombe was forced to hold forth on her situation there, and her position vis-à-vis the men. Sensitive readers had to be accommodated, and the untalked about had to be mentioned. In its posthumous form, the body 'has none of those excretory functions which are here necessary to rid us of the poisons we daily absorb'. He then speculated on sex. 'The sexuality of man and woman consists really in the sexual difference between their souls, which are thence anatomically represented in their bodies.' The writer went on to excite his readers further. Perversions of the sexual relations have been so terrible that the common conception of marriage was far too external, unspiritual, sensuous. Heavenly marriages were chaste, indeed chastity itself. Evil and licentious spirits were blinded and suffocated by this overpowering chastity. However, marriage was better than non-marriage, even in this truncated form, and monks and nuns were reproved for their strange notions that they were wedded to Christ; however, the good among them would be finally delivered from their delusions and in the afterlife would find their conjugal mates.

What about those who were married more than once? Would this not introduce complications into this blissful picture? Not really. These were marriages for 'external and selfish motives', and in the celestial sphere, not marriage at all. No one on earth could possibly know whether an existing legal marriage was a true spiritual marriage or not, and this neatly disposed of the unhappy and ill-crossed marriage (reminiscent to historians of pre-nineteenth-century marriage law when no one could really define what marriage was!). It would seem that with regenerated woman, the attitude towards her husband was symbolical rather than affectionate.

The tenets held by Holcombe were held also by those who were not remotely connected with the spiritualist movement. Some of the tenets could even be held by those of severely circumscribed sects such as the Plymouth Brethren. Philip Gosse and his wife belonged to this strict Calvinist sect. They 'formed a definite conception of the absolute, unmodified and historical veracity, in its direct and obvious sense, of every statement contained within the covers of the Bible'[1]

The Gosses took an intense and painful interest in what was known as the 'interpretation of prophecy', a mode of behaviour similar to that of the spiritualists, except that where the spiritualists sought enlightenment in the jumbled and garbled messages spelled out by medium and planchette, those concerned with prophecy searched 'the dark sayings bound up in the Book of Revelation'. When dying, Mrs Gosse dwelt, wrote her son Edmund, 'on our unity in God; we were drawn together, she said, elect from the world, in a triplicity of faith and joy. . . . My father, I think, accepted this as a prophecy; he felt no doubt of our triple unity; my Mother had now merely passed before us, through a door, into a world of light, where we should presently join her, where all things would be radiant and blissful, but where we three would, in some unknown way, be particularly drawn together in a tie of inexpressible benediction.' Family life would be continued after death as if nothing had happened.

Marriage in the hereafter, perhaps, but what about love and – the Victorian breathed the word suffused in shame and guilt – sex? F. W. H. Myers, longing to join his dead cousin whom he loved and who killed herself when her husband went mad, was unabashed: 'I find that love in its highest – in its most spiritual form is a passion so grossly out of proportion to the dimensions of life that it can only be defined, as Plato says, as "a desire for the eternal possession" of the beloved object – for his or her ever-growing perfection and bliss while removal by death, if no reunion be looked for, at once reduces this life to an act of endurance alone.'[2]

Marriage as a mystical religious state was laid down for the literate public by Coventry Patmore in *The Angel in the House*, which sold a quarter of a million copies. The pursuers of the chimera – marriage and its corollaries in the afterlife – were not an inconspicuous lunatic fringe. Although Patmore was memorably dismissed by Edmund Gosse as 'this laureate of the tea-table, with his humdrum stories of girls that smell of bread and butter', numerous attempts to re-evaluate him are at last meeting with success.

The appeal of *The Angel in the House* – although Tennyson declared that some of the lines seemed 'hammered out of old nails' – lay in Patmore's affirmation that domestic bliss was best and could persist into the great unknown. He contemplated a book called *The Wife in Heaven*, as he felt that he had not spelled out his message clear enough in the earlier book, for 'it must be impressively shown that Felix and Honoria also look to Heaven for the fruition of their love'. His conviction that the truest consummation love is reserved for the afterlife is sometimes declared with unequalled power. Thus his ode *To the Body*:

> Thou needs must, for a season, lie
> In the grave's arms, foul and unshriven,
> Albeit in Heaven,
> Thy crimson-throbbing Glow
> Into its old abode aye pants to go.

In *Religio Poetae*, Patmore wrote: 'The whole of afterlife depends very much how life's transient transfiguration in youth by love is subsequently regarded. . . . Nuptial love bears the clearest marks of being nothing other than the rehearsal of a communion of a higher nature.'

It must be emphasised that this is not reading into Patmore more than is actually there. In *Principle in Art* he is utterly categorical: 'The best use of the supremely useful intercourse of man and woman is not the begetting of children, but the increase of contrasted personal consciousness.' This is echoed by F. W. H. Myers: 'And what possible limit can we assign to the expansion of the noblest joys? . . . the oneness of spirits must be ever more interpenetrating as those spirits bring to the marriage a more eager and incontaminate fire.'[3]

The awareness of a continuous family scene frequently had a not altogether healthy influence on believers such as Mrs M. Vandeleur: 'She was a true Spiritualist, and arranged all her worldly affairs on New Year's Day. She was conscious of the presence of angel friends, and longed for them to take her to the summer land. She leaves one little girl of four in my charge. Her married life was very short but very happy, her husband was so kind and good.'[4] Or the father of Mrs E. Cooper of Liverpool: 'Mother passed away eighteen years ago before father did, two and a half years ago, and, he said, he never broke the link of spiritual communication with her, and in the latter part of his years he often said that she visited him in the night. Of course, we thought this was an hallucination.'[5]

Believers faced with imminent death were even anxious that their loved ones should join them there and then. Josephine Butler was one of the most remarkable women of the nineteenth century; she did more than anyone to stop the noxious trade in twelve-year-old virgins to brothels in Brussels, and fought a life-long battle against the physical degradation of women. She married a man who happily played second fiddle to her, a good well-meaning clergyman who because of certain character weaknesses failed to secure high office. It was March 13th 1890 and George Butler knew that he was dying: 'About four o'clock in the afternoon, just before the end, appearing to feel that he was starting on a long journey, he turned his head to me and took my hand, and said rather anxiously, "You will go with me, beloved, will you not? you will go with me?" The appeal went to my heart; I saw his mind wandered a little. I answered without hesitation, "Yes I will! *I will go with you.*" '[6] However, her promise took a long time to fulfil. She died in 1906.

Reunion was seemingly sometimes a mixed blessing. Like many of the aristocracy, Lady Norah Bentinck was a dabbler in spiritualism, and she described her run of the mill seances as though she had been singled out for special treatment. She got through to a dead friend:

Exceedingly surprised, I went on:
'Are you in the vision of God?' – 'No.'
'Have you seen It?' – 'No.'
'Are you happy ' – 'Fairly.'
'Are you with your husband?' – 'Yes.'
'Where are you?' – 'In Hell.'
'Oh, how dreadful! What an awful answer! ...'

It is not recorded whether indignation cut her any ice in the beyond.

20. Theosophy: The Break-away Movement

Helena Petrovna Blavatsky was born in 1831, the daughter of Colonel Peter Hahn, a member of a Mecklenburg family settled in Russia. When she was seventeen she married a Caucasian official many years her senior; according to her the marriage was never consummated. They separated after a few months, and Madame Blavatsky went globe-trotting.

Ten years of her life she diligently cloaked in mystery referring to the period as the veiled part of her life, and she spoke vaguely of a seven year stay in 'Little and Great Tibet', or alternatively in a Himalayan retreat. She came out of her seclusion in 1858, when she revisited Russia and caused a great stir as a spiritualist medium, and by 1870 she had became one of the leading spiritualists of the United States, where she lived for several years and became a naturalised subject. In 1875 she summarily ejected the controls who had been operating during her spiritualist period, and with Colonel Olcott she founded the Theosophical Society in New York. In 1878 the headquarters moved to India, and theosophy made a good deal of progress among educated Indians. In 1881, A. P. Sinnett, a forty-one-year-old roving journalist, published *The Occult World,* a book which caused a considerable stir in English occult circles, and this he followed with *Esoteric Buddhism.*

The basis of theosophy was this: there exists in Tibet a brotherhood whose members have a power over nature denied to ordinary men, and they have committed themselves to a special relationship with the Theosophical Society, and performed many marvels for it, and particularly for Madame Blavatsky, who claimed to be a *Chela,* or disciple, of this mysterious brotherhood, the members of which were called *Adepts* or Mahatmas. The *Mahatmas* were reputed to be able to cause apparitions of themselves to appear wherever they willed, to communicate with those whom they visited, and to observe whatever was going on.

They were also said to be able to instruct the *Chela* in these enterprises and the projection of the so-called astral form, and to transport solid objects, including letters, as well as being able to 'precipitate' writing and drawings on blank paper.

The resemblances between theosophy and spiritualism can be seen to be close, but there was one crucial difference between the two beliefs. Theosophy had a person of great personal magnetism at the head of it, spiritualism had none. When Madame Blavatsky died in 1891, the Theosophical Society split into two parts, each claiming Madame Blavatsky, or HPB as she was known, as the rightful progenitor.

The phenomena which were reported in India connected with the Theosophical Society intrigued the Society for Psychical Research, and in November 1884 Richard Hodgson went on the behalf of the society to India to see for himself, returning next April, having carried out the best bit of detective work yet accomplished on behalf of psychical research. The voyage was sparked off by an intriguing series of letters in the *Madras Christian College Magazine* of September and October 1884, purporting to have been written by Madame Blavatsky to Monsieur and Madame Coulomb, who had occupied positions of trust with the society but who had been expelled in May 1884. It was a case of thieves falling out. The letters, if genuine, made it plain that the marvels of theosophy were frauds, that the Coulombs were at least cognisant that they were frauds and possibly associated with Madame Blavatsky in their accomplishment. Madame Blavatsky declared that they were forgeries. The editor of the Madras magazine had made an effort to check on the letters, but was frustrated by a lack of experts. He entrusted some of the letters to Hodgson who had them examined by Mr Sims of the British Museum. He had no hesitation in certifying them as genuine.

Hodgson also looked into the mysterious business of the broken saucer. A theosophist opened the door of the shrine; a saucer was leaning against the door (how could it have been leaning if it had not been placed against the door from behind?); the saucer fell, and broke, but was magically reconstituted inside the shrine. Madame Coulomb showed Hodgson the broken fragments and the reconstituted saucer, manifestly a pair. The shrine had been in the Occult Room. Hodgson found signs of fresh plastering to destroy any evidence of double-dealing. The alcove in Madame Blavatsky's bedroom had been fronted by a wardrobe, in the back of which was a sliding panel.

Confronted by this bare-faced mechanism, the local theosophists maintained that it was all done by the lying Coulombs out of revenge, and they even instituted their own inquiry into the matter, but it was a bluff that was doomed to failure. Hodgson never saw the shrine, as it had been destroyed by three theosophists, anxious to preserve the theosophical image.

Hodgson also probed the astral journeys of Madame Blavatsky's confrères, and found them ludicrously unconvincing, founded on lying and credulity and self-deception. He also looked into the theosophical phenomena outlined by Sinnett in *The Occult World*. The introduction of a letter by the *Mahatma* Koot Hoomi into a sealed envelope struck him as utterly unconvincing, the length of the flap on the envelope being long and stuck only on the tip so that a letter could be inserted without the necessity of steaming open the envelope. Sinnett's prize piece was the account of the instantaneous transportation of a fragment of plaster plaque from Bombay to Allahabad. One evening Sinnett returned home to find a telegram, in which was a note from a *Mahatma* telling him to search in his writing room for a fragment of bas relief that the *Mahatma* had transported from Bombay. The fragment was found in the drawer of his writing-table (fortunately there were witnesses, including Colonel Olcott himself). A document signed at Bombay declared that about this time there was the sound of something falling and breaking in Madame Blavatsky's writing-room, heard by guests as they sat in the verandah adjoining this room. The room was empty, but the bas relief was found broken; the plaque was reassembled, but one piece was missing. Madame Blavatsky went into another room, and reappeared with a paper. The *Mahatma* who had sent the note to Sinnett had written that the missing piece had been despatched to him. Naturally, the fragment in Sinnett's possession fitted perfectly. All the witnesses were impressed, but when one realises that none of them had examined the plaque before its fortuitous fall, the whole episode is meaningless.

But India was a long way away. The idea of theosophy appealed in Britain, the doctrine of reincarnation, the seven principles starting from the gross body and going upwards, the theosophic path to Nirvana, and whatever shifty devices Madame Blavatsky was resorting to in India, and whether or not, as was believed, she was a Russian agent using theosophy as a front to undermine British rule, these were of no account to British occultists, finding spiritualism lacking in something and theosophy a more coherent way of life (irrespective of the fact that theosophy was a conglomerate of systems, Brahminism, Buddhism, with a dash of spiritualistic mayhem).

Those who met Madame Blavatsky in London were impressed despite themselves. She had dropped some of the furnishing gimmicks of her New York period – the stuffed monkeys and baboons, the snake on the looking-glass, the lion's head above the door – but she was still a compelling figure with her face deeply pitted with smallpox, her imperious summoning of astral bells (she wore, said Madame Coulomb, a device round her person for producing these sounds), her crafty sleight-of-hand. She was visited by occult-minded young men who had read Sinnett, such as W. B. Yeats, who called in 1887. Yeats contemplated her, an obese powerful woman nearing her end. 'All her life is but sitting in a great chair with a pen in her hand.'[1] Yeats's fellow-poet, Henley, looked at it all laconically. 'Of course she gets up fraudulent miracles, but a person of genius has to do something; Sarah Bernhardt sleeps in a coffin.'[2]

Madame Blavatsky moved to Holland Park, and sat before a green baize table scribbling occult symbols in chalk, contemptuous of her visitors – 'O you are a flapdoddle, but then you are a Theosophist and a brother.'[3] She informed one of her followers that there was another globe stuck on to this one at the North Pole, so that the earth really had a shape like a dumb-bell. She had no time at all for orthodox science. At her New York home, the stuffed monkey wore a cravat and spectacles, and carried a copy of *Origin of the Species*.

Spiritualists let theosophy insinuate itself before they realised what a danger it was to themselves. When Sinnett's *The Occult World* appeared, they reviewed it amiably, and W. H. Harrison, one of the more reliable spiritualist journalists, acknowledged that Madame Blavatsky was a medium of great talent, her ability to conjure up articles from nowhere being reminiscent of Mrs Guppy. He seized on the fact that when she was a spiritualist medium one of her controls was 'John King', a control that appeared many times in Britain to a wide variety of English mediums. Harrison was not so taken with Colonel Olcott or his mediumistic gifts.

There proved to be a doublepronged threat from theosophy. First of all, theosophy threw off the shackles of Christianity (this had made spiritualism unappealing to secularists) and thus had a non-sectarian appeal. Secondly, one particular aspect of theosophy could not be reconciled with spiritualism. This was reincarnation. In pre-theosophical days reincarnation was an optional extra, simply because spiritualists had not worked out the implications. But how could the basic belief that the dead retain their individuality untarnished if rarified fit in with the theosophists' claim that the spirit would come back to life in another form? Both sects had progress as their goal, but spiritualism did not countenance progress being worked out in a succession of earthly lives. Mrs Emma Britten, 'the able historian of Modern Spiritualism', wrote of the doctrine of reincarnation: 'doctrine which of itself, being utterly destructive of personal identity, is a tantamount to annihilation, and hence is almost universally and should be universally, rejected by Spiritualists. Furthermore, it is an unproved doctrine, the assertion of its advocates that all the millions of spirits that deny it are "low spirits", without knowledge, and the few that teach it are "high spirits", who have knowledge, being too assumptive even to admit of comment or argument.'[4]

Despite the laboured phraseology, the burden of the spiritualists' spokesman is this: the theosophists think they know better than we do, but they don't. There are further implications: the spiritualists were once happy to extend a friendly hand to theosophy; now they were not. Outsiders might see a prime example of the pot calling the kettle black in this claim that theosophy was 'an unproved doctrine'.

By the late 'eighties, spiritualism had been around for forty years, but it was no nearer to formulating a workable programme than it was at the outset. The British National Association of Spiritualists had been formed in 1873 to rectify this, but nothing tangible had come about. Supporters considered that it was the 'only doctrine which (1) presents a straightforward philosophy of the survival of the human spirit in a personal and individual form (2) which gives a definite and substantial existence to the spirit world (3) which allows for the straightforward and un-interrupted progress of the human spirit from the elementary conditions of human life on this earth, up to, and through the higher phases of existence in the spirit world.'[5]

Conan Doyle maintained that spiritualists were 'roughly united' on seven main principles: Fatherhood of God; Brotherhood of Man; Communion of Saints and Ministry of Angels; Human survival of physical death; Personal responsibility; Compensation or retribution for good and evil deeds; Eternal progress open to every soul.

But the most cursory glance through spiritualist literature of the period shows that this simply not so. The only principles that all would accept are those that were accepted too by the theosophists.

The theosophists rather enjoyed the dilemma, and when Madame Blavatsky took the trouble to analyse the failings of the spiritualists she could be very cutting indeed. She herself, when taxed, smilingly admitted tricks – what was one to do when man's very stupidity invited trickery, when the more gross the phenomena the more likely it was to succeed? Spiritualism represented a systematisation of popular beliefs and superstitions, and the typical atmosphere of the seance chamber involved morbid credulity, blind prepossession, and emotional contagion.

Theosophy had one thing in common with spiritualism – it could be made to look ridiculous in the popular press. *Punch* in September 1891 parodied of a Mahatma letter:

I AM KOOT HOOMIBOOG. There are more things in my philosophy than were ever dreamed of in heaven or earth. You are POONSH. You are a Thrupni but you are not a Mahatma. Be a Mahatma, and save your postage expenses. But you must be discreet; and you must be exceedingly vague. A Mahatma is nothing if he is not vague. You must also be elusive. Can you elude? It is no light matter to prove one's spiritual capacity by materialising a cigarette inside a grand piano.

Although the phenomena in India crumbled sensationally when prodded by a diligent sceptic, although the occurrences in Britain (letters found in odd places, 'astral bells', strange unearthly music seeping through the room) were bettered by spiritualist mediums, theosophy flourished, and Madame Blavatsky had a firm following of 100,000. It was the hippy movement of the last quarter of the nineteenth century, and emancipated girls with college education went into it, cocking a snook in the face of their square elders. One mini-biography is characteristic of many: 'After leaving Girton, she applied herself to the study of the occult side of Theosophy. Then she married a black magician in the platonic fashion common to Occultists, early Christians, and Russian Nihilists, and since then she has prosecuted her studies into the invisible world with ever-increasing interest.'[6]

Even those who felt that theosophy was an undigested hotch-potch of stock Eastern ideas, mysticism for the masses, had a soft spot for Madame Blavatsky's roguish effrontory, and those who were prepared to reprimand her were stumped by her willingness to admit that she had played tricks on theosophists. No matter what disasters overtook her, she popped back for more. In an area where the saccharine and the lugubrious toddle hand in hand, Madame Blavatsky's brazen insolence comes as a distinct relief.

21. The Spirit of Enquiry

'A reverent, earnest mind gains for itself that information and instruction which it is capable of receiving. The self-conceited flippant, ignorant, and curious receive only what they seek, and are sent away without reply, or with such as suits their query. Flee such. They are empty and foolish.'[1]

The tone of this statement by one of the spirit controls of Stainton Moses was typical of a certain kind of spiritualist who equated curiosity with flippancy, and the mindless reverence that such spiritualists expected from newcomers to the fold succeeded in antagonising many worthy people who approached spiritualism with an open mind. It is not surprising, therefore, that many of these people over-reacted, and took arms against spiritualism with some ferocity.

In an article in the magazine *The Nineteenth Century* a writer said, 'I have always expected most from inquirers who had no great personal interest, religious or irreligious, in this matter . . . whose faith in the unseen was already solidly based on moral considerations, and whose object as investigators was merely to conquer for science a small strip of neutral ground.' But such enquirers were few and far between, and even the founder members of the Society for Psychical Research were suspect. 'Seen at all close the methods of the Society for Psychical Research are extremely repulsive. What it calls evidence is gossip, always reckless and malignant; what it calls discrimination is too often the selection from gossip, all worthless, of those portions which fit best into the theory it happens to be advocating.'[2]

The Society for Psychical Research held its first meeting in 1882. A number of its members were members of the British National Association of Spiritualists, established in 1873, renamed the Central Association of Spiritualists in 1882. In the rooms of this association Professor Barrett of Dublin proposed the idea of the Society for Psychical Research. The Council of the Central Association of Spiritualists was understandably cool about the project, which was either a rival or an enemy. In the event, it was indeed an enemy. Fortunately for the health of the Society for Psychical Research some of the more reactionary of the spiritualists associated with the Central Association did not join.

The president of the new society was Henry Sidgwick. Born in Yorkshire in 1838, his grandfather was a cotton spinner and his father a clergyman. From Rugby he went to Trinity College, Cambridge, where he was a fellow from 1859 to 1869, praelector of Moral Philosophy 1875–83, and then professor. His *Methods of Ethics, Elements of Politics,* and *Practical Ethics* are worthy, rather dull books. In July 1863 he and a college friend, J. J. Cowell, had a series of sittings with a professional medium which were inconclusive. Cowell discovered that he could perform automatic writing; at sittings with Sidgwick the automatic writing was interspersed with raps.

At Cambridge, Sidgwick was regarded with a slightly hostile awe by the undergraduates as he stared through them with a distant and frigid air, chewing his beard. He did much for the higher education of women, and was in a large measure responsible for the founding of Newnham College. He was a man of great probity and distinguished position, and no better man could be found for the role of the first president of the Society. His wife, Eleanor, whom he married in 1876, proved the most astute of all the early investigators.

On the council were four especially able men, W. F. Barrett, Edmund Gurney, Frank Podmore, and F. W. H. Myers. Barrett is chiefly interesting as a commentator and as a populariser, steering a middle of the road course, being upset when there was flagrant imposture and being taken in by the cleverer fraud. Gurney was a man of great energy and persistence, and his major work *Phantasms of the Living* is a monument to Victorian scholarship, 702 cases in 1,300 pages. He accomplished this despite a 'constitutional lassitude' that often made all effort distasteful.

Like Sidgwick, Gurney went to Trinity College and got his fellowship in 1872. He was a member of artistic, musical, and philosophical sets, friends with the two great authorities on English law, Pollock and Maitland, a frequenter of the literary salons held by Mrs Hertz in Harley Street. Between 1874 and 1878 he attended a great number of seances, 'an alien, formidable figure, courteous indeed to all, but uncomprehended and incomprehensible by any'.[3] As the honorary secretary of the SPR he found a sort of niche.

Although *Phantasms of the Living* was supposed to be a joint project, Gurney did all the hard work, writing as many as sixty letters a day. He died alone in a Brighton hotel on June 23rd 1888, from an overdose of chloroform. Three days later Henry James wrote to brother William: 'Suicide is *suspected* I gather – from the strangeness of the form of his death. But he was only *generally* unhappy, and was even "cheerful" up to the last. Therefore it seems improbable.' The present stringent researches being undertaken by G. W. Lambert, a Past President of the Society for Psychical Research, may do much to clear up the enigma of Gurney's death.

Less is heard of Frank Podmore than his better-known colleagues at the Society for Psychical Research, though he is unquestionably the most cogent writer of them all, free from the self-conscious cleverness of Myers and possessed of a sharp succinct style. It is impossible to overrate his work on hallucinations, and his contributions towards checking and counter-checking of cases were invaluable.

Like Sidgwick and Gurney, Podmore was the son of a clergyman. Born in 1856, he was educated at Oxford, where he did well. He pursued a career in the General Post Office. By 1907 he was on a salary of £650 per annum, after twenty-eight years. In 1907 he suddenly resigned and moved to a place near Kettering where his brother was Rector. He had married in 1891 but was estranged from his wife.

In August 1910 Podmore arrived at a cottage near Malvern Wells as a paying guest; the owner of the cottage believed that Podmore had an unnamed male friend staying with him. A few days after his arrival Podmore brought back a young man, who left at nine in the evening by bicycle in the direction of Worcester. At ten-thirty Podmore went out, and did not return. His body was found in a lonely pond near Malvern Wells on August 19th; he was fully clothed, and his gold watch and a few pounds in cash were with him, though his walking stick was a yard from the bank.

It is generally believed that Podmore was a homosexual. Did he commit suicide? It is very strange that no member of the Society for Psychical Research was at his funeral; nor was his wife, nor was his brother Claude. The eerie fate of Frank Podmore, dying in the manner of a case on the haunted houses register, deserves a close scrutiny, and certainly the cold-shouldering by his colleagues at the society has no apparent reason.

F. W. H. Myers was the most flamboyant of the Cambridge group. Born in 1843, he was educated at Cheltenham and Trinity College. Whereas Gurney and Podmore had narrow interests (much as Gurney would have wished it otherwise), Myers was a man of wider culture, a poet, a writer on Virgil and Wordsworth, and although he was frequently intoxicated by his own cleverness he brought into his writings on psychic matters adventurousness and exuberance. Unfortunately his personality did not match his innate ability, and he lacked the integrity of Podmore, Gurney and Mrs Sidgwick. When he was swayed by personal motives he lost his objectivity, and could be fooled by fraudulent mediums if they were pretty and deferred to him.

In 1873 Myers had his first spiritualistic experience, coinciding with his falling in love with his cousin, Annie Marshall. Her husband was behaving oddly, and in 1876 he was placed in a lunatic asylum in Ticehurst. Soon afterwards Annie Marshall drowned herself. Myers was desperate to marry, but he was now in his mid-thirties and no longer the imperious figure of his youth. He settled for Eveleen Tennant, a beautiful thirty-two-year-old woman, whom he married in 1880. He was convinced that he would meet up with Annie Marshall in the hereafter, and his conception of a supramundane nuptial life owes something to Coventry Patmore. The labour force of the SPR was too small to cope with the mass of spiritualistic phenomena then being produced, and concentrated on certain projects. The mainstream of spiritualism deliberately ignored the emergence of a genuine spirit of enquiry, but especially in the metropolis well-known mediums such as Eglinton curbed their excesses and the number of materialisations dropped dramatically.

Earlier enquirers had made their judgments on the spot; there was either fraud or there was no fraud. There had been no attempt to collate and sift data. From 1882, information was collected, analysed, and compared, and fraudulent phenomena might well remain in the files for several years before a reasoned judgment was made upon them. This happened in the Creery case, which was investigated soon after the SPR was inaugurated.

Mediums could no longer be sure that they were definitively bamboozling their audience, and at any time in the future they could be exposed. However, the more cunning mediums delighted to hoodwink the SPR, and two clairvoyants who succeeded in doing it for a long time were A. J. Smith and a Mr Blackburn. This was a case in which Myers was involved, and he wished the clairvoyance to be genuine; when an outsider, Dr Crichton-Browne, considered it all a fraud, Myers accused him of 'offensive credulity'. In 1908, Blackburn owned up, writing in the magazine *John Bull* that 'only the pronounced friendly prejudice of a Myers would have credited [the clairvoyance] as successes'.

Materialisation mediums declined with the coming of the SPR. Sidgwick was anxious to investigate physical phenomena, especially those occurring in private circles, and in the course of his first presidential address hoped that a vast array of new material would arise for the society to look into. The old stalwarts were no longer in operation; Stainton Moses had ceased production about 1880, and Home had retired into private life. There was one medium eager to go on, Slade – but he was on the Continent and dared not come to England as legal proceedings were pending against him.

Those materialisation mediums reluctant to go out of business found that there were greater prospects overseas. Australia in particular welcomed English spiritualists. Nevertheless, there was still the danger of exposure by those who were sceptical of materialisation, and in October 1894 at Sydney, Mrs Mellon was seized impersonating the spirit of a little black girl. It was a damning exposure; Mrs Mellon was on her knees, with her feet bare, a black mask on her face and her shoulders draped with muslin. Her cabinet was examined, and a false beard and other articles were discovered.

Sidgwick and others were disappointed by the disappearance of the materialisation phenomena, but in 1893 their hopes rose. A peasant woman, Eusapia Palladino, was doing great things in Italy before distinguished observers, and in 1894 members of the

Society for Psychical Research were invited to go and see. These included Myers and Oliver Lodge, a distinguished physicist and a welcome recruit to the Society's ranks. He was impressed by the woman, though when reports came through to other members of the Society they were less sanguine. In the summer of 1895, Eusapia (for she was always referred to by her Christian name only) was brought to Britain for a series of sittings.

She had a wide programme. There were raps on walls, ceilings and floors, levitations of furniture and of herself, spirit imprints in damp clay, elongations of her body by four inches, and the playing of instruments by remote control, plus the materialisation of spirit forms, especially additional limbs. Lodge purports to have seen this.

Unfortunately this programme did not operate in the aseptic atmosphere of Myers's Cambridge house in the presence of Professor and Mrs Sidgwick, Lodge, Myers himself, and the extremely sceptical Richard Hodgson. Myers was eager for manifestations, and on one occasion 'Myers, who thought it good policy to encourage mediums at the commencement of a seance, jumped up and said he had been hit in the ribs'.[4] The Cambridge experiments of 1895 were a failure.

The success of the Italian seance was put down by Hodgson and others to the ability of Eusapia to break the circle without the other sitters realising it. During rapid spasmodic movements she managed to release one of her hands and make the other do duty as two; the sitter on the left held one part of the hand, the sitter on the right was touched by the fingers of the same hand. After she left England, a group of French investigators held sittings with her, and proclaimed astounding marvels, but test conditions were slack, and with a degree of dexterity Eusapia could still have extracted her hands and feet from her neighbours' supervision. She was not given credit for simple cunning; she was invalid, illiterate, and deemed incapable of getting the better of her superiors. So astonishing was her reputation on the Continent that in 1908 the Society for Psychical Research tried again.

Eusapia was up against a new generation of researchers; Myers and Sidgwick were dead, and were replaced by W. W. Baggally and Everard Feilding. Baggally had been investigating physical phenomena for thirty-five years, and had found nothing but fraud.

Feilding had been investigating for ten years, but he too had drawn a blank. Eusapia did not encourage them to change their minds. In 1910 she admitted to an American reporter that she had cheated, claiming that sitters had 'willed' her to do so.

This Italian peasant-woman represents the Indian summer of the materialisation medium. The furore that was generated about her can be attributed to wish-fulfilment. But conditions had changed, and the golden age had gone for good.

22. The Scientific Case

In the nineteenth century, science was, to use a contemporary catch-phrase, all the go, and it is surprising that it was not used more to investigate supernatural occurrences. The most obvious of the scientific instruments to document odd happenings was the camera, but photographers had their own ideas about what to record, and they were particularly interested in photographing spirits in their own studios, to the delight of their sitters and to the benefit of the photographer's pocket. The camera could and did lie.

For the most part, investigation of psychic happenings was on an amateur basis. At its most primitive level, investigation consisted of surreptitiously dropping tin tacks on the floor for an alleged spirit to walk on, or squirting cochineal at a ghost, or requesting the spirit to put its hands in water that would leave a stain on spirit hands, or simply grabbing the spirit. Except when the spirit managed to wriggle away, or the investigator was set upon by a confederate (it must be remembered that confederates sometimes made up the larger portion of the audience) the spirit always turned out to be the medium.

Scientists who believed in spiritualism were in a minority, and sceptical scientists were constantly being coaxed to give spiritualism a trial. Faraday did so, and came out against it, Galton was intrigued but uncommitted, Huxley was hostile, and Darwin was not greatly interested. The biologist W. B. Carpenter gave the matter a good deal of attention and came out against spiritualism. It needed a brave scientist to use the tools of his trade to investigate spiritualism when he intuitively believed in it, and honours go firstly to William Crookes, and secondly to Cromwell Varley.

Crookes was born in 1832, studied chemistry and became a person of some importance at the Royal College of Chemistry, went into the meteorological department of Radcliffe observatory,

Oxford, lectured on chemistry at Chester, and founded the *Chemical News* when still in his twenties.

The most cursory glance at his distinguished scientific career will indicate that William Crookes was a man of uncommon ability. He is the most important witness on the side of spiritualism. If what he recounted is true, then accepted natural laws no longer hold sway; if he was hoodwinked, then almost anyone could be hoodwinked. Some maintain that he deliberately allowed himself to be taken in because of an amorous attachment to Florence Cook, the medium.

As Crookes was one of the inner circle of spiritualism, he did not have to be impressed, he was accepted, and could operate in a free and easy atmosphere. Mediums complained about the attitude of most scientists. Francis Galton wrote: 'I really believe the truth of what they allege, that people who come as men of science are usually so disagreeable, opinionated and obstructive and have so little patience, that the seances rarely succeed with them.'[1] Crookes was happy to go along with whatever was happening, to allow the medium to flower in a congenial environment, though Galton affirmed that Crookes was thoroughly scientific in his procedure when dealing with D. D. Home.

One of Home's set pieces was the self-playing of an accordion purchased from Wheatstone's of Conduit Street. Crookes constructed a cage from two wooden hoops, twelve narrow laths, fifty yards of copper wire, and a string mesh. Home sat on a low easy chair, legs astride the accordion, his feet covered by neighbours' feet. The body of the accordion was encompassed by the cage, and the accordion was held by Home the opposite end to where the keys were. Home had one hand on the table. Home lifted his hand, and the accordion played, plunging and floating inside the cage. There were chords, runs, and sweet and plaintive melody. Crookes grasped Home's arm below the elbow, and touched the accordion; Home was not moving a muscle.

'If Home was a conjurer', wrote Frank Podmore in *Modern Spiritualism,* 'Mr Crookes was probably in no better position for detecting the sleight-of-hand than any other man his equal in intelligence and native acuteness.' Professional magicians were more scathing and outspoken: 'As a believer Mr Crookes is all very well,' declared J. N. Maskelyne; 'as an investigator, he is a failure.' And Harry Houdini in *A Magician among the Spirits* was equally forthright: 'There is not the slightest doubt in my mind that this brainy man was hoodwinked, and that his confidence was betrayed, and his reasoning faculties so blunted by his prejudice in favour of anything psychic or occult that he could not or would not, resist this influence.'

The electrical tests in which Crookes took part were dreamed up by Cromwell Varley, a distinguished electrician.

As Varley and his wife were ardent spiritualists, it was natural that his expertise would be utilised. He selected Florence Cook as the subject for investigation, and the object of the exercise was to determine whether the spirit-form 'Katie' was really outside the cabinet while Miss Cook was inside. The idea was simple: Miss Cook was to be put in an electrical circuit. A mild electrical current was to be passed through her body while the manifestations were going on, and a reflecting galvanometer in the next room would indicate changes in the circuit. A spot of light would travel across a gauge. Varley was encouraged to use Florence Cook by her backer, Charles Blackburn. A number of attacks had been mounted against her, and Blackburn was uncertain whether these accusations of fraud were justified. Florence Cook had cheated, and would cheat again, but she agreed to the conditions, and the experiments were carried out at the house of J. C. Luxmoore, another rich enthusiast.

Crookes was present on the first evening, in 1874. A piece of blotting paper moistened with a solution of nitrate of ammonia was placed on each of Miss Cook's arms, a sovereign was placed on each of the pieces of blotting paper, connected by wire to a battery. The sovereigns were held to the arms by elastic. The galvanometer was placed in the circuit, plus two sets of resistance coils. On the floor of Luxmoore's house where the experiment took place, there were two drawing-rooms, divided by a thick curtain, the rear drawing-room serving as the cabinet. Light for the other room, in which the observers sat, was a turned-down paraffin lamp. The galvanometer was put on the mantelpiece about ten feet from the dividing curtain.

Platinum wires led up to her shoulders from her arms, so that Miss Cook was permitted certain use of her limbs, and were then attached to covered copper wire which terminated in the battery. Before she became entranced, Miss Cook was asked to move her arms to determine what the difference in registration was. Throughout the session there were movements on the galvanometer as the blotting paper slowly dried, but had Miss Cook broken the circuit the result would have been dramatic, even if she had broken it for a mere one tenth of a second.

The seance began at 7.10 in the evening. Miss Cook was in circuit, and the galvanometer registered 220. Shortly before five minutes were up, the medium shifted her position, and the meter dropped to 210; ten minutes later, she moved again, and the figure dropped to 191, and fluctuated a matter of four degrees. The most dramatic fluctuation came a couple of minutes later when there was a drop of thirty-six divisions in one minute. Miss Cook, said Varley, had evidently shifted her position and maybe moved the sovereigns slightly. Two minutes later, the spirit Katie looked out from under the curtain, three minutes later, she showed her hands, and in ten minutes she was out and about amongst the audience, putting her hand on Crookes's head, and permitting Varley to grasp her hand. (It was cold and clammy; when Varley took Miss Cook's hand when urging her from her trance it was warm and dry).

At 7.42, Katie asked for pencil and paper, and began to write. The audience heard Miss Cook moaning like a woman in a nightmare. During the writing the galvanometer did not vary. This was considered by Varley to be especially significant.

Podmore was not convinced: "There is really nothing in the record to forbid the supposition that Miss Cook left her seat and promenaded as "Katie" with the wires still attached to her arms.'[2] Modern writers on psychical research have gone into the matter in depth, particularly C. J. Stephenson.[3] Mr Stephenson visited the location, or as near the location as makes no matter (Luxmoore's house is no longer there, but the house next door is), and discovered discrepancies in the description of the layout of the rooms relating to doors and so forth. He also questioned Varley's assumption that the gradual decrease in the galvanometer readings was caused by the drying-out of the soaked blotting-paper, as experiments have demonstrated that this is not the case. So the evidence is not so cut and dried as Varley seemed to think.

Then there were the sovereigns. There are no details as to how firmly they were affixed, though Varley's contention that the drop of thirty-six divisions early in the seance was due to

Miss Cook shifting her position and possibly moving the sovereigns would seem to indicate that they were not set hard against her flesh. Where were the sovereigns? Were they on the arm palm-side or the other side? If they were on the palm-side, and if the spirit form was Miss Cook approaching with the sovereigns attached they would be more easily spotted. It is evident that the light level was low. Varley found it difficult to see anything, having been dazzled by the bright spot of light that marked the galvanometer reading. It was a common practice at seances to make it appear that there was more light than was the case.

It is also clear from a scrutiny of Varley's meticulous time-table that towards the end of the session, the observing became slack. Varley confessed that the seance had taken a lot out of him, and bowed out of future experiments, leaving them in the capable hands of William Crookes. The last reading Varley made was at 7.48. It was then that he approached the spirit and found her hand cold and clammy, but if he went back to the galvanometer he did not mention it, nor did he take cognisance of a crucial time when one would have thought the galvanometer reading would prove most instructive: when the medium came out of her trance. It has been speculated that at this time darkness was absolute, and the investigators were relying entirely on their sense of touch.

If Miss Cook and spirit Katie were one and the same, and common sense strongly favours this supposition, why did her hands appear cold and clammy, then warm and dry? There are three hypotheses: Varley had spent nearly forty minutes in a state of tension, and his hands may well have been cold and clammy, in the metamorphosis Katie – Miss Cook, the operator would have been extremely busy, and the hands may well have dried off naturally; Miss Cook, realising the psychological effect of two kinds of hands, and knowing full well that if she offered a hand to Varley it would be eagerly grasped whether she was in the role of Miss Cook or Katie, had deliberately made her Katie-hands cold and clammy by applying eau de Cologne or cold cream.

Varley was insistent that there was absolutely no chance of Miss Cook escaping from the circuit even for one tenth of a second without this being detected by the galvanometer, and to give Varley his due, his galvanometer was a sophisticated instrument, superior, modern experts say, to many modern galvanometers.

But with credit given to Varley for providing an ingenious toy, once again the human element is seen to have invaded the field of pure science. Even the chronological table of events, so impressive at first glance, is not above suspicion. The seance was mocked-up at Cambridge in the mid-nineteen sixties, and it was discovered that the amount of time did not allow the detail shown on the table. W. H. Harrison, editor of the *Spiritualist*, was taking the notes. As a working journalist, he may have been using shorthand; or he may have written up the notes after the seance. In any event, there is an opening for error in the transcription. Whatever happened early in 1874, there was little difficulty in circumventing the conditions.

A year later Crookes used Varley's machine to test Mrs Fay. Annie Eva Fay had come to Britain from America in 1874, and had impressed a good many people.

On the evening of February 19th 1875, Mrs Fay arrived at Crookes's house, unaccompanied. Crookes had a number of scientific men with him, and there was general conversation while Crookes' precautions were examined. The equipment was looked over, cupboards were looked at, desks were opened, and strips of paper were fixed· over the window fastenings, sealing them with their signet rings, though there is little evidence that confederates climbed through windows to assist the medium in tricks. There were two doors to the seance room, and one was sealed up, while the other led to Crookes's laboratory where he and his guests remained. In place of sovereigns on the medium's arms, Crookes offered two handles for the medium to grasp, brass covered with pieces of linen soaked in salt and water, to help to make a good contact. Two of the scientists were not happy, and by connecting the two handles with a damp handkerchief they succeeded in producing the same effect as Mrs Fay in circuit, though they had to ask Crookes how the galvanometer was reacting for final adjustments. This was not brought out at the time, but proves conclusively that in the sessions with Miss Cook an object between the sovereigns could have passed for Miss Cook in circuit.

Crookes agreed that this would vitiate the experiment, and the brass handles were nailed too far apart for a handkerchief to stretch. Mrs Fay was asked to sit down before the handles, all gaslights were put off but one, which was turned down low. A variety of items were set out of her reach, a musical box, a violin, and a library ladder. Tests began at 8.55, Mrs Fay registering 211 on the galvanometer. It went up three points right away, and a hand bell was rung in the seance room. It went up one point, and a hand appeared on the far side of the curtained door that led from the seance room to the observers' room; the hand was three feet away from the handles presumably still being grasped by Mrs Fay.

The hand showed great dexterity in handing to the various literary scientists who were present copies of their books. (It is not explained how they came to be so handy, for although the seance was taking place in the library, it is very curious that these various books should have been not merely there but grouped for easy distribution.) One of the observers was apparently not a writer, but addicted to what Crookes called the 'fragrant weed', and a box of cigarettes was handed to him. There was also a mantelclock handed out, and that inveterate believer Serjeant Cox saw a full human form, the final coup, as half a minute later the circuit was broken. Crookes entered the seance room, to find that Mrs Fay was unconscious. An odd thing was observed in the seance room: a piece of old china that had been in the drawing-room upstairs, placed on a moulding about eight feet from the ground, was found on top of Crookes's writing-desk. Mrs Fay had been in the drawing-room for about an hour, but Crookes was certain that she had never been there alone. One of the observers (but only one) was positive that the plate had not been on the desk at the start of the experiment.

In the experiments with Miss Cook it would have not been difficult for one of the observers to join Miss Cook and act as a collaborator, but the room at Crookes's house where the audience gathered was not ill-lit. The terminals which Mrs Fay held were nailed down too far away to permit a handkerchief to complete the circuit instead of the medium; but did Mrs Fay perhaps know of another method, a piece of material concealed beneath her clothing and suitably sloshed with salt water? We are not sure what nailing the handles down implies. It was done on the spot, and therefore it may have been bodged. If both handles were freed from their moorings, the appearance of a hand three feet from the original position of the handles would have been easily accomplished, and if there had been sufficient wire the books could have been taken from the shelves (though Crookes pointed out that even he would have found difficulty in finding them in the subdued light from a turned-down gas jet), and the piece of china taken from the drawing-room placed on the desk. One must negate Crookes's claim that for an entire hour Mrs Fay was under scrutiny in the drawing-room.

The professional conjurers were especially merciless on Mrs Fay. Houdini thought that she gripped one handle in the fleshy part of her leg under the knee and thus released one hand to do the tricks. The word was certainly around professional circles that Mrs Fay had boasted about her trickery over the celebrated Professor Crookes, and when she was back in America Mrs Fay was approached to do a tour of England demonstrating how she had bamboozled the scientists. Mrs Fay indignantly turned down the offer, even though, by that date (1877), she was by her own account poor.

An interesting scientific investigation was carried out on Henry Slade in 1877–1878. Slade was a specialist in slate-writing, and had been practising in America for fifteen years before arriving in London on July 13th 1876, sponsored by the theosophists. Madame Blavatsky and her associate Colonel Olcott had been asked by Grand Duke Constantine of Russia to recommend a good medium, Slade was selected, and was therefore en route for Russia. Nevertheless, spiritualism was booming in Britain, the Indian summer of the Golden Age, and Slade took rooms in 8 Upper Bedford Place, giving sittings at a pound per fifteen minute session.

Slade was tall, lithe, graceful, with a dreamy mystical face and a nervous temperament, and he had a host of supporters who believed that he would take over D. D. Home's position as number one medium. He put on a dramatic show; the phenomena came regularly and precisely, and although Slade's speciality was slate-writing, he also produced table-turning, spirit-hands and, taking a leaf out of Home's book, playing a tune on an accordion with one hand; like Home, he produced his effects in broad daylight.

His first sitting was on July 15th, but early in September he had his aspirations dashed in no mean manner. Slade's trial under the Vagrancy Act caused consternation among his followers, and although he did not serve his three months with hard labour (the sentence being quashed on a technicality) his career in England was finished, and he went to the Continent; in Leipzig Professor Zöllner proposed, with selected colleagues, to put him to the test.

Slade came up to expectations, and Zöllner claimed to have observed direct spirit-writing on closed slates, strange lights and shadows, the impression of a naked foot smaller than Slade's on smoked paper, showers of water, smoke and fire which was yet not smoke and fire, movements of objects, the mysterious appearance of objects from outside the room, and the tearing apart of a screen five feet away from Slade held together by half-inch thick wooden screws.

Zöllner's associates were of little help in assessing what had happened. Professors Fechner and Scheibner were both short-sighted and relied on what Zöllner had said, and Professor Weber was seventy-four and admitted that he was entirely ignorant of legerdemain.

On December 17th 1877, Slade purported to produce knots in an endless cord. Two pieces of new hempen cord were used, the free ends being sealed on to a piece of card. The professor had one of the cords slung round his neck. At the end of the session one of the cords had four knots in it. Zöllner asserted that at no time had Slade's hands been out of his sight, and although Slade often touched his forehead, complaining of painful sensations, his attitude was passive. This miracle was too much for the German press to stomach; either Zöllner had been tricked, or he had been party to deception. He was indignant. Either he was a fool or he was a common imposter, and so were his associates who, although not at the seance, had seen the cords sealed.

Accusations that the professor was deranged were put forward, but this was denied by his colleagues after Zöllner died four years later of a cerebral haemorrhage. However, he was certainly not the first or the last scientist to have his judgment twisted by a fixation, and anyone who *expected* two wooden rings to become interlaced would have his sanity questioned; and his statement that this had occurred – in the company of a man who had been detected in fraud – treated with scant respect.

Slade finally went to Australia where he produced full-scale materialisations, phenomena that had lapsed in Britain because of a mania for grabbing spirit forms. In the mid-eighties he was back again in America. Disaster struck him; observers saw him writing on a slate beneath the table and moving furniture with his toes. He and his manager were arrested and released on bail, but no further action was taken. Slade's admirers blamed his debacle on drink and its effect on the sensitive organism. He died in 1905 in a Michigan sanatorium, whence he had been sent by American spiritualists.

One scientist who gave spiritualist phenomena both attention and patience was Michael Faraday, perhaps the most influential scientist of his generation. He investigated table-moving in a thoroughly objective manner, believing that it could be accounted for in nonsupernatural terms.

> You hear, at the present day, that some persons can place their fingers on a table, and then elevating their hands, the table will rise and follow them; that this piece of furniture, though heavy, will ascend, and that their hands bear no weight, or are not drawn down to the wood. The assertion finds acceptance in every rank of society and among classes that are esteemed to be educated. Now, what can this imply but that society, generally speaking, is not only ignorant as respects the education of the judgment, but is also ignorant of its ignorance?[4]

It could also happen with chairs. At another session with Stainton Moses a chair arose a foot or so, touched the skirting board, rose higher, circled, then gently descended. What makes it even odder is that Moses was sitting in the chair at the time. No wonder that the scientific common sense of Faraday boggled at it all.

Faraday did not dispute that tables would move if hands were placed on them, but the movement he put down to unconscious muscular action. Exasperated by the refusal to believe this, he made experiments. He first of all eliminated the idea of electricity or affinity or magnetism. He made plates of the most diverse materials – sandpaper, millboard, glass, moist clay, tinfoil, card-board, india-rubber – into a bundle and placed it under the hands of the operators. The table still moved. Faraday went further. Unknown to the operators he analysed the kind of pressures they were using. Several pellets of cement made with wax and turpentine were fixed on the underside of a piece of cardboard, then placed on the table. The sitters put their hands on the card-board, and the table moved as before. Faraday examined the cardboard; he could see 'by the displacement of the pellets that the hands had moved further than the table, and that the latter had lagged behind; that the hands, in fact, had pushed the card to the left, and that the table had followed and been dragged by it'.

He made further experiments. When people were concentrating on not pushing the table, the table did not move. His conclusion was that the mind becomes absorbed, and that muscles follow the will of the operator without his knowledge. He also com-mented that 'persons do not know how difficult it is to press directly downwards, or in any given direction against a fixed obstacle; or even to *know* only whether they are doing so or not, unless they have some indicator, which, by visible motion or otherwise, shall instruct them.' This difficulty was doubly so when the hand or fingers were cramped or tired, or expectation had let the sitters down.

Faraday's succinct summing-up should surely have spelled *finis* to the moving table as an occult manifestation. But not a bit of it. Fanatics argued that, in respect of the cardboard experiment, the *cardboard* was the mover, the table and hands the moved. Faraday retorted that the card could be reduced till it weighed only a few grains, or even to the dimensions of Goldbeater's-skin.

The spiritualists were desperate to get Faraday on their side. Because he had undertaken a good deal of time-consuming re-search into table-turning, they assumed that he was at their beck and call, ready to devote his great talents towards determining the nature of other spiritualistic phenomena. They had failed lamentably in recruiting Huxley, who had commented, 'Suppos-ing the phenomena to be genuine they do not interest me.' Darwin, too, remained outside the spiritualist orbit: 'I rejoice that I have avoided controversies, and this I owe to Lyell, who many years ago, in reference to my geological works, strongly advised me never to get entangled in a controversy, as it rarely did any good and caused a miserable loss of time and temper.'[5]

In 1864, the Davenport Brothers were producing alleged spiritualist phenomena, and they too were anxious to please Faraday. Faraday wrote to them: 'Gentlemen – I am obliged by your courteous invitation, but really I have been so disappointed by the manifestations to which my notice has at different times been called, that I am not encouraged to give any more attention to them, and therefore I leave these to which you refer in the hands of the professors of legerdemain. If spirit communication not utterly worthless, of any worthy character, should happen to start into activity, I will leave the spirits to find out for themselves how they can move more my attention. I am tired of them.'[6] He put it more bluntly yet elsewhere: 'What a weak, credulous, incredulous, unbelieving, superstitious, bold, frightened, what a ridiculous world ours is, as far as concerns the mind of man. How full of inconsistencies, contradictions, and absurdities it is.'[7]

Psychologists were a good deal more sympathetic towards spiritualism than physicists or chemists, especially regarding subjective phenomena. Francis Galton in his *Inquiries into Human Faculty* made the point that 'a notable proportion of sane persons have had not only visions, but actual hallucinations of sight at one or more periods of their life'. William James declared that every hallucination was a perception 'as good, and true a sensation as if there were a real object there. The object happens *not* to be there, that is all.'

Visions, illusions, hallucinations – all were present in nineteenth-century spiritualism. It was difficult to draw a line between them. To medical men, hallucinations were harbingers of madness, and as spiritualism encouraged hallucinations, spiritualism was a dangerous thing. Dr Forbes Winslow declared in 1877 that 'ten thousand unfortunate people are at present confined in lunatic asylums on account of having tampered with the supernatural'. As at this time the total number of persons incarcerated in lunatic asylums was 81,600, including 29,500 idiots, Winslow's figures are suspect, specially as the 'private insane' amounted to only 16,200.

The divergence of opinion between doctors and psychologists on spiritualism is illustrative of the general lack of cohesion of nineteenth-century science, which was reeling under the shock of Darwin's and Huxley's assaults on orthodoxy. Philosophy was stagnant, epitomised by Spencer's drab systematisation. Psychology was split between the old regime represented by Forbes Winslow and the forward-looking school represented by William James.

The latter group realised that spiritualism was a useful safety valve for mild forms of insanity. The freely expressed fantasies had a cathartic effect, and the process of abreaction had much in common with psychoanalysis, though Freud's studies in hysteria were not published in Germany until 1895, and his name was not known in Britain until the twentieth century.

Generally speaking, scientists thought that they had better things to do than bother with spiritualism. It was difficult not to have preset ideas on the subject, and even those who rated Crookes highly as a scientist looked askance at his meddling with the supernatural. There was also a reluctance to ally oneself with the established church which was condemning spiritualism as a resurgence of witchcraft.

The refusal of many scientists to investigate spiritualism dis-played a form of moral cowardice. Huxley's astonishing statement that even it were true he would not be interested is significant in this context. The aim of nineteenth-century science was to explain everything, and techniques for this purpose had been assiduously cultivated. If spiritualism were true, the whole pragmatic structure of science would topple. It was surely better to ignore the whole thing, and pretend that it had never happened.

23. A Personal Assessment

It is easy enough now to make a sardonic assessment of the Victorian attitude towards spiritualism; but if one had been in the midst of it all, would one have been objective?

We know now how the spiritualist tricks were performed, we know the variety of ways in which spiritualist photographs were fabricated, we know that every medium specialising in materialisations was caught out in fraud. We also know that the heady promise of the 1860s and 1870s was never fulfilled, that the revolution in life styles forecast by nearly every trance speaker came to nothing.

In its impact on everyday life in Victorian England spiritualism compares very poorly with contemporary movements. The Gothic Revival produced many startling buildings; the Nonconformist movement produced vast numbers of squat chapels throughout rural Britain; the Aesthetic movement created a wealth of literature and art. Spiritualism produced nothing but a range of largely unread and unreadable books and a quantity of foxed periodicals. It evoked no architecture, it prompted no literature of any merit, and no art, if one excepts numbers of quaint spirit drawings and paintings.

For a movement that believed that it had proved the reality of life after death it had remarkably little effect on funeral customs. The Victorian cemeteries with their status-symbol tombstones and vaults are there today to prove that to the nineteenth century death was real and earnest, that the smug self-satisfaction of the spiritualists cut very little ice with the majority of the people. When cremation was introduced at Woking in 1885 there was no strong spiritualist lobby to counter it, though cremation was against all the tenets of spiritualism. One must therefore look askance at the spiritualists' claim that there were millions of adherents in Britain.

What was true and what was false in Victorian spiritualism?

Much of the clairvoyance was genuine, even if one disregards the unconscious assimilation of information by an experienced medium – muscle reading etc. Spirit painting and drawing is explained by the emergence of a secondary personality under trance. This is true also of phenomena produced by the planchette, and this was recognised by objective men and women who used the planchette. If Victorian spiritualism rests or falls on the evidence of spirit photography, it must fall. No Victorian spirit photograph convinces.

One is very chary of accepting the evidence of 'apports', if only because their practitioners were suspect in other ways. Their relevance to the spiritualist seems to be nil, and it is difficult to know why apports were inserted into an evening's programme other than to vary the programme or distract an audience from the medium's preparations of other phenomena.

The earliest aspects of spiritualist techniques, table-rapping and table-turning, are more difficult to dispose of. Because they were primitive phenomena, they were easy to produce; but likewise they were easy to investigate. Nothing else in the canon was investigated as thoroughly as table-rapping, and if knee-cracking, rapping on tables with the fingernails, hidden mechanisms in tables activated by electro-magnets, if these could convince shrewd observers like Barrett that the dead were communicating then human gullibility is limitless.

The summit of all spiritualist phenomena, of course, was the spirit materialisation. No seance materialisation of the nineteenth century is free from fraud or the strong probability of fraud, and it is significant that when the Society for Psychical Research wished to investigate attested materialisations the leading materialisation mediums retired or went to Australia.

To sum up, I believe that the evidence for clairvoyance and table-rapping is strong, that the evidence for spirit drawing and painting, spirit photography, apports, and materialisations is thin. The scientific investigations by Crookes and Varley were unsatisfactory and inconclusive. The evidence would be thinner still but for the phenomena surrounding D. D. Home, and I would not hedge my bets but for this piece that will not fit the jigsaw. Home produced astounding phenomena before observers whom one respects; other mediums did so, too, but there is one difference. Home was never detected in any kind of fraud, and in any account of Victorian spiritualism Home must be taken into consideration, an enigma, a giant among pygmies, a man beset by trials and tribulations who never loses his dignity and stature.

In my section *The Tearing of the Veil* I have made a distinction between hallucinations and hauntings. The reader must judge whether this is some kind of linguistic quirk on my part. To my mind, there is a distinction. The hauntings of Victorian England are extremely credible. They have the vestigal unfinished quality of dreams, and an air of understatement. It is a pity that Victorian spiritualism did not have more of this quality.

Bibliography

Viscount Adare	*Experiences in Spiritualism* 1869
Anon	*Scepticism and Spiritualism* 1865
Anon	*Confessions of a Medium* 1882
Sir William Barrett	*On the Threshold of the Unseen* 1917
E. Bennett	*Apparitions and Haunted Houses* 1939
Joseph Braddock	*Haunted Houses* 1956
Emma Hardinge Britten	*Nineteenth Century Miracles* 1884
C. D. Broad	*Lectures on Psychical Research* 1962
John L. Campbell and Trevor H. Hall	*Strange Things* 1968
Hereward Carrington	*The Physical Phenomena of Spiritualism* 1907
	Eusapia Palladino and her Phenomena 1909
J. Coates	*Photographing the Invisible* 1921
J. C. Colquhoun	*History of Magic* 1851
E. W. Cox	*Mechanism of Man* 1876–1879
Sir William Crookes	*Researches in the Phenomena of Spiritualism* 1874
C. Crowe	*The Night Side of Nature* 1848
Charles Maurice Davies	*Mystic London* 1876
A. Conan Doyle	*History of Spiritualism* 1926
E. d'Espérance	*Shadow Land* n.d.
J. S. Farmer	*Twixt Two Worlds* 1886
E. E. Fournier d'Albe	*Life of Sir William Crookes* 1923
Miss Goodrich Freer	*Essays in Psychical Research* 1899
Miss Goodrich Freer and Marquess of Bute	*The Alleged Haunting of B—— House* 1899
Alan Gauld	*Founders of the SPR* 1968

Edmund Gurney	*Tertium Quid* 1887
Edmund Gurney, F. Myers, and F. Podmore	*Phantasms of the Living* 1886
S. C. Hall	*Retrospect of a Long Life* 1883
G. Henslow	*Truths of Spiritualism* 1919
I. W. Heysinger	*Spirit and Matter* 1910
S. Hibbert	*On Apparitions* 1825
D. D. Home	*Incidents in My Life* 1863
	Lights and Shadows of Spiritualism 1877
Mme D. D. Home	*D. D. Home: His Life and Mission* 1888
	The Gift of D. D. Home 1890
A. H. Hopkins	*Magic* 1898
Georgina Houghton	*Evenings at Home in Spiritual Seance* 1881
	Spirit Photography 1882
William Howitt	*History of the Supernatural* 1863
Joseph Jastrow	*Fact and Fable in Psychology* 1901
Andrew Land	*Cock Lane and Common Sense* 1894
	Book of Dreams and Ghosts 1897
F. G. Lee	*Sights and Shadows* 1894
John C. Leonard	*The Higher Spiritualism* 1927
Sir Oliver Lodge	*Survival of Man* 1909
London Dialectical Society	*Report on Spiritualism* 1871
Charles Mackay	*Popular Delusions* 1841
Florence Marryat	*There is No Death* 1892
J. N. Maskelyne	*Modern Spiritualism* no date
Herbert Mayo	*Popular Superstitions* 1849
A Member of the SPR	*Dangers of Spiritualism* 1901
Mrs de Morgan	*From Matter to Spirit* 1863
W. S. Moses	*Spirit Teachings* 1898
F. W. H. Myers	*Human Personality* 1903
	Fragments of Inner Life 1904
Charles Ollier	*Fallacy of Ghosts* 1848
R. D. Owen	*Footfalls on the Boundary of Another World* 1861
	The Debatable Land 1871

BIBLIOGRAPHY

Lady Paget	*Colloquies with an Unseen Friend* 1907
Frank Podmore	*Apparitions and Thought Transference* 1894
	Studies in Psychical Research 1897
	Modern Spiritualism 1902
	Newer Spiritualism 1910
H. Price	*Fifty Years of Psychic Research* 1939
	Poltergeist Over England 1945
W. H. Salter	*Society for Psychical Research* 1948
E. H. Sears	*Foregleams of Immortality* 1858
S. Sitwell	*Poltergeists* 1940
Alfred Smedley	*Some Reminiscences* 1900
W. T. Stead	*Real Ghost Stories* 1897
James Sully	*Illusions* 1881
Cora L. V. Tappin	*Discourses through the Mediumship of Cora L. V. Tappin* 1874
Morrell Theobald	*Spirit Workers in the Home Circle* 1887
Camilla Toulmin	*Light in the Valley* 1857
Ivor L. L. Tuckett	*Evidence for the Supernatural* 1911
G. N. M. Tyrrell	*Apparitions* 1953
Lionel A. Weatherly	*The Supernatural?* 1891
Dr Forbes Winslow	*Obscure Diseases of the Brain* 1861
Horace Wyndham	*Mr Sludge the Medium* 1937

Journals and Periodicals

Journal of the Society for Psychical Research
Medium and Daybreak
Proceedings of the Society for Psychical Research
Publications of the Society for Psychical Research
Spiritualist
Spiritualist Times
Two Worlds

In addition there are numerous references to spiritualism in the ordinary periodical press, such as *All the Year Round, Chambers's Journal, Household Words, Once a Week, Punch* and *Quarterly Review*.

References

1: Mesmerism

1 *The Two Worlds* March 1, 1889
2 *Sights and Shadows* F. G. Lee 1894: p.189
3 *Edinburgh Monthly Medical Journal* June 1851
4 *Magic, Witchcraft, Animal Magnetism, Hypnosis* James Braid 1852: p.84
5 ibid: p.79
6 *Household Words* January 17, 1852
7 *Dreams and Ghosts* Andrew Lang 1897: p.vi
8 *Magic, Witchcraft, Animal Magnetism, Hypnosis* James Braid 1852: 79
9 *From Matter to Spirit* Mrs A. de Morgan 1863: p.49
10 *Mad Humanity* Forbes Winslow 1898: p.301
11 *Mystic London* Rev. Charles Maurice Davies 1875: pp. 262–268
12 *New Letters and Memorials of Jane Welsh Carlyle* 1903 2 vols I p.158
13 *Letters of Elizabeth Barrett Browning* 1897: 2 vols I pp.258–259
14 *Charles Dickens* Una Pope-Hennessy 1947: p.238
15 ibid: p. 464
16 Letter Charlotte Brontë to James Taylor January 15, 1851
17 *Punch* Volume 2 1851: p.104

2: The Birth of Spiritualism

1 *Memoir of Robert Alfred Vaughan* Robert Vaughan 1864: p.139
2 *C. H. Spurgeon* W. Y. Fullerton 1920: pp.90–91

3   *Memoir of Robert Alfred Vaughan* Robert Vaughan 1864:
    p.163

3: Table-Rapping

1   Letters of Elizabeth Barrett Browning 1897: 2 vols II p.99
2   *Memoir of Robert Chambers* William Chambers 1873:
    p.334
3   *Westminster Review* January 1858
4   *Essays in Psychical Research* A. Goodrich Freer 1899: p.14
5   *Life and Letters of Rev. Stopford Brooke* L. P. Jacks 1917:
    2 vols I p.132
6   *Nineteenth Century Miracles* Emma Hardinge Britten 1884:
    p.139
7   *Mad Humanity* Forbes Winslow 1898: p.279
8   *There is No Death* Florence Marryat 1891: p.25
9   *From Matter to Spirit* Mrs A. de Morgan 1863: p.4

4: Seance

1   *From Matter to Spirit* Mrs A. de Morgan 1863: p.4
2   ibid: p.4
3   *Mr Sludge the Medium* Horace Wyndham 1937: p.118
4   *Behind the Brass Plate* Alfred Schofield n.d.: p.304
5   *Chambers's Journal* December 30, 1871
6   *Mystic London* Rev. Charles Maurice Davies 1875: p.250
7   ibid: 338
8   *Eastern Post* July 31, 1869
9   *The Two Worlds* March 15, 1889
10 Letter Nelson Holmes to D. D. Home September 16, 1876
11 *The Vampires of Onset: Past and Present* quoted *Studies
    in Psychical Research* Frank Podmore 1897: p.234
12 *More Ghost Stories* W. T. Stead 1892: p.54

13 *Proceedings* SPR 1886: p.27
14 ibid: p.55
15 *The Two Worlds* April 20, 1889

5: The Appeal of Spiritualism

1 *The Two Worlds* March 22, 1889
2 ibid May 17, 1889
3 *Life of John William Strutt 3rd Baron Rayleigh* Robert John Strutt 1924: p.67
4 Novel *The Medium* serialised in *Spiritual Times* May 7, 1864
5 *The Spiritualist* March 31, 1882
6 *The Two Worlds* March 15, 1889
7 *Frome Times* August 6, 1884
8 *Lights and Shadows of Spiritualism* D. D. Home 1877: p.307
9 *The Two Worlds* March 15, 1889
10 ibid October 4, 1889
11 *Medium and Daybreak* June 13, 1884

6: D. D. Home's Gift

1 *The Gift of D. D. Home* Mme D. Home 1890: p.20
2 *Letters of John Ruskin to Charles Eliot Norton* 1905: p.169

7: Seance Phenomena

1 *Studies in Psychical Research* Frank Podmore 1897: p.197
2 *Fact and Fable in Psychology* J. Jastrow 1901: p.133
3 *Experiences in Spiritualism* Lord Adare 1869 privately printed p.53
4 ibid 154
5 *Proceedings* SPR 1885

6   *Proceedings* SPR 1895 : p.49
7   ibid 51
8   Report of Dialectical Society on Spiritualism 1871 : p.205
9   Report of Dialectical Society on Spiritualism 1871 : p.208
10 ibid 263
11 *Researches in Spiritualism* Sir William Crookes 1874 : p.91
12 *Experiences in Spiritualism* Lord Adare 1869 privately printed p.115
13 Stainton Moses' Notebook January 3, 1874

8: Materialisations

1   Report of Dialectical Society on Spiritualism 1871 : p.298
2   ibid 172
3   *Spiritualist* January 30, 1880
4   *Spiritualist* February 6, 1880
5   Report of Dialectical Society on Spiritualism 1871 : p. 128
7   *From Matter to Spirit* Mrs A. de Morgan 1863 : p.9
8   *The Two Worlds* September 6, 1889
9   *London Society* February 1874
10 *Mystic London* Rev. Charles Maurice Davies 1875 : p.317
11 ibid p.316
12 *Spiritualist* September 28, 1877
13 *On the Threshold of the Unseen* Sir William Barrett 1917 : p.318
14 *Researches in Spiritualism* Sir William Crookes 1874 : p.22
15 *Spiritualist* 1873 : p.83

9: Spirit Writing and Drawing

1   Report of Dialectical Society on Spiritualism 1871 : p.66
2   ibid 1871 : p.143
3   *Light in the Valley* Camilla Toulmin 1857 : pp.127–128
4   *Evenings at Home* Georgina Houghton 1881 : p.112
5   ibid 163
6   *From Matter to Spirit* Mrs A. de Morgan 1863 : p.8

7   ibid 282
8   Proceedings SPR 1887: p.351
9   *Light* October 16, 1886
10 Journal SPR 1886: p.331

10: Spirit Photography

1   *Photographing the Invisible* James Coates 1921: p.48
2   *Spirit Photography* Georgina Houghton 1882: pp.162–163
3   *Human Nature* Stainton Moses 1875: p.152

12: Hallucinations

1   *Haunted Houses* Joseph Braddock 1956: p.46
2   *Strange Things* John L. Campbell and Trevor H. Hall 1968: p.171
3   *Lights and Shadows of Spiritualism* D. D. Home 1877: p.199
4   *Handbook of Psychology* William James 1892: p.302
5   ibid 329
6   *The Philosophy of Insanity* Rev. Mr Walford 1860: p.20
7   *Obscure Diseases of the Brain* Forbes Winslow 1861: p.60
8   *The Dangers of Spiritualism* A Member of the SPR 1901: p.124
9   *Obscure Diseases of the Brain* Forbes Winslow 1861: p.561
10 ibid 106
11 Letter Mr Findlay to Lord Bute March 3, 1897

13: Collective Hallucinations

1   *Manual of Psychology* G. F. Stout 1913: p.554
2   *W. B. Yeats* Joseph Hone 1942: p.70
3   *The Doctor Remembers* Dr J. Crichton-Browne 1938: p.94

4 Proceedings SPR 1890: p.103
5 *Modern Spiritualism* F. Podmore 1902 2 vols II p.264
6 *Collected Essays* T. H. Huxley 1893–1895 9 vols V p.226
7 Proceedings SPR 1894: p.312
8 *Human Personality* F. W. H. Myers 1904: 2 vols I p.263
9 ibid I p.263
10 *Phantasms of the Living* Edmund Gurney 1885: 2 vols II
   p.194

14: The Haunted Situation

1 *Proceedings* SPR 1889: p.229
2 ibid p.229
3 *All The Year Round* August 5, 1871
4 *Essays* W. C. Roscoe 1860: 2 vols II p.437
5 *Mayfair* May 10, 1879
6 *Reminiscences* Lady Dorothy Nevill 1906: p.303
7 *Proceedings* SPR 1889: p.237–238

15: The Haunters

1 *Proceedings* SPR 1889: p.241
2 *Sights and Shadows* F. G. Lee 1894: pp.30–31
3 *Memories of Ninety Years* Mrs E. M. Ward 1922: p.144
4 Journal of Arnold Bennett November 28, 1897
5 *Real Ghost Stories* W. T. Stead 1897: p.133
6 ibid pp.179–180
7 *The Doctor Remembers* Dr J. Crichton-Browne 1938:
   p.301
8 Letter Mr Findlay to Lord Bute March 3, 1897
9 *Real Ghost Stories* W. T. Stead 1897: p.199
10 *Autobiographies* W. B. Yeats 1955: 340
11 *Essays in Psychical Research* A. Goodrich Freer 1899: p.67
12 *Maud* by Alfred Lord Tennyson 1855
13 *The Two Worlds* July 19, 1889
14 *Records and Reminiscences* Sir Francis Burnand 1905:
   p.320

REFERENCES

16: Poltergeists

1 *Essays in Psychical Research* A. Goodrich Freer 1899: p.55
2 *Proceedings* SPR 1889: p.311
3 *Life of Edward Bulwer* Earl of Lytton 1913: p.45
4 *Proceedings* SPR 1926: p.110
5 *Music at Night* Aldous Huxley 1950 edition: p.70

17: The Walking Dead

1 *Lancet* March 17, 1866
2 *The Times* May 6, 1874
3 *British Medical Journal* December 8, 1877

18: The Moment of Truth

1 *Retrospect of a Long Life* S. C. Hall 1883: 2 vols II p.511
2 ibid II p.474
3 *Discourses and Trance Addresses of Mrs Cora V. Tappin* 1875: appendix p.6
4 *Human Personality* F. W. H. Myers 1904: 2 vols I p.230
5 *Discourses and Trance Addresses of Mrs Cora V. Tappin* 1875 appendix p.6
6 *From Matter to Spirit* Mrs A. de Morgan 1863: p.81
7 ibid pp. 307–309
8 *Man's Concern with Death* a symposium 1968: p.253
9 *The Ring* Alfred Lord Tennyson 1889
10 Spiritualist's National Union Hymn Book

19: Family Reunion

1 *Father and Son* Edmund Gosse 1922 edition: p.67
2 *Fragments of Inner Life* F. W. H. Myers 1904: p.35
3 ibid 44

4 *The Two Worlds* February 1, 1889
5 *The Two Worlds* January 25, 1889
6 *George Butler* Josephine Butler 1892: p.478

20: Theosophy

1 *W. B. Yeats* Joseph Hone 1942: p.70
2 *Autobiographies* W. B. Yeats 1955: p.174
3 ibid 175
4 *Medium and Daybread* August 2, 1889
5 *The Higher Spiritualism* John C. Leonard 1927: p.4
6 *Real Ghost Stories* W. T. Stead 1897: p.26

21: The Spirit of Enquiry

1 *Spirit Teachings* Stainton Moses 1933 edition: p.47
2 *The Times* June 8, 1897
3 *Fragments of Inner Life* F. W. H. Myers 1904: p.65
4 *Recollections and Reflections* Sir J. J. Thomson 1936: p.148

22: The Scientific Case

1 Letter, Francis Galton to Charles Darwin April 19, 1872
2 *Modern Spiritualism* Frank Podmore 1902: 2 vols II p.157
3 *Proceedings* SPR 1966
4 *Experimental Researches in Chemistry and Physics* M. Faraday 1859: p.470
5 *Autobiography* Charles Darwin 1929: p.62
6 *Life and Letters of M. Faraday* Bence Jones 1870: 2 vols II p.468
7 ibid II p.307

Index